THE SPRINGBURN STORY

The History of the Scottish
Railway Metropolis

PRIDE IN THE JOB. *Hyde Park men pose on an Indian engine they have helped to build*

THE SPRINGBURN STORY

The History of the Scottish
Railway Metropolis

By

JOHN THOMAS

DAVID & CHARLES: DAWLISH

MACDONALD: LONDON

1964

Printed in Great Britain
by W. J. Holman Limited Dawlish
for David & Charles (Publishers) Limited
39 Strand Dawlish Devon

CONTENTS

ILLUSTRATIONS

9

ILLUSTRATIONS

IN TEXT

NEILSON & CO
HYDE PARK LOCOMOTIVE WORKS
GLASGOW.
Established 1836.

LONDON OFFICE,
PARLIAMENT MANSIONS,
VICTORIA STREET, S.W.

TELEGRAMS "LOCOMOTIVE" GLASGOW.
GLASGOW TELEPHONE Nº 822.

Certificate of Apprenticeship

FROM

Messrs. Neilson & Co.
Hyde Park Locomotive Works
Glasgow. July 1894

This is to Certify that

John Wilson

served with us an Apprenticeship of five years

as a Machinist

from Feb 1889 until Feb. 1894

We consider his attendance to have been

Regular his conduct good and his skill

Satisfactory

He worked thereafter as a journeyman Machinist

from Feb: till this date

Neilson &
Jr & Co

A Neilson Certificate of Apprenticeship. To generations of Springburn men Neilson's 'papers' were a cherished possession.

Prologue

SPRINGBURN BUILT!

If you had been in Glasgow on the first of January in the year 1900, and you had wanted to get to the highest point of the city, you would have taken one of the new electric cars from Mitchell Street to Springburn.

The car set off climbing northwards up West Nile Street, then turned north-east to begin the long straight ascent of Parliamentary Road, a thoroughfare bordered by high stone tenements that made it look like a long, smooth-sided railway cutting. At the top the tram turned north again into Castle Street, dipped under Inchbelly railway bridge and began its whining grind up the steep gradient of Springburn Road towards the heart of Springburn.

The first tram stop in Springburn Road stood opposite No 130, and this unpretentious two-storey building in sooty brick was the office of the locomotive superintendent of the Caledonian Railway, the great John Farquharson McIntosh. In the big front room on the second floor, not five years before, the design of the Dunalastair had first seen the light of day. Behind sprawled the Saint Rollox Works. *Saint* Rollox! That was how the Caledonian styled their locomotive and carriage and wagon establishment. The proud railway company that had appropriated the Scottish national emblem and motto as its very own had no truck with diminutives. In those workshops the craftsmen of Springburn had fashioned McIntosh's beautiful blue engines.

All was quiet at St Rollox on New Year's Day 1900. The

drawing boards were bare, the machines silent. In the erecting shop the newest of the Dunalastair IIIs stood in various stages of completion. The draughtsmen and the smiths, the boiler-makers and the coachpainters were in their homes with their wives and children celebrating the best-loved holiday in the Scottish calendar. It would be the third before the works were open again and ready to bring to life the wonderful things that McIntosh had planned for the new century.

Three tram stops beyond St Rollox the car halted at Spring-burn Cross. There, at the hub of Springburn, two streets diverged from the main road. Cowlairs Road on the left led down to Cowlairs Works, the celebrated headquarters of the North British Railway Company's stud of bronze-green loco-motives. By then a railway workshop had stood on the site for well nigh on sixty years. The holiday quiet pervaded Cow-lairs too, but within forty-eight hours old Matthew Holmes would be on the scene in his grey morning coat superintend-ing the building of his latest engines. All Springburn was aware that anything new in blue turned out by the place down the road would be matched by a bronze-green challenger from Cowlairs.

To the right from Springburn Cross was Vulcan Street; at its foot was the main gate of Neilson, Reid & Co's Hyde Park Works. You knew from your *Glasgow Herald* of the previous day that Neilson's had employed 3,275 men in the locomotive trade in the year just ended—1,258 more than were employed by the next biggest Scottish locomotive works and 1,407 more than the pay roll of their nearest English competitor.

Still climbing through the heart of Springburn the tram passed the shuttered premises of Cowlairs Co-operative Society (which used as an official seal an impression of a Wheatley 4—4—0) to the bridge carrying Springburn Road over the railway at Springburn station. On one side of the railway was Hyde Park Works, on the other the Atlas Works of Sharp, Stewart & Co. During 1899 'the Atlas' had employed 1,581 locomotive builders. Where else *in all the world* could a passenger in a tramcar, in the course of a half-mile journey along a public highway, have found such a concentration of railway interest and railway skills? Two company works, two private builders—and for good measure, two major sheds and a main line cable-worked incline just round the corner!

The tram climbed on the final stage of its journey, past the shop where Chalmers the jeweller displayed a card offering to lend a watch free to any railwayman who gave in his own for repair; past Anderson the hatter who four months ago had been selling cloth caps with a portrait of John F. McIntosh in the blue silk lining. The young gallants of Springburn had worn them at the great Caledonian Excursion to Carlisle in the previous September. Ah, that Caley trip! What a day that had been! On New Year's Day 1900, Springburn was still talking about the 14-Dunalastair, 250-coach outing that had taken 15,000 people (Springburn population, 27,000) over the Border to Carlisle and back for one shilling a head.

The tram lines ended at the foot of Balgrayhill Road. 'The Balgray' defied (and still defies) public transport. To gain the highest point of Glasgow you had to trudge up the hill past the manses of the Springburn ministers and the grand stone villas of the Springburn doctors. At the top you were 350 feet above your Mitchell Street starting point and Glasgow lay below like a map. The cranes of the Clyde shipyards were away to the west. To the north lay a magnificent sweep of open country stretching across the Kelvin valley to the Campsie fells and the first of the West Highland mountains, Ben Lomond and Ben More among them. And right at the top of the Balgray, near enough on the highest geographical point of Glasgow and commanding a vista of city and country embracing seven counties, was Belmont.

Belmont, a great red castle of a place, the newest and largest private dwelling house within Glasgow's boundaries, was a fitting home for the principal proprietor of the largest locomotive works in Europe. Belmont reflected the boundless prosperity of the Reid family and of the locomotive trade.

15

In Springburn the order books were bulging. The expanding mineral trade of the Caledonian had forced McIntosh to farm out the building of substantial batches of his 'Dunalastair goods' to Neilson's and the Atlas and Henry Dübs's Glasgow Locomotive Works. Capacity was at a premium, and three English railway companies had been driven to seek locomotives in America. Hugh Reid sat at Belmont's great table enjoying his New Year dinner secure in the knowledge that any customer who came to him for locomotives would take his place on the waiting list. Before daylight on the next working day he would walk down the Balgray—not on the footpath but imperiously in the middle of the road as was his habit—into the hub of the great railway empire that was Springburn.

What a story Springburn has to tell! Its workshops and tenements and streets are steeped in railway lore. What a cavalcade of railway worthies has passed over its pavements: Benjamin Conner, Brittain, the Drummond brothers, the Uries, those striplings Stroudley and Samuel Waite Johnston gathering experience for great things ahead, McIntosh, Tom Wheatley, Matthew Holmes; characters as diverse as Rous-Marten and George Westinghouse; Walter Neilson, James Reid, Henry Dübs, Edward Snowball, Goodall-Copestake; and many more. And the Springburn engines! For one hundred and thirty years Springburn was the cornucopia from which flowed famous classes for most of our home railways as well as locomotives in infinite variety for the five continents. There were the Conner eight-footers; the Wheatley inside-cylinder, inside-frame four-coupled express engine, the very first of a class that became a British institution; the first British 4—6—0; the immortal Caledonian No 123 and the peerless Dunalastairs. The engines that ran for the Scottish companies in the Race to the North came out of Springburn. There were Scotts and Royal Scots, Atlantics plain and Atlantics fancy, compressed-air tram engines and massive Mallet compounds. There were the brave might-have-beens, from Robert Davidson's electric locomotive of 1842 to the

Reid-McLeod condensing turbine of the twenties and the ill-fated *Fury* of the thirties.

I remember the night the 'Nizam's big engine' went down to the docks. It was 17 March 1933. Although nearly midnight Springburn Road was lined with people. Craftsmen and their wives mingled with youths and girls from a St Patrick's Night dance. The spectators might have been waiting for a royal progress, and so in a way they were. The newest product of the Hyde Park Works, a locomotive for the railways of His Exalted Highness the Nizam of Hyderabad, was about to pass on its way to the docks.

The good folk of Springburn were well used to the spectacle of out-of-gauge engines trundling down Springburn Road in charge of a pair of snorting traction engines, bound for some sun-baked railway halfway round the world. On such occasions the local people were reminded (if they needed reminding) that for seventy years the world had come to Springburn for engines, just as confidently as it had gone to the Clyde for ships. The Clydesider's traditional craftsmanship in marine architecture and engineering was matched by the railway expertise that had developed over the years in Springburn, and the variety of Clyde-built ships ranging the Seven Seas had a counterpart in the variety of Springburn-built engines traversing the world's land masses. There was hardly a country in the world that had not seen one.

About a quarter to twelve the big gates of Hyde Park opened and two traction engines eased the 16-wheel articulated trailer bearing the Nizam's engine out under the arch into Vulcan Street. The engine was a 103-ton 2—8—0 for heavy freight duties, fitted with a North British Locomotive N1 type mechanical stoker, the first of its kind to be manufactured in Britain.

The cavalcade halted outside the Public Library opposite the works. NB officials, policemen, and officers of Glasgow Corporation buzzed about. The top of the boiler was sheeted with rubber because of the tram wires which would be some six inches above it during most of its journey, and representatives of the tramway department were in attendance just in case of accidents. There was also an official from the water department, for had not a Hyde Park engine once sunk down through the road and burst a water main?

Just before midnight the traction engines, their copper-capped stacks billowing yellow smoke, eased their load up the gentle slope of Vulcan Street, round the tricky right-angled bend into the main road. The great locomotive, its boiler as high as the first storey of the surrounding tenements, was trundled townwards at a brisk walking pace watched by the spectators on the pavements, and followed by officials on foot and in vehicles. Wee boys in pyjamas, let out of bed specially for this great occasion, had their faces pressed against the glass of their bedroom windows. Round the elbow bend of Springburn Road and down the hill past Saint Rollox (now St Rollox, LMSR) it went, and at Inchbelly bridge there were precious few inches to spare between the chimney cap and the bottom of the girders.

We will leave the engine to spend the night passing down Castle Street and Parliamentary Road, Sauchiehall Street and St Vincent Street, eventually to arrive alongside the *City of Barcelona* at Stobcross Quay. Inchbelly Bridge is as good a place as any to begin the Springburn story, for here it was, 102 years before that night in 1933, that the railway came to Springburn.

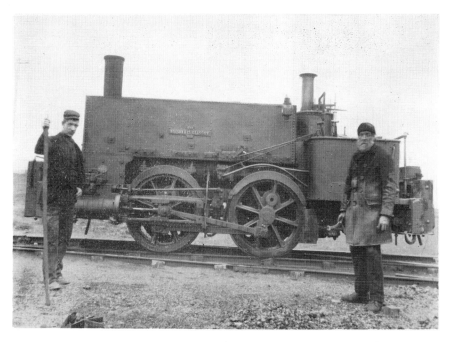

HYDE PARK PRODUCTS. Top: *A Neilson patent shunter of 1862.*
Bottom: *Bengal Nagpur Railway compound Pacific of 1929 at Raipur*

HYDE PARK WORKS. Top: *A general view of the works in 1862.*
Bottom: *The main entrance to the works in Ayr Street, Springburn,
about 1895*

20

Chapter 1

THE RAILWAY COMES TO SPRINGBURN

The main news story on the front page of the *Glasgow Courier* on Thursday, 22 September 1831 concerned a recent case of *plagium*—man-stealing. John Aitkenhead, journeyman chimney-sweep, had abducted one John Campbell aged nine, the lawfully apprenticed climbing-boy of another journeyman sweep John Black, and had set him to climb chimneys in Ayrshire and elsewhere. James Fleming, Magistrate of the City of Glasgow, read down the column far enough to find that the rascal had been found guilty and sentenced to fourteen years transportation before he discarded the newspaper and concentrated on a letter that had been delivered that day. It consisted of a single sheet of paper folded and sealed after the style of the period, and Bailie Fleming noticed that the red circle of sealing wax was marked with the impression of a wheel. The outside, as well as bearing the Bailie's name, carried the inscription 'Rail Way. Hill and Davidson'. He broke the seal and opened the letter.

Sir,

The Committee of the Garnkirk and Glasgow Railway having just resolved to have a Public Inspection of the Railway on Tuesday first the 27th instant, when the principal part of their Works will be opened to the Public Trade; we are directed by them to apologise to you for the unavoidable shortness of this invitation and to request the honour of your accompanying them from the West End of the Line at the Townhead of Glasgow, from which the Locomotive

21

B

Engines and Carriages will proceed, at 12 o'Clock Noon, Eastwards that day and that at all events you will honour them with your Company at Dinner in the Black Bull at Six o'Clock in the Evening of that day.

We are,

Sir,

Your Most Obedient Servants,

Hill and Davidson.

Attached to this letter from the Clerks to the Railway was a green ticket entitling the holder to board the railway carriage displaying a flag of the same colour.

The Garnkirk & Glasgow got its Act in 1826, and the first sod was cut on 28 August 1827. The railway was built mainly to bring coal from the Monkland coalfield, some ten miles east of Glasgow, into a city hungry for it. In 1801 the population of Glasgow had been 77,385; by 1826 the figure had leapt to over 200,000 and thousands were pouring into the city every month to fill the new factories. Much of Glasgow's coal and iron came from the Monklands and its transport was a major concern of the city's industrialists. James Watt's Monkland Canal had brought in most of the traffic. Then, in October 1826, a ten-mile railway line was opened from the Monklands down to the Forth & Clyde Canal at Kirkintilloch. Coal was sent down the Monkland & Kirkintilloch by gravity (the empty wagons were returned by horse haulage) to make a somewhat circuitous journey by barge to Glasgow. But the direct canal service and the rail-canal link together did not meet the city's needs, and a group of far-seeing merchants promoted a direct rail link between the Monklands and Glasgow.

Though the new venture was the greatest of its kind ever mooted in Scotland, practically no notice was taken of it in the press. Railways were still an unknown quantity in 1826, locomotives extravagant novelties that had yet to prove themselves. The solitary steam engine that had appeared in Scotland (on the Kilmarnock & Troon) had impressed nobody. Nevertheless, enough money for the Garnkirk enterprise was subscribed to enable a start to be made, and the company's representative took up residence in a public house at Provan Mill on the line of the proposed railway some two miles from Glasgow to interview prospective contractors. The main contract was let to Grainger & Miller, an up-and-coming firm of civil engineers who had already engineered the Monkland & Kirkintilloch. The Garnkirk & Glasgow was planned to leave Monkland & Kirkintilloch metals at Gartsherrie colliery and strike westwards through Gartloch, Cardowan, Garnkirk, Hogganfield and across the southern edge of what was then the parish of Springburn to a terminus in the Townhead of Glasgow. Immediately east of the terminus the track passed over the earth road that was to become Springburn Road on Inchbelly Crossing; the bridge came later. It was no accident that the Glasgow station adjoined the great Tennant chemical works. They consumed 30,000 tons of coal a year and, not surprisingly, John and Charles Tennant were enthusiastic supporters of the railway.

In the three years that it took to build the railway, the steam locomotive rose in status. The *Rocket*, Rainhill and the success of the Liverpool & Manchester had assured its future, and the very men who so recently had poured scorn on George Stephenson now vied for his favours. It was fashionable for railway promoters to seek the approval of the sage of Newcastle for their schemes and the Garnkirk was no exception. Stephenson was commissioned to build two locomotives for the opening of the line, planned for the late summer of 1831.

The first engine that Springburn ever saw was a Planet type to which the Garnkirk & Glasgow gave the name *St Rollox*, for there had been an ancient church of St Roche or St Rollox near the western terminus of the line. It was a 2—2—0 weighing 4 tons, with 11 in. by 14 in. cylinders and a boiler pressure of 50 p.s.i. The driving wheels were 4 ft 6 in. in diameter and the leading wheels 3 ft 3 in. The Garnkirk paid Stephenson £750 for it. *St Rollox* arrived in Glasgow in the early summer of 1831 and some weeks later it was joined by *George Stephenson*, a bigger and more powerful Planet type. It weighed 8 tons, its cylinders were 11 in. by 16 in. and its wheels were coupled. On 7 July the company organised a private trip for invited guests. *St Rollox* was used and its 20-ton load included a new carriage, *Isabella*, made for the railway by the coach-building firm of Johnston & McNab. This, the first railway passenger vehicle constructed in Glasgow, accommodated 24 passengers in three cushioned compartments. Construction work on the line was still in progress when the demonstration trip was made. On the outward journey the train ran on the wrong line and speed was restricted because the engine was encountering facing points all the way. A passenger, Mr Findlater, made a detailed log of the run, surely the oldest surviving log of locomotive performance made in Scotland, if not in Britain. Here are his figures for the outward trip.

Mile	Minutes	Seconds	Speed (miles and furlongs per hr)	
			Miles	Furlongs
1	4	54	12	2
2	4	52	12	1
3	4	13	12	2
4	3	41	16	2
5	6	39	9	
6	5	30	11	
7	4	45	12	2
8	5	15	11	3
$8\frac{1}{4}$		40	22	4

On the return journey Mr Findlater was offered scope for his recording talents. *St Rollox* picked up 12 loaded coal wagons weighing 66 tons at the east end of the line and set off for Glasgow with Findlater timing the train at quarter-mile intervals.

Mile	Minutes	Seconds	Speed (miles and furlongs per hr) Miles	Furlongs
¼	1	10	12	7
½	1	2	14	4
¾	1	0	15	0
1	1	47	8	8
1¼	1	50	8	1
1½	2	0	7	4
1¾	2	1	7	3
2	2	3	7	2
2¼	2	0	7	4
2½	1	45	8	4
2¾	1	50	8	1
3	1	30	10	0
3¼	1	16	11	7
3½	1	41	9	7
3¾	1	9	13	0
4	1	15	12	0
4¼	1	3	14	0
4½	1	13	12	2
4¾		45	20	0
5	1	10	12	7
5¼	1	33	9	5
5½	1	40	9	0
5¾	1	25	10	5
6	1	25	10	5
6¼	1	30	10	0
6½	1	45	8	4
6¾	1	10	12	7
7	1	30	10	0
7¼	1	30	10	0
7½	1	12	12	4
7¾	1	18	11	4
8	1	15	12	0
8¼	1	2	14	4

Over one quarter-mile stretch Findlater counted the piston strokes; he got 93 and calculated as follows: 4 ft 6 in. x 3.1416 x 93 = 1,315 ft. Since this result was near enough the 1,320 ft in a quarter mile Findlater deduced that the distance had been run without slipping.

On 17 July a more elaborate trial trip took place. It was a gala affair staged as one of the annual Glasgow Fair holiday festivities, and many distinguished ladies and gentlemen were present. The party included three doctors, which was just as well, for their services were to be required before the end of the day. Seven miles out from Townhead St Rollox encountered an obstruction on the line and overturned. Mr Thomson, the manager of the railway, who was riding on the engine, was thrown violently on to the embankment and had his jaw broken. The driver was badly bruised and an employee who was riding with his legs dangling over the front of an open carriage was severely crushed. The passengers escaped injury, except for one lady who took fright and jumped out of her carriage. The derailment was caused by a large stone deliberately placed on the line—apparently road transport's answer to the threat from the railway. Many of the pioneer lines were plagued with similar demonstrations. Both Garnkirk engines had been tampered with since their arrival, and on the day of the St Rollox derailment a waggoner driving towards Glasgow had been heard to say, 'Damn them, they have got their supper, and will not run again for these twa days'. The road hauliers' fear of rail competition must have been great for, if caught tampering with railway equipment, they risked long sentences of transportation. The Garnkirk offered the massive (for those days) reward of £100 for information that would lead to the arrest of the saboteurs.

In the first newspaper accounts of the railway's pre-opening activities the reporters fumbled for words to describe the new method of transport and its equipment. St Rollox was described as 'the Engine-carriage' or simply 'the Carriage carrying the Engine'. The Glasgow Chronicle on 27 September

26

1831, the day of the public opening, printed not a word about the railway, but the *Glasgow Courier* had a better sense of history. It told its readers that the event they were about to see was taking place for the first time in Scotland and only for the second time in Britain, and went on to advise its readers how best to view the pageant. Two trains were to start simultaneously from each end of the line at noon, and about half an hour later would pass in the cutting near Provan Mill. The *Courier* advised its readers to go to the bridge over the railway there to watch the trains approaching from opposite directions. The day was wet to begin with, but the rain did not prevent carriages with ladies and gentlemen and artisans and their families on foot from converging on the line from an early hour. The best vantage points were taken up before dawn, and by mid-morning the press of carriages had produced a traffic jam on the road to Provan Mill. The station at Townhead was packed with people who had come to see the wondrous machines they had been told were on view at the north end of the town. By noon the distinguished guests had assembled. When Bailie Fleming arrived he found *St Rollox* standing at the head of a train made up of four open trucks, with the two barouches *Royal William* and *Royal Adelaide* and the velocipede *Novelty* coupled on at the rear. A band, crushed into the leading open truck, blared out a march. The sun had come out and Townhead station presented a merry, colourful scene. Each carriage was flying a flag of a distinctive colour, and Fleming took his place with the Lord Provost and fellow-magistrates in that displaying the green flag.

It was 12.30 before everyone was seated and the signal was given to start. *St Rollox,* a large green banner with her name embroidered on it in gold fluttering from a flagstaff erected on the tender, eased the train away from the crowded depot to the accompaniment of cheering. Past Tennant's works she went, over Inchbelly crossing and out on to the long Germiston embankment, the coloured silk flags flapping in the breeze. *St Rollox* was greeted all along the line with cries of wonder and approval. 'It darted in many parts,' said an eye-witness, 'with twice the rapidity of the mail coach, and seemed evidently capable of acquiring any additional speed that might have been necessary or safe.' The public were pleased, but horses, we were told, ran away from the railway and hid themselves 'from being witness of a power which rendered the service of their species useless'.

The crowd was thickest at Provan Mill. At the approach of the trains the people 'set up a cheer that rent the air for miles and which along with the rumbling noise of the waggons, had the effect of nearly unhorsing some equestrians'. Then came the exciting moment when the westbound and eastbound trains met and passed. Contemporary accounts are conflicting about who drove what that day. One account says that *St Rollox* was driven by George Stephenson, another that he drove his namesake engine on the Glasgow-bound train. At any rate Stephenson was there and for him this was the triumph of the Liverpool & Manchester all over again. The westbound train of 33 wagons loaded with the produce of the district—coal, iron, freestone, lime and grain—was intended by the company to show the assembled guests, many of them potential customers, what a railway could do. *St Rollox* took one hour and six minutes to reach the eastern terminus, and after the passengers had eaten at the company's expense the engine returned them to the Townhead in 43 minutes. All that afternoon the depot was thronged with people inspecting the engines at close quarters and seeking short trips. Late in the afternoon the engines were put away and railway officers and guests repaired to the Black Bull for the promised celebrations.

That was quite a night. Some 160 guests sat down to dinner. After 'the cloths had been removed' the company settled to a marathon evening of drinking, described glass by glass in the next issue of the *Glasgow Courier*. For three hours every conceivable person and institution connected with the railway, however remotely, was toasted. The guests were invited to 'drain a bumper' to Charles Tennant. They were exhorted to 'dedicate a bumper glass' to the directors of the Garnkirk & Glasgow. A toast to the Scientific Institutions of Glasgow was drunk 'amid deafening cheers' and that to James Watt 'in solemn silence'. The toast to Mrs Sprott, who had cut the first sod of the railway, was drunk 'most rapturously'. When Lawrence Hill, the clerk to the railway, came to reply to his toast late on in the evening his remarks were inaudible; which is not surprising. The chairman, maybe by then in his cups, asserted that the Liverpool & Manchester was inferior to the Garnkirk & Glasgow. The *Courier* report concluded, 'the company, which was of the most exhilarating description, did not separate until a late hour'.

Bailie Fleming wrote this inscription on the bottom margin of his letter of invitation to the day's festivities. 'Went to the East end of the Railway in one of the Carriages with the Lord Provost and other Magistrates, and returned to the Townhead all safe from accident. Dined with the Committee in the Black Bull Inn in the evening, a large party and all happy and pleased.' The Bailie's letter has survived, and can be seen in the Glasgow Room of the Mitchell Library. On the back is a fragment of the original seal showing the wheel impression. Fleming's green ticket is still attached to it.

The railway settled down to a bread and butter existence. There were modest administrative premises at Townhead and a shed and small workshops were built near the depot to house and service the locomotives. In anticipation of a steady rise in traffic the directors ordered two more engines. They did not go back to Newcastle for them, probably because of the cost of transporting them from Tyneside to Glasgow. Instead, they ordered the engines from small local firms of general and marine engineers who were trying their hands at locomotive building. The *Glasgow* was built by Johnston & McNab, and ran on the railway for the first time on 1 February 1832. The *Statistical Account* notes that the engine 'hauled a train of 56 loaded coal waggons eight and a quarter miles, a gross weight of about 145 tons, in one hour and seven minutes, thus carrying a load of twenty times her own weight. This was the first locomotive made in Scotland on the improved construction.' A few months later the *Garnkirk* followed from the Hill Street (Glasgow) workshops of Murdoch & Aitken.

The great railway rivalry that was to dominate Springburn life for generations had its roots in the earliest days of the locomotive. The Garnkirk & Glasgow competed directly with the Monkland Canal and the Monkland & Kirkintilloch Railway. From the beginning the M & K and the G & G were at loggerheads, till in time the former became a constituent of the North British Railway, and the latter were incorporated into the Caledonian. It was not until they heard that engines had been ordered for the opening of the Garnkirk & Glasgow that the directors of the M & K decided to exercise their powers to use locomotives. Accordingly they instructed George Dodds, the little-known engineer of the adjoining Ballochney Railway (another of the small Monklands coal railways) to design two engines capable of pulling 60 tons at 4 or 5 m.p.h. This he did, and bravely by-passing Newcastle the directors gave the first order ever placed for a locomotive in Glasgow to the untried firm of Murdoch & Aitken. It is easy to believe that the M & K management were influenced in their choice of designer and builder by the fact that George Stephenson was a known friend of the Garnkirk & Glasgow. Murdoch & Aitken began work on the first engine in February 1831 and delivered it on 10 May.

This was a remarkably good performance considering that locomotive work was entirely new to the builders. But they had trouble with the second engine, and it was not until 10 September that it was put in service. Both, however, were at work on the Monkland & Kirkintilloch before the official opening of the Garnkirk & Glasgow.

That the M & K directors were well satisfied with their purchases is evident from one of the company's annual reports. During an eighteen-month trial period when the two locomo-

tives handled all the traffic they 'proved themselves the most
efficient engines of their kind ever made in the kingdom,
being capable of taking 10 tons more on a level railway than
any engine yet made of the same size of cylinder with a pressure of fifty pounds to the square inch upon the boiler'. That,
no doubt, was window-dressing for the shareholders. The
Murdoch & Aitken engines were basically Killingworth engines with a few improvements. 'The locomotives,' continued
the report, 'never required a single horse to assist them, and
they were never off the road for one day except on two occasions when injured by the malice or carelessness of certain
waggoners of the road. On the other hand the engines procured from England by an adjoining railway company have
repeatedly been taken off the road on account of needing
repairs. Hundreds of people about Glasgow have frequently
seen this engine standing hard fast on the Garnkirk Railway
with a load which one horse could have taken away with ease.
It may be asked, where was the power of the other three and
twenty horses at the time? In the stable, it is presumed.' It is
doubtful if an account in a rival company's report is a reliable
indication of the Stephenson engine's performance. That it
gave trouble is true enough, and the Garnkirk soon got rid of
it at less than half its original cost.

As a commercial proposition the railway was only moder-
ately successful. Passenger traffic did not develop on the scale
that the proprietors had hoped for. Except on public holidays
when large numbers of Glaswegians rode on the railway for
the fun of it, the four trains each way a day seldom ran with
more than three carriages. So sparse was the passenger traffic
that the company did not consider it worth their while to
erect buildings at the intermediate stations. The Garnkirk
operated on a shoestring. Some of the carriages had built-up
sides and windows only on the side exposed to the prevailing
wind, the other being entirely open. In summer all the carriage sides were removed and stored. It is said that parts of
the line were ballasted with refuse by local collieries. They

must have had some fun from time to time when hot coal fell out of the locomotive ashpans. One can visualise the railway ablaze from end to end, especially since the sleepers were of red Scots pine! The company grew their own boundary fences in the form of quick-growing hedges.

Traffic was sufficient for the Garnkirk & Glasgow to add to their locomotive stock from time to time. In 1833 Murdoch & Aitken supplied *Gargill* which, at 13 tons, was much heavier than the earlier locomotives. In 1835 *Jenny* from Murdoch & Aitken and *Frew* from a small foundry at St Rollox were added. The early Garnkirk engines burned coke. However, with a view to exploiting the large deposits near the railway at Robroyston the company experimented with peat. Experiment showed that twice the amount of peat was required to produce the same volume of steam as a given quantity of coke; also the light fuel was sucked through the boiler tubes only partly consumed and tended to drop between the firebars. There is no evidence that the engines were specially adapted for burning peat. Later in railway history good results were obtained with peat-fired locomotives in Ireland and Sweden when the engines were fitted with broad, short grates and the firebars were set closer together.

In 1839, when Francis Whishaw visited the Garnkirk, the company were operating with six engines; *George Stephenson* and the five Glasgow engines. Of the passenger stock Whishaw wrote, 'These carriages are by far the most unsightly and uncomfortable we have met with on any passenger railway in the United Kingdom.' According to him the average time spent by trains at intermediate stations was .62 of a minute. Either there were very few passengers to be accommodated or station work on the Garnkirk was uncommonly efficient.

In 1822 James Cleland prepared his map of the northern environs of Glasgow. That map hangs today in Provands Lordship, Glasgow's oldest house, a ten-minute walk away from Inchbelly bridge. On it can be picked out many names that were to achieve significance in the railway age: Eastfield,

Cowlairs, Sighthill, Balornock. But there is no mention of Springburn. Indeed, you could sift through a whole library of Glasgow books without finding its name. History is written round people and events rather than round places and until the railway came only a handful of uninteresting people occupied the spot that was to become Springburn.

The Garnkirk workshops and the Tennant chemical factory marked the northern limit of industrial Glasgow in 1831. From the railway crossing the open road climbed up the slope to the north and disappeared over a wooded ridge. It was a pleasant, pastoral scene. Opposite the spot where the Caledonian Railway works were to rise stood an inn with the odd name of Lodge My Loons. Half a mile further on, a few cottages inhabited by weavers and quarrymen clustered round the bend of the road that was to become Springburn Cross. A path leading off to the left gave access to the mansion house of Cowlairs and to Springvale Farm. The district was one of lush meadows, wooded hills and running streams, and studding this rural landscape were the mansion houses and estates of the Glasgow merchants. All this placid beauty was soon to be swept away.

The main topic of conversation at the Garnkirk opening had been the prospect of extending the line to Edinburgh. 'A grand railway linking the cities and the seas' was one of the toasts at the celebration dinner. The men with the money bags who were present that day did not need much imagination to picture the traffic potential of a railway connecting the political and commercial capitals of Scotland. Much money and time were devoted to pushing rival inter-city schemes. There was a North Line and a South Line, both of which climbed over the high ground between the two cities. George Stephenson had an interest in the South Line, which was planned to gain access to Glasgow over the metals of the Garnkirk & Glasgow. In the end a different scheme, a Grainger & Miller plan that avoided the high ground, won the day. That was a fateful decision for Springburn. The Edinburgh & Glasgow Railway curved in a 46-mile parabola to the north of the high ground, taking in Linlithgow and Falkirk in its course and coming down into Glasgow from the north-east along valleys and contours already followed by the Forth & Clyde and Union Canals. At its western end the line passed between Cowlairs House and Springvale Farm and within a quarter mile of the cottages at the bend of the road.

By the late thirties the quiet Forth-Clyde valley was occupied from end to end by a raucous, itinerant army of railway navvies, Irish almost to a man, with English overseers. Some found lodgings in the Springburn cottages; most lived in hutted camps made available by the contractors.

The Edinburgh & Glasgow was conceived on a grand scale. The Romans would have built it if they had come to Scotland in the railway age (after all, they built their Antonine Wall on the same route). Grainger & Miller carried their line almost as level as the parallel canals. They tunnelled or sliced their way through hills and when they encountered depressions they filled them. They crossed the formidable valley of the Almond on an embankment 90 ft high containing half a million cu. yd. of earth leading to a viaduct of thirty-six arches containing 1,105,000 cu. ft of masonry. At Croy they cut 70 ft deep into the hard whinstone to let the railway pass through a hill on a level course, and they cut an even deeper and longer defile in the rock mass immediately to the north of Springburn. But on the level ground at Springburn, with easy access to the heart of Glasgow seemingly assured, the canal pitched its last battle against the railway—and won. This victory brought into being one of the most interesting civil engineering features on Britain's railways: Cowlairs Incline.

When the Edinburgh & Glasgow (in its paper stage) reached Springburn the line stood a mile and a half short of the city centre and 150 ft above it. Grainger & Miller, who aimed above all to preserve the easy gradients of their trunk line right to the terminus, planned to take it down a long, gradually-sloping embankment to a high-level station in the city. This plan envisaged railway arches crossing the Forth & Clyde Canal at Port Dundas, and, though the canal was to be doomed from the day the railway opened, the proprietors pleaded that a railway viaduct would restrict future canal development.

Such was their standing that their plea was upheld. To win a central terminal site the railway promoters would have to drop it down a terrifying gradient, varying from 1 in 41½ to 1 in 50, most of it in tunnel. There was pessimism among the shareholders, and the timid ones had visions of their trains roaring out of control down the slope and piling up in the streets of Glasgow. But a central terminal was essential, and a start was made on the construction of Cowlairs Incline. The canal proprietors had hung a millstone round the necks of the railway administration.

For four years the skippers of the canal boats making their leisurely cross-country passages saw the great railway taking shape. The Union Canal was forced to sell its own land to the railway proprietors so that they could bring the railway close to and on a line parallel with the canal. Quarrymen worked day and night hewing stone and there was plenty of work for the waggoners who carried the stone to the sites of the great railway viaducts, and for the stonemasons who dressed the rough blocks. The central belt of Scotland with its motley temporary population of 15,000 railway navvies was a hurly-burly of activity.

On a summer evening in 1841—it was Thursday 13 May—an open cart containing a partly-assembled scaffold passed northwards through Springburn. Walking alongside the cart, acting as guards, was a company of infantry, preluding an astonishing day in the social history of railway building. The scaffold was taken out to a point on the Edinburgh & Glasgow Railway a mile and a half beyond Bishopbriggs in readiness for the execution next day of two railway navvies.

In the previous December a foreman ganger on the railway, an Englishman by the name of John Green, sacked an Irish labourer named Doolan for insubordination, and ordered him to clear off railway property. Doolan lodged in a cottage at Auchinairn along with his brother Dennis, a man named Hickie and another Irishman, Patrick Redding.

That night the Irishmen plotted revenge on the English overseer. On the following day when they went to work Redding and Dennis Doolan had iron bars tucked up the sleeves of their jackets. They found Green superintending operations at a temporary wooden bridge over the railway cutting near Crosshill Farm.

Green was civil enough, for he remarked to the men that it looked like being a wet day. When he leaned over the parapet of the bridge to inspect some feature of the line below Doolan ran up behind him and felled him with a blow of his iron bar. As the Englishman collapsed both Irishmen rained blows on him and battered him into senselessness. Green was taken on a cart to the infirmary in Glasgow, but died long before they got him there.

Doolan and Redding were arrested and lodged in Glasgow jail that same night, and their subsequent trial for murder was one of the most celebrated in the annals of the Scottish courts. The men were found guilty.

It was then the practice for felons to be hanged in public in front of the court buildings in Glasgow. On this occasion the authorities and the railway directors were bent on giving the great mass of railway navvies a lesson and a warning. Doolan and Redding were ordered to be taken to the scene of their crime and there executed.

At eight o'clock on the morning of 14 May the convicted men were brought from the jail shackled by the feet to face a Glasgow determined on a gala day. Doolan and Redding were put on an open parcels cart with the rough coffins in which they would make the return journey and a priest of the Roman Catholic Church. This improvised tumbril was surrounded by a mass of excited citizens who were held in check by the largest assembly of soldiers seen in the town for many

EARLY DAYS

Top:

An advertisement for Murdoch, Aitken & Co., builders of the first Glasgow locomotive.

Bottom:

A large American-type 4—4—0 built in the middle 1850s at the old Hyde Park Works by Walter Neilson after his return from America

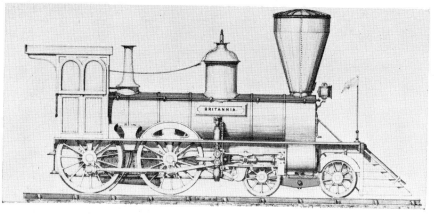

SPRINGBURN SCENES. Top: *Springburn Road about 1910.*
Bottom: *Springburn Road in 1963. Cowlairs Road branches off
to the left*

a day. When the procession was ready to move off on the six-mile march it was made up as follows:

Cavalry—a Body of 1st Dragoons
City Marshall
Cavalry
Sheriff Allison
Culprits
Strong Guard of Cavalry
Executioner
Magistrates of City.

All this for two railway navvies! The reason for the show of force was a rumour that the railway workers intended to rush the scaffold and rescue their compatriots. An organisation called the United Hibernian Labourers, to which most of the men belonged, was said to be arranging a mass demonstration to take place at the execution site, so a force of 1,200 infantry was dispatched in advance to patrol railway property near Crosshill Farm.

Vast crowds watched the pageant pass up the High Street of Glasgow into Castle Street, and saw it cross the Garnkirk & Glasgow Railway at Inchbelly and begin the climb to the village of Springburn. The condemned men were seen to be engaged in devotions with their priest and they paid no attention to their distinguished escort or to the spectators. By the time the procession had cleared Springburn thousands of people were trailing behind it. At Crosshill a mob of six thousand surrounded the scaffold so that the soldiers had to clear a path for the official party. But there was no sign of the railway navvies; to their credit they registered their protest by staying away.

Doolan and Redding mounted the wooden steps to the scaffold together. Before the hangman placed them on the drop and adjusted the ropes he turned them so that they looked directly down upon the bridge where they had committed their crime. They showed no emotion. But the spectators were wildly excited. The *Glasgow Argus* reported, 'The

39

c

people turned out in unexpected numbers to see a rare and novel spectacle, but with hearts as light as if it had been a mere holiday pageant. Even those who repaired to the place of execution, and saw the dreadful exit of the two culprits, had their feelings of horror speedily superceded by the thousand and one attractions which excited their attention on a country road crowded with every description of person and teaming with objects of amusement.' Of the actual execution a newspaper reporter wrote, 'On being thrown off Doolan struggled with dreadful violence, but Redding seemed to die instantaneously.' As the hangman himself remarked, 'The other rope came down kindly enough.'

It took 500 men working in continuous shifts two and a half years to create Cowlairs Incline. Almost 280,000 cu. yd. of rock were excavated to make the tunnel. When the Incline was finished an observer who stood on the flat ground at Cowlairs a hundred yards from the start of the slope saw the rails suddenly plunge over the edge and disappear. They dipped dramatically straight downwards on a gradient of 1 in $41\frac{1}{2}$, which eased to 1 in 44 and then to 1 in 50. The line burst out of the lower end of the tunnel on to the space that had been cleared for a station at the corner of West George Street and Dundas Place. It was unthinkable that such an incline could be worked by adhesion. Rope haulage was called for, and the directors gave the job of designing and erecting a winding engine to the firm of Kerr, Neilson & Co at Stobcross down by the Clyde. An imposing stone engine house with a 90 ft chimney was built at the top of the Incline, and by the winter of 1841 the Neilson twin-beam engine was installed. It had two 28 in. by 72 in. cylinders and steam at 50 p.s.i. was supplied by eight boilers. Power was transferred by a system of drums and pulleys to the endless hemp rope that ran over sheaves between the rails on the up and down lines. Descending trains were to be put in charge of specially-constructed brake wagons and these, attached to the rear of ascending trains, were also to provide brake power in the event of a

40

failure of the rope.

The railway directors took the vital step, for Springburn, of buying Springvale Farm and building workshops on its site at the top of the Incline. William Paton was appointed to take charge of this establishment. He might well have called it Springvale, but instead he chose to name the works after the mansion house of Cowlairs, whose policies adjoined railway property, and so a name was introduced that was to become famous in railway history. To Miller the engineer of the line fell the job of ordering locomotives for the opening of the line. He could have done worse than give the order to Kerr Neilson, who had just started to build locomotives, but he by-passed the Glasgow builders and ordered fourteen passenger engines, seven each from Bury and Hawthorn, and six goods engines, three from each of those makers. The Bury passenger engines were 2—2—0s and the Hawthorn engines 2—2—2s. The Bury goods were 0—4—0s and the Hawthorn 2—4—0s. Paton was thus assured of a range of motive power to meet a variety of passenger and freight requirements.

The Edinburgh & Glasgow had hoped to open their railway with a flourish of trumpets at the New Year 1842. However, a short stretch of line near Dullatur was not ready and the grand opening was postponed. But the citizens of Glasgow were not, after all, denied their holiday treat, for on New Year's Day 1842 the Edinburgh & Glasgow opened Cowlairs tunnel for public inspection. The populace was invited to a Grand Promenade there, and the response was staggering. All day hundreds of people queued up in Queen Street for the privilege of entering the great railway tunnel, and at the end of the day hundreds more were turned away disappointed. Those who were fortunate enough to get inside found themselves in an imposing white-washed cylinder, inclined upwards and lit throughout its length with 43 gas lamps fitted with the latest fan-tail burners and reflectors. The guides pointed out the device by which the lamps would be shielded from the draught of passing trains, and special mention was made of the new galvanic telegraph, the first in Scotland, that was used to convey messages from Queen Street to Cowlairs. Some of the visitors may have noticed here and there the curved metal plates fitted as an afterthought to the roof of the tunnel to deflect seeping water into the gutters.

SECOND GRAND PROMENADE.
PAISLEY RELIEF FUND.

PUBLIC EXHIBITION OF THE
GREAT RAILWAY TUNNEL AT THE HEAD OF
NORTH QUEEN STREET.

IN consequence of numerous Parties having been disappointed in Visiting the TUNNEL on SATURDAY, on account of the Shortness of the Notice given, the DIRECTORS have agreed to throw it Open for a
SECOND PROMENADE,
THIS DAY, (MONDAY).
The arrangements for permanently lighting it with Gas being completed, and the whole interior being whitewashed, the public will have an opportunity of examining this important Work under a Brilliant Light, with the Apparatus for the Electric Telegraph, the Station with its large Shed, Carriage Vaults, &c.
The proceeds of the Exhibition are to be applied, one-half to the Paisley Relief Fund, and the other half for the benefit of the Workmen, &c. injured on the Railway.
AN INSTRUMENTAL BAND WILL BE IN ATTENDANCE.
Hours of Admission from 11 Morning to 8 Evening.
Admittance—Ladies and Gentlemen. 1s.; Trades' People, 6d.; Children under 12 years of age, Half-price.
The Public will enter from North Queen Street, and depart by the Gate in Dundas Street.
Edinburgh and Glasgow Railway Office. ⎫
    North Queen Street,   ⎬
    Glasgow, 3d January, 1842. ⎭
N.B.—Policemen will be stationed to prevent the entrance of disorderly persons.

The Edinburgh & Glasgow's advertisement appeared in the *Glasgow Argus* alongside an announcement of the first publication in serial form of certain of the Waverley novels. This publishing venture was designed for 'Intelligent Correspondents among the Working Classes who have yet to form the acquaintance of Baron Bradwardine, Dominie Sampson, Edie Ochiltree, Rob Roy, Meg Merrilies and numberless other immortal creations of the Prince of Novelists'. The Glaswegians who read their *Argus* as they stood in the queue waiting to get into the tunnel that day hardly could have guessed that in time North British Scotts and London & North Eastern Directors bearing just those names would be passing up and down the tunnel.

The public opening of the railway was advertised to take place on Monday 21 February 1842, with a ceremonial private opening on Friday 18 February. The directors were public-relations minded, and made the most elaborate plans for introducing their enterprise to the citizens. The open, north end of the Glasgow terminus was blocked off with curtains of pink calico, and the other three walls were curtained and festooned with Grecian drapery. The rails were boarded over and on the flooring banqueting tables were placed. The Edinburgh & Glasgow were so pleased with their effort that they opened the improvised banqueting hall to the public on the Thursday evening. Once again the citizens of Glasgow flocked to North Queen Street. The festive tables, already set, glittered under thousands of gas jets. High on the south wall, above the platform reserved for the most distinguished guests, was the outline of a locomotive in perforated gas-pipes, and this pioneer of illuminated signs glowed with tiny pin-points of flame.

In their effort to impress the public at the opening ceremonies the directors severely handicapped their operating department. With the station given over entirely to social activities, Paton had to marshal his rolling stock in the small space between the station and the tunnel mouth, and in the tunnel itself. The ceremonial first train was due to leave for Edinburgh at 8-30 in the morning. So great was the confusion at the station in getting the invited guests placed in their carriages that the first section did not get away until 9-40. The whole train consisted of 30 first class carriages, each with three compartments seated for six passengers. The interior upholstery was of fawn cloth, and the windows were draped with crimson silk curtains. It took three lifts of ten carriages each to get the train to Cowlairs. There the three sections were combined and the 30-carriage train set off for Edinburgh with three engines at its head. It took 1 hr and 53 min. to reach Falkirk, where a fourth engine was attached, and the train eventually arrived in Edinburgh at 12-10. At the Edinburgh terminal a train loaded with local guests was waiting to depart for Glasgow. It left at 1 o'clock and was followed at 2 o'clock by the returning Glasgow train. This train was reported as arriving at Cowlairs at 4-30 with three engines in front and two in the rear. All the passengers from both trains took their places in the banqueting hall and the waiters advanced on the tables with, among other things, 120 tureens of various soups, 400 dishes of potatoes, 30 roast turkeys each stuffed with a bullock's tongue, 40 boiled rounds of beef 'richly glazed and ornamented', 60 dozen lobsters and 600 tartlets. Quite a party.

When the feasting was over all that remained was for the railway to transport the Edinburgh guests back to the capital. There was delay and confusion because of the restricted space available for the carriages, and it was late evening before the third section of the train was attached to the rope and had begun its ascent to Cowlairs. It had almost reached the north end of the tunnel when the rope broke. It was an awkward moment. However, the special brake wagons at the rear proved their worth; they held the train until engines came down from Cowlairs and lifted the train in two halves. Dividing the train on so steep a gradient must have been a tricky business. Glasgow, and particularly the railway company, never would have lived down the scandal if they had let ten vehicles of Edinburgh gentry run away to pile up in the abandoned banqueting hall. The directors were sufficiently perturbed about this first day's mishap to go into the tunnel themselves, taking Mr Miller of Grainger & Miller with them, to inspect the damage to the rope. A somewhat ambiguous statement was issued to the press suggesting that the rope had not broken, but had the appearance of having been cut

44

deliberately.

The day of celebrations ended with the carriages being coupled up and dispatched from Cowlairs. An eye-witness who saw the departure wrote, 'The whole of the carriages—seemingly about 30 in number—having their lamps lighted, the *tout ensemble* was very striking and, when the immense mass moved away, preceded by a pilot engine, with its deep red light, the effect was extremely beautiful.'

Chapter 2

SUPERINTENDENT OF LOCOMOTIVES

William Paton was not just a locomotive superintendent; he was the Superintendent of Locomotives. A guard on the Edinburgh & Glasgow was Guard of the Train and on the most important trains he was helped in his duties by an Assistant Guard of the Train. The company liked to dignify its servants. By the opening date Paton had received fourteen of the twenty engines ordered, seven from each maker, and the remaining six arrived within the next few weeks. The passenger service, initially four trains each way a day, was soon stepped up to eight. In the opening weeks the Edinburgh & Glasgow was purely a passenger railway.

Paton must have been hard put to find staff for his new works and competent crews for his locomotives. Engineers for Cowlairs would not be too difficult to come by, for Glasgow already had a tradition in engineering. But where did Paton find trained locomotive men? One wonders if he did some judicious poaching on Garnkirk and Monkland & Kirkintilloch preserves. Traffic staff would present less of a problem. There were stage coach men who understood passenger handling and who were willing enough to become railway guards, and mastery of the rudimentary signalling system was well within the scope of the Springburn quarrymen and weavers. A new community of railwaymen blossomed round Cowlairs works. Paton installed himself in a house at Springvale overlooking the works and the railway. Workers' cottages were built on either side of the track (soon to be called Cowlairs

Road) that had led to Springvale Farm, and round the winding engine house at the top of the Incline were built cottages to house the enginemen and splicers who were concerned with the transport of trains from Queen Street to Cowlairs.

Drivers on the Edinburgh & Glasgow were expected to observe strict footplate discipline. 'During the whole of the journey the Engineman shall keep *a sharp look-out forward* so as instantly to observe any obstruction which may be on the road or signal which may be made for his guidance,' said the rule book. 'He shall on no account sit down, or allow the Fireman to sit down on either the Engine or Tender. The Engineman shall not allow any person whatever to light tobacco at the Engine fire or lamps.' Except when he was firing, the fireman was required to stand on the footplate keeping a sharp look-out *backwards* and ready to act on any signal from the guard. The Engineman was forbidden without the order of the Superintendent of Locomotives or his assistant 'to have more pressure of steam than 55 pounds on the square inch, and that only when required; and on approaching the end of the journey he shall reduce the pressure to 40 pounds'.

A Guard of the Train had to report at Queen Street in time to assist in the dispatch of the train *before* his own. He was obliged also to assist in the manhandling of carriages out of the station carriage vaults. These were recesses in the west wall of the station at right angles to the tracks, where carriages were pigeon-holed and removed as required, turnplates being provided to help this manœuvre. The Guard of the Train had to meet cabs arriving at the station and escort passengers to their carriages, ensuring that they were safely seated. When the first train had been drawn off into the tunnel he prepared for the reception of his own passengers, assisted of course by the guard of the *next* train. Before departure he had to lock all off-side doors, and see that the luggage was properly stowed on the carriage roofs. The Guard of the Train and the Assistant Guard of the Train took up posts at opposite ends of the train, where they were required to sit facing each other throughout the journey. If there was trouble with a hot box the guard had the regulation 'small box of grease' in his pocket with which to anoint the offending member. The procedure for handling a drunken passenger was clearly set out in the rule book; the Guard was obliged not merely to put him off the train but 'off the line'. On arrival at Edinburgh the Guard of the Train had to await the arrival of the *following* train 'to open the doors and assist with the light luggage and to make themselves useful and obliging to passengers by getting Cabs for them and the like'.

The porters, too, were busy chaps. A porter had to report for duty at his station one hour before the first scheduled departure and his day did not finish until one hour after the last. From the beginning the Edinburgh & Glasgow resolved to discourage ticketless travel. Each station was so planned that the only lawful approach was through the booking office, and it was the porter's job to see that passengers entered by the approved route. If anyone attempted an unauthorised approach the porter had authority to detain him until such time as he could 'be taken before a Justice of the Peace'. On the approach of a train the porter was expected 'to have the roof ladder and luggage sliding board on the arrival and departure platform and ready for instant use'. He was specifically instructed to pay the *utmost attention to passengers,* and to see that they left the station via a prescribed exit gate and not through the booking office.

When he was not serving his employers in his capacity of porter and policeman, the porter had to act as signalman. The standard signal on the Edinburgh & Glasgow was a board, red on one side, green on the other, mounted on a post. The porter had to exhibit the red aspect for ten minutes after the departure of every train. There was also a white portable board which indicated to a driver that he had to proceed through a station without stopping. A 'bonnet held steadily outstretched' was acceptable in lieu of a white board. If a porter had a message for an engineman he was not permitted to stop the train to deliver it. He had to display a green board and wave a green flag up and down beside it, this being the signal for the driver to reduce 'to such a slow speed as will enable the Porter to run alongside the Engine and communicate the circumstances to the engineman'.

That the Edinburgh & Glasgow's faith in its signalling system was not absolute is seen in a curious instruction given to its earliest gangers. Foremen in charge of permanent way works were instructed to lift rails in lengths of not more than 20 ft. They were further instructed to raise the track so that both rails were raised equally and that the ascent created by the lifting would be against any approaching train. This procedure ensured that if a train got through the signals and surprised gangers at work it would have 20 ft of uphill gradient to help stop it!

Once its teething troubles were over the railway settled down to give a reliable service of eight trains a day operated on a regular-interval timetable. Departures from Glasgow and Edinburgh were at the same times throughout the day, fast up mail trains being balanced by corresponding down trains running to precisely the same timings in the reverse direction; mixed trains and stopping trains were similarly balanced. Journey times ranged from $1\frac{1}{2}$ hours by express to $2\frac{3}{4}$ hours by mixed train. Return fares from Glasgow to Edinburgh were 16s, 12s, 8s or 5s according to the accommodation occupied. There were ten intermediate stations: Bishopbriggs (called Bishop's Bridge in the early timetables), Kirkintilloch, Croy, Castlecary, Falkirk, Polmont, Linlithgow, Winchburgh, Ratho and Gogar. The Edinburgh & Glasgow promoters had expected 340,000 passengers to use their trains in the first full year. In the four and a half month period between the opening day and 30 June 1842, 205.268 passengers were carried. Passenger revenue was £27,285 6s 9d and the profit on operations £16,449 4s 2d, which justified the company in declaring a 5 per cent dividend within seven months of the line's inauguration.

The social implications of the opening of the railway were enormous. Hitherto the citizens of Edinburgh and Glasgow had seen little of each other, for it had been all but impossible for a return visit to be made in one day. All that was changed dramatically on 30 June 1842. John Leadbetter, who was the first chairman of the Edinburgh & Glasgow, was also the president of the Glasgow Mechanics' Institution, a body consisting mainly of the better type of Glasgow artisan. Leadbetter decided to take some 600 Institution members and their families on 'a whirl along the line of railway'. Tickets were provided at half price and the party set off on a 23-coach train. For the first time in history Glasgow working people descended *en masse* on genteel Edinburgh. At first the Edinburgh citizens were suspicious of the invasion. Some stared at the Glaswegians 'as if an hostile attack on the castle had been meditated; but then the men looked peaceful and the fear vanished. At length the information spread that it was a body of Glasgow citizens just imported per railway, and it forthwith became the settled opinion that a fast had been proclaimed in Boeotia.' Of the outing and its participants a contemporary newspaper (admittedly a Glasgow one) was able to report, 'Throughout the day the most perfect propriety was observed; their bearing in all the Institutions in Edinburgh laid open for their examination, was quiet and gentlemanly. In those respects the most fastidious modern Athenian could have found nothing to cavil at, and we may further mention to the honour of the whole party that when the time of returning to Glasgow by the evening train arrived not one individual showed the slightest symptoms of even having tasted spirits.' Later in the year the Edinburgh Mechanics visited Glasgow. Those pioneer excursions set a pattern that has survived until the present day. On public holidays Edinburgh and Glasgow traditionally exchange a substantial proportion of their populations, and many of the excursionists still travel by rail.

It is pleasing to picture a Bury 2—2—0 at the head of an Edinburgh & Glasgow express pounding down through Ratho and Gogar in the winter gloom with the driver peering intently ahead and the fireman peering just as intently backwards. From opposite ends of the train the guard and his assistant would look down on the carriages, the first class with the luggage strapped to the roofs, the open thirds, mere boxes with neither seats nor handrails, their standing occupants huddled together seeking what shelter they could find from the cinders and smoke that showered down on them from the Bury's tall stack. If the visibility was impaired the driver would be sounding his regulation whistle blast every half mile. The whistle on the old Burys was mounted on the top of the haycock firebox. It consisted of a pipe from the boiler which directed a jet of steam into an inverted metal cup, and it was the steam impinging on the rim of the cup that produced the warning note. It was said to be a most disagreeable sound. It must have been something to hear the shriek of a Bury as it approached Haymarket on a December night with its load of frozen, soaked humanity standing in the open carriages behind the tender.

First-hand accounts of travel in the early days of the Edinburgh & Glasgow are hard to come by, but one turned up in the pages of *The Scottish American,* a periodical circulating among Scots in the United States, in 1906. A Mr Barrowman, then living in Buffalo, New York, told of his experiences as a third class passenger. 'Lucky was the traveller,' he wrote, 'who got his back up against the front end or the back end to steady himself. There were no straps to hold on by. Middle men dunched against their neighbours. The only advantage I ever saw in them was it gave a lad a good excuse to support his lass.'

An interesting account of a mishap to a mixed train in the early days appeared in the *Glasgow Argus.* The train was made up of a cattle box next to the tender, a luggage wagon, and the usual open third class vehicles. The cattle box was aptly named. It was a box with its sides built up higher than those of the open thirds. On this occasion it carried not cattle, but a domestic removal including furniture and feather beds. As the train rattled on its journey the passengers in the open carriages became aware that the engine smoke that enveloped them as a matter of course was laced with something more acrid than coke fumes. The furniture in the cattle box was burning! Passengers all along the train shouted at the enginemen and waved their hats and umbrellas. The guard waved his flag. The enginemen took no notice. Fragments of burning bedding blew back along the train, and the passengers were mortified to see the fire spreading to their own luggage in the second vehicle. Not till Castlecary was the train stopped and the outbreak doused under a water column.

The newly built parish church of Springburn was opened on 3 July 1842, barely five months after the opening of the railway. No record now survives of the first sermon preached, but it is not unreasonable to suppose that the minister denounced the Edinburgh & Glasgow Railway and all its works. The Glasgow Presbytery had instructed all the ministers within its jurisdiction 'to discountenance the Company so far as may be in their power'. The directors of the Edinburgh & Glasgow brought a hail of fire and brimstone down on their heads when they announced that they hoped to run trains 'on the morning and evening of the Lord's Day'. A meeting of the Presbytery was summoned and after a fiery session a delegation of ministers waited on the general manager of the railway company. They protested that 'the Presbytery regard the carrying into effect of this resolution (to run Sunday trains) as a flagrant violation of the Law of God, as expressed in the Fourth Commandment, a grievous outrage on the religious feelings of the people of Scotland, a powerful temptation to the careless and indifferent to abandon the public ordinances of Grace, and most disastrous to the quiet of the rural parishes along the line of the railway, by the introduction into them every Sabbath, of many of the profligate and dissipated who inhabit the cities of Glasgow and Edinburgh'.

The controversy dominated the newspapers for weeks. At a

time when the Corn Laws debate was at its height the entire front pages of both Edinburgh and Glasgow papers were given over to news and opinion about Sunday rail travel. The directors expressed themselves cautiously. 'There ought to be a train in the morning and evening,' they said, 'but under such regulations as shall enable the servants of the Company, and all persons travelling by the railway, to attend Divine Service.' The E & G Rule Book *required* its employees to turn out for Sunday duty, but the relevant rule expressed a hope that the hours of duty would allow the employees to attend church. That was an age when men who worked on Sundays, however necessary their job, were looked down on by their fellow men, and there was uneasiness among the Springburn railwaymen over the prospect of Sunday duties. Nor were the directors themselves unanimous. There was in the board room 'the Sabbath party' led by the chairman, John Leadbetter, which flatly opposed Sunday trains in any form. But it was in the minority, and the board decided to advertise Sunday trains. Then a massive campaign was undertaken to discredit the railway. Meetings, in some cases attended by thousands, were held up and down the country. Prominent industrialists declared publicly that they would never send their goods by a railway that operated Sunday trains. Petitions were organised and signed and eventually 214,113 protesting signatures were lodged at the railway office.

The Sunday service began on 13 March 1842. Members of the press were at Queen Street to see the first train 'filled with peaceful and respectable persons, gliding quietly away on its mission'. Everything went so smoothly at the station that 'within a few minutes of the departure and arrival of the trains, the Servants of the Company were at perfect liberty; and so quick was their release, that they themselves were astonished at the short space of time required for their services'. The train was met at Edinburgh by a thundering divine who ranted at the detraining passengers, and reminded them that they had bought tickets to Hell. The great Sunday train controversy proved to be a damp squib. The tumult quickly died down and the Sunday trains continued their quiet existence; although for many years there were people who considered them not quite respectable. John Leadbetter resigned his chairmanship over the decision, being a man of principle. The same could not be said of Bailie Johnstone, who had led the anti-railway campaign in Edinburgh, and had urged all and sundry to boycott the railway. While he was thus engaged as a private citizen he was, as a business man, publishing the official guide to the Edinburgh & Glasgow Railway, a work dedicated to the directors. This was the guide by Willox which contained the celebrated description of Queen Street station. It is worth quoting again. 'The astonished traveller,' wrote Willox, 'finds himself transported into an almost fairy palace; this is the Passenger Shed at the Glasgow terminus. This spacious and splendid erection, which is elegant as well as commodious, is furnished with a beautiful passengers' parade on each side, covered in by a roof supported on forty-eight columns arranged in double rows, besides the principal roof between them, a light and elegant fabric of the great span of sixty-four feet.' Willox also described the view that confronted the passenger when his train emerged from Bishop-briggs cutting as being dominated by the chimney of the Cowlairs enginehouse. 'The engine-house being surmounted by a handsome chimney-stalk upwards of ninety feet in height has a fine effect on the brow of the steep bank.' Printed vertically in the margin of each page of descriptive matter was a figure giving the rise or fall of the line at the place being described. Thus the railway is shown climbing away from Edinburgh on a gradient of 1 in 5,280 and falling into Glasgow on a gradient of 1 in 42.

*   *   *

September 1842 found William Paton experimenting with an electric locomotive. Robert Davidson's experiments with electro-magnetism as a motive power were given their first public airing in a letter sent by Dr Forbes of King's College,

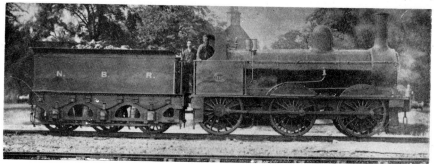

CONNER AND WHEATLEY. Top: *A Conner long-boilered mineral engine.* Middle: *Wheatley standard goods No. 127 in original condition at Lennoxtown.* Bottom: *A Conner eight-footer at West Walls, Carlisle, in 1869*

NORTH BRITISH PUGS. Two generations of Springburn men doing the same job. Top: *A Neilson pug at Queen Street in the 1880s with William Graham on the footplate.* Bottom: *Holmes's pug No. 9 at Queen Street about 1900*

Aberdeen, to Faraday on 7 October 1839. In this letter Forbes described how Davidson, a fellow Aberdonian, had used electricity to supply power to a small lathe and to a 'locomotive carriage'. The electric locomotive was capable of carrying two persons across a rough wooden floor. Davidson spent his private fortune on his electrical experiments and, helped by Dr Forbes, he tried to interest railway managements in his locomotive, without success until 1841 when Davidson held an exhibition of his inventions in Edinburgh which included, in addition to his lathe and locomotive, a saw-mill and a printing press, all electrically operated. The influential people who inspected the locomotive included representatives of the Royal Society of Arts and of the Edinburgh & Glasgow Railway, then nearing completion. Davidson was given money by both bodies, with which he built an enlarged version of his locomotive suitable for propulsion on rails. The finished machine was described in a contemporary journal as a 'large and massy carriage'. It was, in fact, a four-wheeled open truck 16 ft by 6 ft and weighing five tons. The vehicle was very low-set, the axles passing *over* the flooring. Three parallel iron bars were fastened to each axle, and eight magnets were fixed to the floor, two on each side of each axle and pointing inwards towards it. The application of current from batteries housed in boxes at each end of the vehicle produced rotary motion in the axles.

The Edinburgh & Glasgow directors were far-seeing in putting up money for the development of Davidson's locomotive. Most of them could remember when steam had been considered doubtful as a prime mover for locomotives, and there was no knowing what potentialities were held by this new source of motive power. A successful electric locomotive would have advantages. The public, especially those faced with the prospect of having a railway in their district for the first time, were afraid of the noise and dirt of the steam engine. The electric locomotive promised to be clean and noiseless. Moreover, six months of operation had shown the Edinburgh &

57

D

Glasgow that the Cowlairs Incline rope was not working satisfactorily. The climate of the West of Scotland was unkind to
the hemp and breakages, with their attendant delays, were
frequent. Might there not be a solution in Davidson's engine?

David Mackie, C.E., Lecturer in Mechanical Philosophy,
thought there might be a danger to the passengers from
hydrogen gas escaping from the batteries. However, he was of
the opinion that the hydrogen could be collected and made
available for producing light and heat. A proposed alternative
source of light was a piece of carbon inserted in the circuit
which when ignited would afford 'the most intensely brilliant
light imaginable'.

In tests carried out on the Edinburgh & Glasgow the electric
locomotive *moved,* but that was about all that could be
claimed for it. More batteries were added, and a top speed of
four miles an hour was achieved. Davidson had the right idea
but, like many of the early experimenters with electric traction, he lacked the means of supplying current in sufficient
quantity to enable the engine to do a useful job of work.

A month after the experiments with the electric locomotive
a new rope was delivered, made by Haggie of Gateside. It was

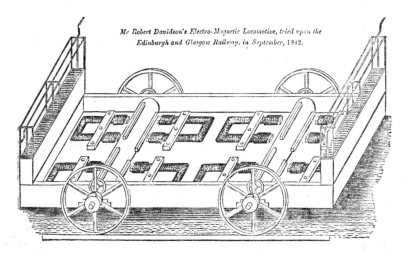

Mr Robert Davidson's Electro-Magnetic Locomotive, tried upon the
Edinburgh and Glasgow Railway, in September, 1842.

three miles long and weighed fifteen tons, five tons heavier than any rope previous made. To get it from Leith docks to Haymarket station it was laid in a longitudinal coil on a 'train' of six carts coupled together and hauled by nine horses. At the railhead it was transhipped to railway vehicles and duly delivered at Cowlairs. By the middle of 1843 it was clear, however, that the efficient working of Cowlairs Incline by means of a hemp rope was virtually impossible, for breakages and wastage led to heavy expenditure and made a mockery of the timetable. Paton decided to try locomotive haulage. This time the Superintendent of Locomotives did not go shopping, perhaps because the private manufacturers had nothing to offer that suited him. Paton needed a special engine, one that was powerful and *safe,* one that would dispel the prejudice then prevailing against relying on adhesion alone on steep inclines. Paton knew that he would have to design such an engine himself; it was the first Cowlairs-built locomotive.

Paton's engine appeared from Cowlairs Works in January 1844. Paton named it *Hercules.* If there was at that time a more powerful engine anywhere in the world there is no record of it. It was a six-coupled tank with 4 ft $3\frac{1}{2}$ in. wheels and it weighed $26\frac{1}{2}$ tons.

Special attention was given to brakes. The centre pair of wheels had a handbrake operated by a screw arrangement from the footplate. The after pair were mechanically braked —an innovation far in advance of the times. The brake was similar to that devised by Peter Robertson and demonstrated on the Glasgow & Ayr Railway in the previous year. The upper segment of the wheel was covered by a semi-circular metal band hinged at one end and fixed at the other, the application of steam pressing the metal band on the tyre. The rails in the tunnel were more often than not wet and greasy; Paton therefore equipped *Hercules* with two hot water jets in front of the wheels and two cold water jets behind them to wash the rail surfaces. The cold water jet was directed by air from a small air vessel. As a further safeguard sandboxes under the control of the fireman were provided on either side of the smokebox. Coke was carried in a small box on the foot-plate and a 200 gallon water tank contained enough water for two return trips.

Hercules did everything that its designer hoped. The cost of working the Incline by adhesion fell to one-third the cost of rope haulage. *Hercules,* according to one account, could take a 12-coach train weighing 54 tons up the Incline at 15 miles an hour. Paton was so pleased with his handiwork that he built *Sampson,* identical with *Hercules* except that the cylin-der diameter was increased by one inch to $16\frac{1}{2}$ inches. It appeared in October 1844, and during the following month did 435 'lifts', in the course of which it took 28,775 tons of passengers and freight traffic up the Incline. The rope equip-ment was dismantled and Neilson's engine was prematurely (but not, as we shall see, permanently) retired.

Monday 19 May 1845 was a day of travail for the Edinburgh & Glasgow, but one significant for the historian, for its events illuminate the operation and management of locomotives of the period.

There was a prelude in the afternoon when the engine of the 1.30 from Glasgow, after losing time consistently through-out the journey, failed completely at Gogar. There the train waited until the arrival of the 3 p.m. from Glasgow, when the two trains were combined and taken forward to Edinburgh by the engine of the latter. During the wait at Gogar a pompous and impatient passenger in the 1.30 entered the station office and asked for the complaints book. When he was told there was none, he asked for a sheet of writing paper. There was no writing paper either, but on being handed a time sheet printed only on one side, he wrote on the back an epistle to the management demanding an explanation of the delay.

About the time the 3 p.m. was getting into Edinburgh the Bury *Napier* was limping into Cowlairs with a train of stone from the quarries at Bishopbriggs. Her driver had had a day of it. In truth she should not have been out at all, even on a stone train, for she had been scheduled for shopping on the previous Saturday. However, the railway had been so short of motive power on Monday that *Napier* had been pressed into service to work the Bishopbriggs and Kirkintilloch stone traffic. The boiler tubes had leaked all day, and it had taken the enginemen all their time to keep enough steam in her. The men were thankful to get her back to Cowlairs shed at the end of the shift. Now *Napier* could be put into the works.

Napier was no stranger to Cowlairs Works. New Year's Day that year had seen her in the shops, and she did not emerge until 2 February. During that time 10 workmen had spent a total of 18 days 4 hours on her. In spite of this attention *Napier* featured all too often in the complaints book at Cowlairs shed in the first two weeks of February, the complaint invariably being 'leaking tubes'. She was again put into the shops on 14 February and did not reappear until 1 April. On 9 April she was again reported with leaking tubes. On 16 May she was shopped yet again and three hours' work were booked against her. When on 17 May her performance was no better Paton decided to withdraw her from traffic, and now on the 19th she stood at Cowlairs, her active life ended for the time being; or so it seemed.

About 5.30 that evening one of the big engines came up the Incline from Queen Street with a one-coach special for Edinburgh. What had happened was this. Thomas Cooley, a wine merchant, arrived at Queen Street about 5.15 expecting to board the 5 p.m. express for Edinburgh. Not surprisingly, it had departed. Cooley was booked to travel from Edinburgh to Newcastle on the 8 p.m. *Quicksilver* coach, and the next regular train would not make the connection. He offered the stationmaster at Queen Street one pound if he would send him on an engine to overtake the 5 p.m. When he was told that this was impossible he offered £50 for a special train. The manager of the E & G, when consulted, pointed out to Mr Cooley that the fee for a special train was £10, but the railway were content to accept £5 since they were confident that the special would overtake the 5 p.m. at Falkirk. Consequently, Cooley was installed in a first class carriage, a porter was delegated to act as guard as far as Cowlairs and the carriage set off propelled (according to a contemporary report) either by *Hercules* or *Sampson*.

The arrival of Mr Cooley at Cowlairs set a problem for Mr Cooper, Assistant Superintendent of Locomotives. There were only two engines in steam. William Chicken was preparing *Archimedes* to take out the 7.30. The other engine was *Napier*; Cooper had no alternative but to order *Napier* out with the special. The driver who had been with her all day flatly refused to go, but the regular fireman, Henderson, agreed to fire on the trip, and was joined by Richard McNab as driver. In giving McNab his instructions Cooper told him, 'You have to catch up with the 5 o'clock at Falkirk or Linlithgow,' to which McNab replied, giving *Napier* a wry look, 'Aye, that will be when it is on the road back.' The E & G rules required that a driver should see that his engine was provided with the regulation lamps and that they were lit if the journey was likely to extend into the hours of dusk or darkness. The special left Cowlairs a few minutes before 6 o'clock on that summer evening, and it never occurred to McNab that the trip to Edinburgh would not be completed before dusk. *Napier* in fact carried one lamp on the tender. It was of the bulls-eye type, red on one side, white on the other, and could be used either as a headlamp or a tail-lamp. There was no tail-lamp on the passenger coach nor was a guard provided beyond Cowlairs.

For the first mile or two *Napier* behaved tolerably well, but by the time she got to Kirkintilloch the tubes were leaking badly, the coke fire was low and the engine was moving at walking pace. Later on Henderson was to tell the court how, throughout the trip, he had heard the water 'bizzing' in the fire. Nevertheless *Napier* got as far as Falkirk, where McNab and Henderson worked hard to improve the fire. They were watched in their efforts by a porter and by Mr Cooley himself who remarked, referring to *Napier,* 'She is like a spring well.' The train made fitful progress beyond Falkirk. Mr Cooley, peering from behind his pink curtains at the overcast sky and the slowly-passing landscape, knew there was no hope of catching the *Quicksilver,* let alone the 5 p.m. At Winchburgh there was another prolonged stop for steam raising. Cooley went forward and told the enginemen he would make the Edinburgh & Glasgow pay dearly for the delay, but he assured McNab and Henderson that he would commend them for their efforts to keep *Napier* going.

Napier continued her slow cross-country progress with speed at times down to 2 m.p.h. At last, just short of Ratho, came the ultimate indignity. The engine failed completely and McNab and Henderson got down and *pushed* her along the track. According to the driver's subsequent testimony in court they pushed her and her vehicle 'for a good bit'. By a combination of manual and steam power *Napier* arrived at Ratho. There McNab obtained a supply of coal which he knew from experience gave better results than coke when tubes were leaking. The coal did the trick. For the next mile or two the engine steamed reasonably well and some progress was made. On the Edinburgh side of Gogar she failed again and the enginemen had to resort to a further stint of pushing. They had just got the engine restarted when McNab, looking back, saw the 7.30 from Queen Street passing Gogar bridge about a mile behind them. 'Take a lamp and warn Chicken,' he called to Henderson. But there was no hand-lamp on the engine, and no time to light the bulls-eye lamp on the tender. The fireman grabbed a red flag and ran back along the track towards the approaching passenger train.

It was about 9.15 when Driver William Chicken passed through Gogar with *Archimedes* at the head of the 7.30. The porter at Ratho had told him that the special was 15 minutes ahead of him, and he was running at reduced speed and keeping a sharp look-out for the special's tail-lamp in the gathering dusk. It was not until the last moment that he saw Henderson standing at the side of the line waving a red flag. Chicken reversed his engine and whistled for brakes. But before these measures could take effect *Archimedes* crashed into the rear of the special and the two engines ran on for 40 or 50 yards with the crushed and splintered carriage sandwiched between them.

When McNab saw the wreckage his first remark was 'Oh! the man.' There was no trace of Cooley. He had fallen on to the track when the coach disintegrated around him, and the engine and coaches of the 7.30 had run over him. Henderson found him lying between the rails near the spot where he had exhibited the red flag. All the severely injured man said was, 'Good Lord!' That was his last protest against the iniquities of the Edinburgh & Glasgow, for he died before help could be got. When Henderson got back to *Napier* he found McNab removing the unlit lamp from the tender. 'This lamp will damn us both,' he said, whereupon he climbed over the stone boundary wall and threw it into a shallow pool. There was no nonsense in those days about removing an engine from traffic after it had been involved in an accident. *Napier* limped into Edinburgh and, after receiving some attention, worked the early morning parcels train back to Glasgow.

The Edinburgh & Glasgow got an extremely bad press over the Cooley affair. The *Glasgow Argus* called it 'the most shameful case of the kind that has occurred since the establishment of railways. There has been gross and culpable negligence—so gross that it is extraordinary that the lives of the passengers in the ordinary train were not sacrificed as well as that of the sole occupant of the extraordinary one'. The year, it will be remembered, was 1845. The railway mania was at its peak, and railway matters dominated the newspapers. It was hard to find a page in an 1845 newspaper that did not exhibit a prospectus for a new railway or report an item of railway news. The account of and comments on Mr Cooley's death were widely read and they made considerable impact on the public. The E & G directors held an emergency meeting on the day after the accident, but no statement was issued. The absence of an official announcement angered the *Argus*, which was campaigning for the establishment of coroners' courts in Scotland so that accidents could be investigated in public and the blame, if any, apportioned. As the weeks passed in silence the *Argus* returned again and again to the attack. 'Mr Cooley,' said a leader, 'placed himself in the hands of the Railway Company to be conveyed to a particular destination, under circumstances which might be supposed to have seemed to him a more than ordinary amount of protection, and his life was sacrificed either through gross mismanagement or most unaccountable carelessness.' But neither the accident nor the adverse publicity kept passengers away from the trains. During the week of the Glasgow Fair in July, Queen Street station set up a record by dispatching 13,901 passengers, 4,659 being handled on the Fair Saturday—a prodigious number considering the modest facilities available.

On 16 July two of the company's servants were indicted to stand trial at the High Court of Judiciary on a charge of culpable homicide—the Scottish equivalent of manslaughter. They were Richard McNab, the driver of *Napier,* and William Paton, Superintendent of Locomotives. The trial occupied two days, 3 and 4 November 1845. McNab was charged with having taken his engine out in an unfit condition, and with having failed to observe the company's rules regarding the provision of lamps. The charge against Paton was that he permitted an engine in an unfit condition to be used in traffic. The trial was an extremely serious matter for the accused; on conviction the likely penalty was a long spell of transportation.

Paton was questioned in detail about the condition of *Napier* in particular and the Edinburgh & Glasgow engines in general, and conceded that all his engines suffered from leaking boiler tubes from time to time. Persistent cross-examination brought out every detail of *Napier's* disreputable past. On the second day of the trial the court proceedings started at 9 a.m. and went on until 10 p.m. when the jury retired. It was nearly midnight when the jury returned, to announce a verdict of 'guilty, by a large majority'. One can picture the Superintendent of Locomotives and his driver, tired and anxious after their long ordeal, standing in the dock of the sombre, gas-lit court waiting for the sentence. But they were to be kept in suspense for several more days. The railwaymen were ordered to return to the court on 8 November to hear their sentences read. On the fateful morning, the Lord Justice Clerk began by delivering a 'high eulogium' on Paton's character. Nevertheless, he sentenced him to twelve months' imprisonment in Glasgow Jail, and for nine of those months McNab kept him company.

By present-day standards the men had a rough deal. McNab had erred over the matter of the lamps, and his shoddy attempt to get rid of the unlit lamp (it was recovered and produced in court) did him no good with the jury. The poor man was so distraught that night trying to get movement of any kind out of *Napier,* that it is no wonder that the lamps did not enter his mind until too late.

As for Paton, he was doing his best to run a railway with engines that were not very good when they were new, and that were indifferently maintained by a largely inexperiencd staff. Anyway, the Edinburgh & Glasgow had to manage for the next year without the services of its first Superintendent of Locomotives.

We began this account of the happenings of 19 May 1845 with the passenger who wrote to the management on the back of a time sheet demanding to know why the 1.30 was late. The company replied that the delay to the train was caused by 'an accident to the machinery of the locomotive at Croy'. He wrote back to say that this explanation was unsatisfactory, and demanded to be given details of the failure. The E & G informed him that the breakdown was due to 'the loss of one of the valves and the risk of this was not forseen on a careful examination which was made previous to the engine starting from Glasgow'.

It is remarkable that, in their time of trouble, the management had the patience to reply to this pompous pest.

The Edinburgh & Glasgow prospered and the directors would have been contented men had it not been for the running costs of Cowlairs Incline. The big engines *Sampson* and *Hercules,* which had held so much promise at the start, proved to be a disappointment. They were *too* good, for civil had not kept pace with mechanical engineering. If broken ropes had been Paton's headache before, broken rails were his worry now. The 58 lb. rails with the sleepers at three-foot centres crumbled under the assault of the mammoths. It was said too that the daily hammering of their exhausts on the tunnel roof damaged the fabric and water seeped in from the canal overhead.

There was nothing for it but to revert to rope haulage. Neilson's beam engine at the top of the Incline was renovated, its 28 in. cylinders being replaced by those of 36 in. The enginemen, splicers and brakemen were recalled to their jobs and the engine began winding trains up the Incline on 4 March 1847. It was to go on winding for 62 years.

The Incline now used one of Robert Stirling Newall's patent untwisted wire ropes. Newall was born in Dundee in 1812 and patented his wire rope in 1840. The publicity which followed its appearance on Cowlairs Incline resulted in more than one engineer claiming to be the wire rope's true inventor. Newall's main challenger was Andrew Smith, a civil engineer of Dumfries, who claimed to have experimented with wire ropes as far back as 1828 and to have taken out a patent for one in 1835. Smith and Newall engaged in a series of lawsuits over the matter.

The Rope was to become as much a part of Glasgow as Sauchiehall Street or the Tolbooth Steeple. Regular travellers from Queen Street spoke of it almost with affection. It was a delight to generations of railway enthusiasts and small boys. People got to know its habits.

Latecomers who arrived at Queen Street to see their train

pulling out of the platform were not dismayed; they knew it would stop again for the attachment of the Rope. Intending passengers in the refreshment room did not gulp their drinks when they heard the departure bell; they were well aware that the train would be waiting for them at the tunnel mouth.

All trains leaving Queen Street stopped at the entrance to the tunnel, where the foreman in charge of the Rope attached the 'messenger', consisting of a short chain attached to an equally short hemp rope. The rope end of the messenger was secured to the cable and a link of the chain was passed under the engine's drawhook, which was inverted. The engine then set back a few feet to take up the slack of the messenger and prevent the chain from slipping off the drawhook. A signal was sent to Cowlairs and if the road was clear the winding engine was started and the train began the ascent. When the engine reached the top the driver put on steam so that the engine ran slightly faster than the cable. The messenger rope slackened and fell off the inverted drawhook on to a boarded four-foot way. The locomotive, freed of the cable, continued on its journey and the engineman stopped the winding engine.

Trains did not go down on the cable. Incoming trains stopped at Cowlairs where the locomotive was replaced by two or more of the special Incline brakes. These were robustly-built four-wheeled trucks weighing fourteen tons, each wheel having two brake blocks. No down train, whatever its weight, was allowed to leave Cowlairs without at least two brakes with a brakeman in charge of each. When a train was ready to descend it was given a push to the edge of the Incline, either by the train engine which meantime had run round, or by the station pilot, and the journey down to Queen Street was then completed by gravity. The brakes came up the Incline again on the rear of the train. As soon as the locomotive was free of the cable the head brakeman uncoupled his vehicle and allowed it to freewheel into Cowlairs station. His mate mean-while detached the messenger from the cable and placed it in the brake for delivery to Queen Street on their next descent.

The enginemen in the big engine house were a race apart. Neilson's great beam engine was a thing of beauty as well as of power. Passengers in the passing trains got a glimpse of a gleaming mass of metal behind a polished wooden balustrade, for everything was spit and polish. The engine house had a large window facing down the hill, and through it the engineman on duty watched the ascending trains. Long before the train appeared he knew just where it was. Fixed on the wall of the engine house was a large circular dial with a pointer which the engineman put to zero before he started his engine. The pointer began to rotate in a clockwise direction when the cable began to move and indicated on the dial the train's position on the Incline. The enginemen used to say that they could name the driver on the footplate of an ascending locomotive by the 'feel' of the winding engine. Some gave their engines more steam than others, and experienced enginemen could sense the subtle difference in the tension on the cable. An engineman's first sight of an ascending train was a plume of smoke rising above the horizon line 180 yards from the engine house where the rails dipped suddenly over the crest. Then the chimney appeared, followed by the smokebox, until eventually the engine came bounding past the engine house. The characteristic 'clunk' of the messenger chain hitting the wooden boarding between the rails was his signal to shut off the engine.

On one occasion the engineman was tardy in stopping the cable, with sad results. The train was the 9.10 a.m. from Queen Street to Perth and Beagrie, the engineman was not one of the regular engine house staff, and kept the engine running after the messenger had dropped. The chain went clanging and bumping along underneath the moving train, and eventually looped itself round a broken plank and tore away a section of the boarding, throwing it under the carriage wheels. The vehicles escaped derailment, but they lurched so violently on passing over the obstruction that four passengers received injuries that required hospital treatment. The Perth was not due to stop at Cowlairs, but Henderson the driver felt the jolt and stopped his train. Meanwhile, the two brakes had been detached from the rear and McNiven the head brakeman, not expecting the train to stop, was coasting briskly towards Cowlairs platform. The result was a sharp collision with the back of the train.

In spite of the hazards involved in working Cowlairs Incline it remained remarkably free from even minor accidents. Indeed, it was not until the days of the London & North Eastern Railway, powerful engines and continuous brakes that the Incline was to witness anything of disaster proportions. The enginemen and brakemen in the days of the Rope were alert to the dangers of their daily task. Rules were obeyed. If any descending train had more than 16 vehicles, regulations required three brakes to be attached, and more could be added at the discretion of the head brakeman. A peculiar rule was that any train that was preceded down the Incline by a fish train was limited to 20 vehicles. The top speed permitted on the descent was 12 m.p.h. and 8 minutes were allowed for the journey. Very occasionally an Incline man nodded—as did head brakeman James Jackson one day in the spring of 1899 when he took over the 11.30 ex-Waverley at Cowlairs. The train's 8 vehicles weighed 101 tons and Jackson used two brakes—more than adequate power. But he came down the Incline in six minutes instead of eight and rammed the buffers. Nobody was seriously hurt.

The Rope inspired mischief among small boys, and railwaymen dreaded the school holidays. A favourite ploy was to push barrel staves or lengths of wood between the spokes of the pulleys when the cable was stationary. When it started up it was fun to see the wood being crushed and splintered between the pulley and the cable. Once such an obstruction brought the Rope and the train it was hauling to a standstill. Another trick was to fill the wooden cases in which the pulleys were enclosed with ballast. When the winding engine was started the revolving pulley crushed the stones and scattered them far and wide. And there was fun to be had by dropping earth clods from the overbridges on to the heads of the completely exposed brakemen. Punishment was salutary. A local paper gave this description of the scene in St Rollox Police Court when eight schoolboys who were rash enough to allow themselves to be caught were ordered to be given eight strokes of the birch each. 'While the whipping sentences were intimated the youthful culprits cried and sobbed, some of them howling and begging for mercy, assuring the officer at the bar subsequently that if only they got away the offence would never again occur.'

Life on the Incline could be unpleasant for the brakeman. It was a sight to see a heavy train rolling down the slope with three brakes in front, a brakeman in each hanging on to his brake wheel and sparks flying from the grinding blocks. In winter the brakemen soared down the Incline enveloped in snow flurries only to be plunged, halfway down, into the hot sulphurous maw of the tunnel. It became a fashionable ploy for writers to ride with the brakemen. 'It is a somewhat dirty business descending,' wrote one such passenger, 'or about as bad as going down a deep colliery.' It was a far cry from the Grand Promenade of 1842. Still pursuing the coal mine analogy the writer remarked that if the brakeman lost control on the Incline the result would be 'somewhat equivalent to the overtaking of colliery cages'.

The cost of running Cowlairs Incline worried the management. In their first report the Edinburgh & Glasgow gave the cost of working the Incline separately and their successors continued the practice. During that first half year it was £545 13s 6d; by the last six months of 1886 it had risen to £2,438 7s 3d. A rope lasted from a year to 15 months and in that time it hauled some 28,000 trains. With each new one the pulleys over which it ran had to be replaced, for the rope could eat through their rims in its own lifetime.

The Incline was several times worked by adhesion both of

necessity and by design. In October 1899 the winding engine suffered the only major failure of its long career and for the three days and nights that Cowlairs worked to repair the damage all trains were locomotive hauled. Contemporary accounts speak of three engines being used on each train. Three years later trials took place, mainly during the night, with locomotive-hauled empty stock trains. It is known that the 11.30 from Queen Street to Edinburgh on 3 September 1903 set off from Queen Street double headed and without the assistance of the Rope. Why the railway company elected to conduct this experiment on a Saturday, and a Trades Holiday at that, remains a mystery. After some preliminary slipping on the notorious wet patch just inside the tunnel mouth the engines settled into a steady ascent, but the climb took five minutes longer than normal. It was about this time that the Glasgow papers published reports of a scheme to use electric locomotives, the current to be supplied from the recently abandoned tramway power station in Springburn. Matthew Holmes, the locomotive superintendent of the time, was cagey when he was interviewed. While admitting that 'the problem of bringing traffic up the Incline is one that has long engaged and is presently engaging the directors', he denied that there was a plan to use electric locomotives. The directors even at that late date were scared of adhesion. It was not until 31 October 1908 that the management got over its timidity, and the Rope was abandoned, a system of banking trains with powerful tanks being substituted. And almost at once there was a terrifying runaway. That is a tale for another chapter.*

Meanwhile, let us return to 1846 and pick up the thread of the Springburn story.

---

* In the first half of 1909 the operation of Cowlairs Incline cost the North British £554 10s 11d. The expenditure on the same item for the first half of 1908 had been £2,049 10s 3d.

ENGINES OF THE NINETIES. Top: *No. 602 at Lennoxtown on 11 March 1890 with the crew who had manned it a week earlier at the opening of the Forth Bridge.* Middle: *Drummond 4—4—0 on a Caledonian West Coast express.* Bottom: *No. 123 and Caledonian coaches at Ayr in 1958*

SPRINGBURN PERSONALITIES. Top left: *James Reid*. Top right: *Walter Neilson*. Bottom left: *Dugald Drummond*. Bottom right: *J. F. McIntosh*

Chapter 3

A PATTERN EMERGES

By the middle of 1846 Springburn was firmly established as a railway centre, two railway communities being separated by half a mile of country road. One was the railway settlement, now 15 years old, round the Garnkirk terminus. The Garnkirk had extended eastwards to Coatbridge, and had changed its name to the Glasgow Garnkirk & Coatbridge Railway, but it was still very much a local line whose main business was the transport of minerals. The Edinburgh & Glasgow was the great railway of the day, and it was round the Cowlairs establishment that urban Springburn evolved.

In that same year the fate of the Edinburgh & Glasgow, seemingly so important and impregnable, was sealed, and the Glasgow Garnkirk & Coatbridge surrendered control of its affairs to a grand new railway still being built, the Caledonian. A new name was heard in Springburn. It was in 1846, also over on the eastern side of Scotland, that another new line came into Edinburgh from the south: the North British. The events of 1846 were to have a profound effect on Springburn's future. The roaring, rumbustious railway age had reached the peak of its momentum. Hudson and his cohorts were striving to push great trunk lines up the East Coast into Scotland while a rival group of financiers were building the competitive West Coast route; out of this tumult Springburn, in the end, was to do rather well.

The Caledonian Railway was planned to run northwards from Carlisle for 84¾ miles to Garriongill in Lanarkshire to

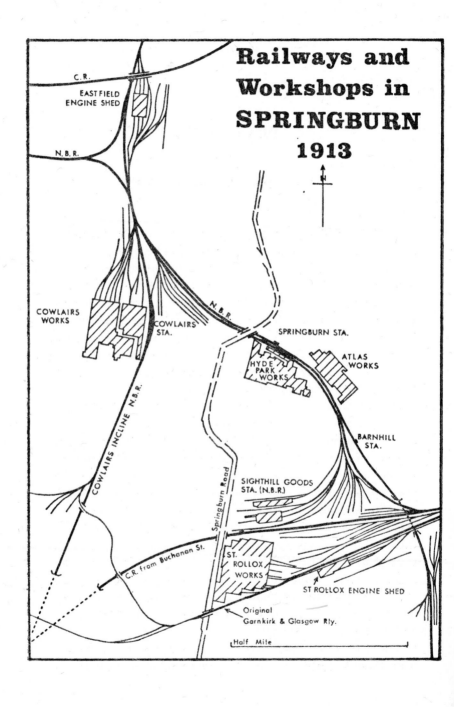

Railways and Workshops in **SPRINGBURN** 1913

C.R.

EAST FIELD ENGINE SHED

N.B.R.

COWLAIRS WORKS

COWLAIRS STA.

N.B.R.

SPRINGBURN STA.

HYDE PARK WORKS

ATLAS WORKS

COWLAIRS INCLINE N.B.R.

BARNHILL STA.

Springburn Road

SIGHTHILL GOODS STA. (N.B.R.)

C.R. from Buchanan St.

ST. ROLLOX WORKS

ST ROLLOX ENGINE SHED

Original Garnkirk & Glasgow Rly.

Half Mile

meet the complex system of small mineral railways in the
Monkland area. The promoters then proposed to buy their
way over $11\frac{1}{2}$ miles of three of these to reach Garnqueen on
the northern fringe of the Monklands, whence ten miles of
new Caledonian metals would take the line to Castlecary to
bisect but not join the Edinburgh & Glasgow. From Castlecary a series of four end-on-end railways took the West Coast
route right on to Aberdeen. Ostensibly independent, these
railways were engineered by Joseph Locke of the Caledonian
and financed largely by the same backers as the concern that
was already calling itself 'the National Line'. The finished
route was visualised as a great trunk railway running
diagonally through Scotland for $240\frac{3}{4}$ miles from Carlisle to
Aberdeen.

Railway	Starting Point	Mileage
Caledonian	Carlisle	$84\frac{3}{4}$
Wishaw & Coltness	Garriongill	9
Glasgow Garnkirk		
& Coatbridge	Whifflet	$1\frac{3}{4}$
Monkland & Kirkintilloch	Gartsherrie	$\frac{3}{4}$
Caledonian	Garnqueen	10
Scottish Central	Castlecary	45
Scottish Midland	Perth	$32\frac{1}{2}$
Arbroath & Forfar	Forfar	7
Aberdeen Railway	Guthrie	50

From the main line at Carstairs a $27\frac{3}{4}$-mile branch was to
strike off to Edinburgh. Access to Glasgow was over the Glasgow Garnkirk & Coatbridge to the ready-made 1831 terminus
at Townhead. For the privilege of gaining control of their line
the Caledonian guaranteed the Garnkirk shareholders a dividend of five per cent.

The Edinburgh & Glasgow board room viewed the coming
of the Caledonian with apprehension, and made plans to meet
and if possible thwart the brash newcomer. First they tried to
get control of the strategic Monkland group of railways,
especially the Wishaw & Coltness, but the Caledonian offered

the Wishaw & Coltness shareholders an extravagant 10 per cent dividend, as against the 5 per cent they were then being paid, and the Edinburgh & Glasgow could not compete. Next the Edinburgh & Glasgow concentrated their attack on Castlecary. This little village suddenly assumed great significance in the Scottish railway scene. The E & G's main line passed through it from east to west, the Caledonian came up to it from the south, and the Scottish Central went off to the north. The Edinburgh & Glasgow directors flirted with the Scottish Central and when the little railway agreed to the E & G building a spur at Castlecary linking the two systems, the E & G directors saw themselves getting a foothold in the route to the north. The Scottish Central was the key, and whoever held it could send traffic through to Aberdeen. Again the E & G were beaten by Caledonian money. The Caledonian (along with its partner the London & North Western) offered the Scottish Central 7 per cent and the Scottish Central said *yes*. West Coast control all the way from London to Aberdeen was assured.

In spite of its prodigality with money the Caledonian lost the race to be first into Glasgow with London passengers to the Edinburgh & Glasgow. Fifteen minutes after midnight on 1 July 1847 a handful of travellers who had left London at 9.25 the previous morning stepped on to the platform at Queen Street. For the first time in history the journey from London to Glasgow had been made in one day. Four separate trains had carried the pioneer travellers. From London the first and longest lap had taken them to Gateshead. Then they had spent half an hour crossing the unbridged Tyne to join a train on the newly-opened Newcastle & Berwick Railway. They had reached Tweedmouth and their first sight of Scotland by 8.25 in the evening, where forty minutes were allowed them to cross the Tweed. At Berwick they had taken their seats in the North British train to Edinburgh and the link with the Edinburgh & Glasgow Railway. Not until 10 September 1847 did the first West Coast rail passengers arrive in

Glasgow, the last 55 miles from Beattock being accomplished by stage coach. The Caledonian was opened throughout from Carlisle to Glasgow and Edinburgh on 15 February 1848. The Scottish Central was opened on 22 May 1848 and on 2 August the Scottish Midland ran its first public train. Five days later, on 7 August 1848, the missing link, the Caledonian section between Garnqueen and Castlecary, was opened, thus completing the longest continuous stretch of railway in Britain— $509\frac{1}{4}$ miles from Euston to Dubton. The remaining $38\frac{1}{2}$ miles of the Aberdeen Railway from Dubton to Aberdeen were ready by 1 April 1850. Thus came into being the great route over which generations of Springburn engines were to try their paces.

The old terminus of the Garnkirk in Glebe Street was a cramped and inadequate place for a concern as grand as the Caledonian Railway, and was too far from the city centre for the convenience of passengers. The Caledonian therefore built a new line branching off from the original Garnkirk line near Provanmill bridge and coming in towards Springburn on a falling gradient. This passed under Springburn Road some two furlongs north of Inchbelly crossing, then dropped in a cutting towards the city. To get into it the railway had to pierce the same hill through which the canal owners had forced the Edinburgh & Glasgow to take their line. There was no canal opposition this time. The Caledonian threaded their line between the canal above and the Cowlairs tunnel beneath to emerge into 'a temporary wooden shed' which was Buchanan Street station. (The shed remained until 1933!) Buchanan Street was opened on 12 August 1849 and remained the Glasgow terminus of trains from the south for many years.

With the advent of the Caledonian and the North British the Edinburgh & Glasgow became a relatively minor railway, though still important, as any line connecting the two main cities of Scotland must be. The North British and the Caledonian glowered at each other from their respective strongholds in the east and west; the North British determined to reach Glasgow, and the Caledonian just as determined that they should not.

The Edinburgh & Glasgow, with their fine inter-city route, had not anticipated a serious challenge for inter-city traffic from the Caledonian. They were wrong. By running trains from Glasgow down to Carstairs and then back up to Edinburgh the Caledonian had a route of sorts, though a poor one. Not only was it longer by 10 miles than the E & G, but it was steeply graded in places. Nevertheless the Caledonian struck again with the money weapon. The E & G were still charging their original fares of 8s, 6s and 4s single, for first, second and third class respectively, when the Caledonian advertised corresponding fares of 6s, 4s and 3s. The E & G retaliated by reducing their fares to the same level. Successive reductions brought the single fare by either route down to the ridiculous and ruinous sum of 6d. When the fare war proved indecisive the rivals used speed as a bait to attract passengers, and for the first time the Edinburgh & Glasgow ran non-stop trains between the two cities. Light, fast trains became the order of the day on both systems, and on the locomotive superintendents fell the task of providing motive power to operate these wasteful services. By 1848 William Paton had doubled the original stud of locomotives with which the Edinburgh & Glasgow had begun operations. Except for the two Incline engines, all were obtained from outside builders, but in 1848 Paton built at Cowlairs *Orion* and *Sirius,* express passenger engines with 6 ft driving wheels and 15 in. by 20 in. cylinders. These engines, and six rather similar machines that had been built by Sharp in 1847, handled the principal expresses.

At the beginning of the fifties there was a passing craze among railway managements for fast inter-city lightweight trains hauled by small, light engines. Paton therefore ordered a 2—2—2 well tank from the principal light engine specialist, George England. This was delivered in 1850. George England claimed many virtues for his Little England engines, his main boast being that they would consume no more than 10 lb. of coke per mile. He offered one to the Edinburgh & Glasgow for £1,200, the engine to be accepted and the purchase price paid only if tests on the line satisfied the directors. If not, England undertook to remove his engine and reimburse the railway company for the expenses incurred in the tests.

On its arrival at Cowlairs, Paton arranged to run the England engine in comparative trials against his newest and most powerful engine, his own *Sirius*. First reports of the trials gave a glowing account of the light engine's performance. With a seven-coach train it did the round 95-mile trip from Glasgow to Edinburgh and back on 8.3 lb. of coke per mile, and with the load reduced to five and four coaches the coke consumption fell to 7.4 and 6.5 lb. per mile respectively. A speed of 60 m.p.h. was said to be commonplace, and during the great gales of January 1851 the engine was the only one on the line that ran to time. Indeed, it was so often before time that the driver was told to ease the speed to avoid possible accident. During a test on the Campsie branch the engine took a loaded eight-coach train up a three-mile bank to such a tune that the banker detailed to assist in the rear was left behind. With results so spectacular it is remarkable that Paton did not scrap his existing Cowlairs stud and flood the railway with George England products. It seems more than likely that the claims made for the engine were based more on advertising matter put out by the manufacturers than on the results of carefully observed tests. The wonder engine performed no better, if as well, as its shed mates. Good, solid old *Sirius* continued to give excellent service on the E & G and outlasted its flighty rival.

The workshops of the Caledonian Railway were in Greenock and William Paton's Caledonian counterpart was Robert Sinclair, a refined young Englishman, a Charterhouse boy, a fine engineer who yet seemed out of place in the busy world of railway engineering. He had the task of providing engines for the National Line, engines that would do battle with their Cowlairs rivals. Sinclair was no stranger to Greenock. He had served his engineering apprenticeship in the shipyard of Scott, Sinclair & Co., the Sinclair of this concern being his uncle. Then he picked up railway experience on the Liverpool & Manchester, at Crewe and in France, and in 1844, when still only 28, he came back to Greenock as general manager of the new Glasgow Paisley & Greenock Railway, with special responsibility for the locomotive department. Sinclair had superintended the production of 15 locomotives and three more were in course of construction when in 1846 the GP & G fell into the Caledonian sphere of influence. Sinclair was appointed locomotive superintendent of the Caledonian, and his three new engines were numbered Caledonian Nos. 1, 2 and 3. They were based on Alexander Allan's Crewe design, 2—2—2s with $14\frac{1}{2}$ in. cylinders and 6 ft wheels.

Shortly after his own appointment Sinclair engaged as his foreman at Greenock young Joseph Goodfellow, and on the day that No. 1 was steamed took his foreman out to lunch (this same Joseph Goodfellow was to serve six successive Caledonian locomotive superintendents; he lies buried in Springburn beside John Lambie, the last of his chiefs). Those were busy days for Sinclair and Goodfellow. Inside four years they built no fewer than 30 Allan-type engines in the small, cramped workshop at Greenock, and Sinclair ordered three more from his uncle's shipyard. Later Goodfellow was to tell how in those early Greenock days he met the chief draughtsman of Caird's engineering establishment, a young Ayrshireman from Kilmaurs, one James Reid, who was having his first taste of locomotives. Both Goodfellow and Reid were to gravitate to Springburn, Goodfellow as Caledonian works manager, Reid as the sole proprietor of the largest locomotive works in Europe.

Greenock was jubilant over the rise of a locomotive industry within its boundaries. It had come just at the right time, for the town had been dealt a crushing economic blow by the sudden collapse of its staple trade—shipbuilding in wood. In 1841 there were nine shipyards in Greenock. Then, suddenly,

came the age of the iron ship, and within a year only three
were open. But Greenock was a bad geographical location for
the workshops of a railway that called itself the National Line.
The Caledonian looked for a new site, and found it in Springburn. In 1856 new locomotive and carriage works—St Rollox
—were laid out in Springburn Road in the angle between the
original Garnkirk line and the new main line down to
Buchanan Street. And so it came about that the Edinburgh &
Glasgow found its rival established in spacious new workshops
on its own doorstep. The works at Greenock were closed and
unfinished engines were brought up to St Rollox. The first
Caledonian engine to be steamed in Springburn was No. 174,
one of Sinclair's 2—4—0 Crewe-type goods engines, the first
of which had been turned out in 1854. However, Robert
Sinclair's connection with Springburn was brief. St Rollox
had been in production for only a few months when he went
south to become locomotive superintendent of the Eastern
Counties Railway, taking with him a souvenir in the shape of
a Scottish wife, daughter of the Greenock customs officer.

The rapid spread of the national railway network demanded
more and more locomotives, and led to the rapid expansion of
the private locomotive manufacturing industry. By the accident of history the pioneer manufacturers had built their
factories on Tyneside and Merseyside, but it was not to be
expected that the city that had seen James Watt at work
would ignore the steam locomotive. In the forties and fifties
there were a score of firms in Glasgow and the West of Scotland trying their hand at locomotive building. These were
marine and general engineering concerns, for whom locomotives were an experimental sideline. Most were two or three
engine firms, and after their tentative experiments all except
one firm with premises in the Stobcross district down by the
Clyde reverted to general engineering. In its formative years
this firm was known by several names. In 1836 it traded as
Mitchell & Neilson from an address in McAlpine Street. A
year later a factory was opened in Hyde Park Street in the

same neighbourhood, and the directory listed the firm as Kerr, Mitchell & Neilson. In 1841 its works supplied the winding engine for Cowlairs Incline. By 1845 the firm had become Neilson & Co.

Walter Montgomerie Neilson joined the firm *as a partner* when he was a boy of seventeen. 'Wee Walter' his workmen called him, and 'Wee Walter' he remained for many a day. Walter Neilson had rich engineering blood in his veins. His father was James Beaumont Neilson, the inventor of the hot blast method of iron manufacture which revolutionised the iron industry. His uncle was John Neilson of Oakbank Foundry, who built the first Clyde iron ship.

Walter had enthusiasm and a gift for organising; above all, he believed in the future of the locomotive. Neilson's first order was for three engines for the Garnkirk. Orders from other companies followed and before long locomotives in prodigious numbers were taking shape on the floor of the little factory among the marine engines and the rum pans that were the firm's bread and butter lines. It did not take Neilson long to establish himself as a locomotive builder of the first rank, to whom railway managements at home and abroad came for engines.

It is not quite clear when Neilson took the decision to abandon marine and general engineering and concentrate wholly on locomotives. It was probably in 1855, for at that time he built a new foundry and boiler shop in Finnieston Street and made the Hyde Park Street factory a machine shop. The last order for a marine engine may have been taken that year (marine engines and locomotive works numbers were lumped together) but construction of marine engines was still going on four years later. William Wallace, who spent all his working life at Neilson's, recalled when he retired in 1901 that he did marine work as an apprentice in 1859, and also remembered the excitement among the workers when Neilson got an order for twelve locomotives for the Caledonian Railway.

During the eventful fifties Neilson attracted an amazing galaxy of young men destined to make names for themselves. Benjamin Conner was his works manager. James Reid came from Caird's of Greenock to spend a year or two with him before moving temporarily to Sharp, Stewart of Manchester. One of Neilson's works managers at this period was William Tait, who later went to Mather Dixon of Liverpool to erect for them the Great Western 10-footers. Another Neilson works manager was Henry Dübs. Dübs in turn used his influence to secure the services of Sampson George Goodall-Copestake as chief draughtsman for the firm. Patrick Stirling worked for Neilson before going on to do great things at Kilmarnock and greater things at Doncaster. So did Robert Band Pope, who is credited with being the first man to suggest fitting weather protection cabs to locomotives.

Glasgow in those days was a meeting place of the railway giants. The Institution of Engineers in Scotland was founded in the city in 1857, and to attend its meetings Conner came from St Rollox and Paton from Cowlairs. Alexander Allan came down from his Scottish Central headquarters at Perth, and Patrick Stirling came up from Kilmarnock. Walter Neilson, James Reid and William Tait were there from the Hyde Park Street foundry. In such an assembly there must have been fascinating conversations. Listen to Patrick Stirling speaking in an argument on the relative merits of inside and outside bearings.

'I prefer that all the bearings be inside and do not agree that outside bearings increase stability. The stability depends on the width of the base which in the locomotive is 4 feet $8\frac{1}{2}$ inches, the gauge of the wheels. The weight above should be kept as much within the base as possible, and the lateral spreading of the weight consequent on the use of outside bearings is injurious rather than beneficial.'

A member pointed out to Stirling that if he carried out his theory to its logical conclusion the perfect engine would have only one bearing right in the middle of the axle! Alexander

Allan spoke about his duplex spring buffer and his 'drip pipe fountain lamp' for carriages. So successful was this lamp, said Allan, that one important railway company had fitted it to their engines and it had easily withstood the vibration.

There were exciting nights when Walter Neilson, newly returned from America, showed the drawings he had brought back with him, and told of the huge eight-coupled freight engines he had seen on the Baltimore & Ohio. Neilson was greatly impressed by American locomotive building practice and by American locomotives in operation, especially the 4—4—0. This he described as 'a gay, jaunty-looking vehicle— very different from the sombre, business-like machine of the old country'. He went on to say,

'The extraordinary amount of bright brass and bright-painted ornamentation one is scarcely prepared for. Yet the care with which all this gaudy decoration is kept clean gains our admiration of and interest in the machine, the effect being somewhat favoured by a generally clear and dry climate. The ordinary form of locomotive engine used all over the States has driving wheels before and behind the firebox coupled together; the fore part of the engine being carried on a swivel four-wheeled truck or bogie. It is worthy of remark that in America they seem, with a sort of common assent, to have agreed as to the best form of engine suitable for their purpose, while we in this country, if we may judge from the variety of engines to be seen, would appear not to have arrived at this step towards perfection. The American eight-wheeled truck engine is a beautifully balanced and steady machine remarkably easy on a bad road and much safer than an English engine under similar circumstances.'

William Tait had no faith in the bogie engine.

'I think the small wheels are objectionable as they will sink into the concavity formed in the rail by the weight of the locomotive, and be constantly moving up a never ending incline, the effect of which will be worse on the smaller wheel. I think that many of the American locomotives, presenting a confused mass of stripes of paint and brass, are the flimsiest pieces of mechanism in existence, and that for work and durability they are not half the worth of ours.'

But Neilson was unshaken in his faith in American workmanship. 'We may predict that the time is not far distant,' he declared, 'when we may look to our friends across the Atlantic with the expectation of learning something from them even in railway engineering.' Neilson forthwith proceeded to build a large American-type 4—4—0.

As early as September 1849 Walter obtained a patent for a 2—2—2 saddle tank. The tank covered the entire boiler barrel and smoke box and extended right down to the frames, although the specification stated that a smaller tank supported on the boiler only could be supplied if desired. Water from the tank was fed to the boiler at the smoke box end, the idea being to take advantage of the smoke box heat. The coal bunkers were on either side of the firebox, and the driving wheels were flangeless.

The respect with which Neilson was regarded by senior railway officers even in the early days is nicely illustrated by an incident which took place in 1851. Neilson had built a tank engine for a coal owner near Kilmarnock and when it was completed the customer refused to accept it on the grounds that it was not powerful enough to meet his requirements. Neilson knew well enough that the engine was fit for the job for which it had been designed, but in the cramped space of his Stobcross factory, with no railway connections, he had no facilities for staging a full-scale test. Accordingly he sought help from the Caledonian, who were more than willing to co-operate in staging a test. Joseph Goodfellow arranged the details, and a senior officer acted as arbiter. In addition the Caledonian called in for a second opinion no less a person than Mr William Johnstone, engineer and manager of the Glasgow & South Western Railway (this throws an interesting light on Caledonian—South Western relations at that time).

The Neilson engine, Walter Neilson himself, the doubting customer and the judges were duly taken to a point on the Caledonian line near Cambuslang. A down mineral train from Motherwell to Gushetfaulds was stopped on the Glasgow side of Cambuslang station. The Caledonian engine was detached and the new Neilson product substituted for the remainder of the journey. It performed its task perfectly, and the coal owner was satisfied that he had got what he had paid for.

By the end of the fifties the works at Stobcross were barely able to cope with the flood of orders, and delivery was becoming a problem. Overseas orders were easily dealt with; the engines were loaded on ships that tied up at the quay wall only a few hundred yards from the works. Deliveries to home railways were much more difficult. The finished engines had to be manhandled over public roads to the nearest railhead, and as they became bigger and heavier the task of moving them became more complex. Neilson employed a local contractor, Matthew White, to transport the locomotives, using a huge, multi-wheeled lorry. A familiar sight in Glasgow was White's juggernaut, complete with a new locomotive, trundling slowly through the main streets of the city with up to fifty horses pulling it, and excited schoolboys dancing behind it. Once a boy fell under the wheels and was crushed to death.

Among the boys who watched Neilson's engines passing through Glasgow was a fifteen-year-old printer's apprentice, William Graham. Many years later Graham was to recall the scene.

'The carters,' he wrote, 'wore a special suit in honour of the occasion, including moleskin double-breasted vests with sleeves and mother of pearl buttons, and Kilmarnock bonnets. One man had charge of the whole procession. He sat on the bogie of the engine and at his signal the thirty horses set off in grand style. The hill at West Nile Street was taken at a gallop, and the sight here usually attracted large crowds.'

Neilson looked for a site for a new factory and, like Robert Sinclair, he found it in Springburn. In the middle of that district of hills, half a mile north of St Rollox and a quarter of a mile east of Cowlairs, was a pleasant meadow bounded on one side by the Sighthill branch of the Edinburgh & Glasgow Railway and with the Caledonian main line from Buchanan Street not far away. This was exactly what Neilson wanted—space and access to railways—and he allotted to Henry Dubs and Copestake the job of laying out the new factory. On the eve of the move to Springburn, in 1861, the machine shop at the old works was equipped as follows:

6 planers	1 nut mill
5 slotters	19 lathes
6 shapers	3 nut lathes
2 screw-cutting machines	

There were two steam hammers in the forge and one in the smithy. This machinery was dismantled, loaded on carts and dragged to Springburn by horse teams, at times assisted by Neilson employees manning long towing ropes. Neilson took the name of the street the old works had graced for his new Springburn factory, Hyde Park; so was established another illustrious name in locomotive history.

In the year that Neilson came to Springburn, William Paton left Cowlairs. He had given the Edinburgh & Glasgow twenty years of excellent service, and left the railway with a fine stock of locomotives. Paton had had strong Manchester leanings as far as engines were concerned. Those he did not build himself he got from Sharp, Stewart or Beyer Peacock, although he did put some small orders in Neilson's way. One Neilson order was for three small, light 2—2—2 well tanks rather similar in design to George England's light tanks, one of which, No. 5, lasted in various forms into the twentieth century. Another was for four 5 ft 0—4—2 goods engines. But at the end of 1861 the principal passenger trains on the Edinburgh & Glasgow were hauled by Beyer Peacock singles of 1856 or the new (1860) 2—4—0 from the same maker, and most freight traffic by Beyer Peacock 0—4—2s. Paton's place at Cowlairs was taken by William Steel Brown. His works manager was William Stroudley, and one of his foremen was a young unknown, Dugald Drummond.

Neilson had produced engines for his other Springburn neighbour, the Caledonian, from time to time. He had built, among others, twelve of Benjamin Conner's 0—4—2 goods engines. But the engine that was attracting most attention about Springburn at the time was Conner's great 2—2—2 eight-footer, the first batch of which had been at work on the Glasgow—Carlisle expresses for two years. There was nothing very original about the eight-footer. It was Allan's Crewe-type pure and simple, but the Allan engine had never looked more impressive. The towering 28-spoke, 8 ft 2 in. driving wheels encased in their slatted, paddle-box splashers, and the general elegance of the engine in its glorious Caledonian blue made it a sight to remember. The cylinders were 17 in. by 24 in., heating surface was 1,169 sq ft, and the engine weighed 30 tons 13 cwt, no less than 14 tons 11 cwt of the weight being on the driving wheels. The boiler was so low set that the shell was recessed underneath in two places to allow for the play of the eccentrics.

The new Hyde Park was established while preparations were taking place for the holding in London of the great International Exhibition of 1862. Eleven years earlier the Great Exhibition of 1851 had demonstrated a new technique in promoting trade by gathering together under one roof for all to see the finest products of British industry. At the latest exhibition it was planned to have a section housing the largest collection of exhibition locomotives ever assembled at one place, and Walter Neilson was determined to be represented. The engine he selected was the Conner eight-footer. Neilson was on excellent terms with his old works manager and Conner readily agreed with Neilson's suggestion that he build one of the class at his works especially for the London exhibition, the arrangement being that Neilson would sell the

COWLAIRS INCLINE. *The Neilson winding engine with George Jack who was in charge of it for 52 years*

WORKSHOP INTERIORS. Top: *Drummond and Holmes engines in Cowlairs erecting shop about 1903.* Bottom: *Carriage building in wood at St Rollox about 1900*

engine to the Caledonian after the show.

Exhibitors were required to present their exhibits at South Kensington not later than 31 March 1862. Neilson's engine was not ready by then, partly because of the builder's lateness in deciding to make the entry, and also because the steel tyres, ordered from Krupp, had not arrived. Robert Blackburn, who worked on the exhibition engine, recorded that it was finished 'in a superior manner'. It carried a nameplate inscribed 'Caledonian Railway Co. Exhibition Engine made by Neilson and Co. Glasgow, 1862'. Nevertheless, it was not to see the Caledonian.

The engines that went to the Crystal Palace in 1851 were hauled through the streets of London by thirty-horse teams. In 1862 Bray's traction engine pulled them from their respective railheads to South Kensington. The journeys at first were performed in daylight hours, but the snorting traction engine terrified the working horses of London and after several mishaps the authorities decreed that the locomotives were to be moved only between the hours of 8 p.m. and 9 a.m.

The Conner was one of the last to arrive, and so had to travel during the hours of darkness. The Londoners were thus deprived of the spectacle of a blue Caledonian engine making a progress through the streets of the capital.

Locomotives, fixed engines and other heavy machinery were to be shown in a building called the Western Annexe. It was built of wood with glass skylights let into the roof, and was little more than a shanty. Moreover, it was showing signs of collapse and had been secured by hastily devised props. Of the building the *Engineer* wrote, 'The roof would doubtlessly prove a most valuable acquisition to a market gardener largely engaged in the cultivation of cucumbers. It is hoped that the building may stand until the Exhibition is over. At the same time it need not excite any surprise to hear any day that the whole affair has tumbled to the ground with the loss perhaps of several lives.'

F

In these unimposing surroundings Neilson's men and the Conner found themselves in April 1862. The grounds surrounding the Western Annexe were a clutter of locomotives and machinery waiting to be placed. Four lines of rails ran into the building and on them a beautifully turned out Manning Wardle tank bearing the coat of arms of the City of Leeds and a steam crane were working to place the exhibits. The tank had arrived as an exhibit, but had been steamed and given this job of work by the exhibition authorities. The official in charge of the Western Annexe was an ex-Cowlairs man, Daniel Kinnear Clark, who had fitted Paton's *Orion* and *Sirius* with Ivison's patent coal-burning firebox with its steam jet that was supposed to improve combustion. Clark had also induced Conner, as a result of a conversation at a meeting of the Institution of Engineers in Scotland, to try out his system of steam jets on a Caledonian engine. Conner had abandoned coke for Wishaw coal; this raised steam quicker than did coke, and pressure was well maintained, but excessive smoke proved a nuisance. Clark's idea was to get an abundance of air into the firebox so that combustion would be complete and smoke eliminated. Air jets entered the firebox slightly above the fuel level and were directed at right angles to the ascending gases. Fine steam jets, only 1/16 in. in diameter, were used mainly when the engine was standing.

All too slowly the chaos and confusion at the Western Annexe were overcome, and the locomotives were placed in position. The interior was hot, stuffy and noisy with the hiss of steam escaping from an elaborate system of pipes that conveyed live steam from a central boiler house to the various working exhibits. An Armstrong four-coupled goods for the East Indian Railway was placed immediately ahead of the Conner. This engine had left the works unpainted and it was actually painted on its exhibition stand among the bustle and dust of the pre-opening days. On the other side of the Conner stood *Manchester,* a five-foot six-coupled freight engine from Sharp, Stewart. Among the British engines were two from the

London & North Western, one of them Ramsbottom's *Lady of the Lake*. George England exhibited his *New England*, a light tank of the type he had supplied to the Edinburgh & Glasgow more than a decade earlier. Perhaps the engine that most intrigued the Springburn men was Robert Sinclair's entry for the Eastern Counties Railway. The Sinclair and the Conner, if not sister engines, were cousins. Both carried the plain conical chimney that Sinclair had introduced on the Caledonian. Neilson had built twenty engines of the class for the Eastern Counties, but that on show, No. 327, was the first of the Armstrong Whitworth batch, and not new. Indeed, it had run 44,950 miles, and had been given nothing more than a repaint for the Exhibition.

The Conner, viewed from ground level, must have been a sight to behold. One can imagine the visitors crowding round that great wheel and looking up at the shining blue of the boiler. 'The outward finish of the engine is plain but neat,' wrote the reporter from *The Engineer,* 'and all but the finished ironwork and the smokebox and chimney is painted a deep and rich blue. Altogether, Messrs Neilson and Co's engine is one of the finest examples of locomotive construction in the Exhibition.'

Across one wall of the Western Annexe hung a banner inscribed 'Each climate needs what the other climes produce'. Perhaps Said Pasha, Viceroy of Egypt, took this motto to heart when he went to South Kensington shopping, so it is said, for a locomotive 'capable of travelling at 70 miles an hour'. Out of the eight or nine express engines from various countries and makers from which he could take his pick he chose the Conner. Neilson sold it to him there and then, its Caledonian nameplate and number notwithstanding. Was the Viceroy captivated by the engine's big wheel or the Caledonian blue, or was there an extra glib salesman on the Neilson stand? Kinnear Clark afterwards wrote, 'Its striking appearance with its magnificent wheel—the largest in the Annexe—secured for it the choice of his late Highness.'

The Engineer was not so sure that the Viceroy had got a bargain. A leading article considered that the benefit of Conner's big wheel was more apparent than real, and that, using six-foot wheels, the same boiler supplying 15 in. by 24 in. cylinders would result in an engine weighing only 24 tons yet as powerful as 'the big engine which the Viceroy will soon have packed off to Egypt'. Said Pasha must, however, have been satisfied, for he gave Neilson an order for two further engines of the class. The Exhibition Conner ran for 35 years on the Egyptian Railways, and was one of four engines chosen to embellish a commemorative stamp issued by the Egyptian Government in 1935 to celebrate the International Railway Congress held that year in Cairo. Another stamp in the series illustrated an express engine delivered to Egypt by Neilson's descendant in 1932.

There is a very beautiful model of Conner eight-footer No. 76 in the Royal Scottish Museum in Edinburgh. The motion operates at the touch of a button. Looking at the great wheel revolving the modern visitor can well visualise a Conner gliding gracefully at the head of a West Coast express of a century ago.

The Conner eight-footer was not the sole Neilson representative at South Kensington. Also on view was a model of Nathaniel Grew's ice engine *Rurik,* the original of which was built for Russia in 1861. This peculiar locomotive was a five-foot single with 10 in. x 22 in. cylinders and a pair of steel runners like large skates mounted in front of the driving wheels where one would expect a bogie to be. This 'bogie' could be steered from a platform above the buffer beam. The connecting rods drove an intermediate shaft coupled to the driving wheels, which were spiked like a runner's shoes to give them a grip of the ice. *Rurik's* job was to haul a three-coach passenger train (the coaches had runners instead of wheels) over the ice from St Petersburg to Kronstadt. Grew's model is still in the Science Museum at South Kensington, at one stage in its long history having been rebuilt by Neilson!

While Neilson and the Caledonian were enjoying their joint triumph in London the Edinburgh & Glasgow, in a single evening, suffered a catastrophe that cost the company half its total passenger revenue of the half year in which it occurred. The 5 p.m. from Glasgow to Edinburgh and the 6 p.m. Scottish Central train from Edinburgh to the North met in head-on collision near Winchburgh, the biggest calamity that had occurred on Scottish rails up to that time. For months the cream of the Scottish bar was engaged in presenting claims for compensation and before the Winchburgh account was closed the Edinburgh & Glasgow had admitted 129 claims and paid out £40,000. The life of Mr Howie, the manager of the Oakley Iron Works, was assessed at £4,200, that of a soldier in the Scots Greys at £150. The value of the life of Fireman John Cunningham, 'whose death appeared to have been the most painful of all the many deaths that night', was put at £50—plus funeral expenses. A Miss Lonie, whose betrothed was killed, claimed on the grounds that the accident had deprived her of the chance of marriage *or* her chance of obtaining damages for breach of promise. Her claim was rejected.

In their search for guilty men (or scapegoats) the Crown cast a wide and indiscriminate net. No fewer than six members of the Edinburgh & Glasgow staff were arrested and charged with culpable homicide. They were Mr Latham the general manager, J. B. Thomson the traffic superintendent, Alexander Rennie, inspector of permanent way, and his assistant Alex Forrest, Newton the pointsman and, surprisingly, Davidson the driver of the pilot engine. Only two, Latham and Thomson, were put on trial, and after eight hours' examination of witnesses had established that the accident was the result of a tragic but honest mistake by óne man, the Lord Advocate directed the jury to return a verdict of not guilty. An interesting feature of the accident was that the track was cleared in little more than twelve hours and the morning trains next day ran past the spot without interruption. The track was practically undamaged, which says a lot for the stability of E & G permanent way at that time. A contemporary wrote, 'Not a rail, not even a joint or spike was displaced by the terrific collision. How great, how painful is the contrast constantly furnished on the Chatham and Dover.'

If the High Court had convicted J. B. Thomson, the Edinburgh & Glasgow Railway Volunteers would have lost their major. E & G men of the 'sixties were proud to wear the dark green uniform of their own army unit. On parade days Springburn men would be seen polishing their leather belts with their brass buckles in the form of 'a large representation of a locomotive' before taking the train down Cowlairs Incline to their parade ground—George Square. Occasionally Major Thomson took his unit out into the country for field exercises, and on such occasions a special troop train conveyed the railway's own troops to Lenzie Moss. On one such exercise Thomson was directing operations from horseback when his mount and himself became embedded deep in the bog. The entire company spent the rest of the day extracting their commanding officer and his horse from the Moss.

At the east end of Lenzie Moss, $6\frac{1}{4}$ miles from Glasgow, was Campsie Junction where the branch to Kirkintilloch and Lennoxtown left the main line. On the site there was a station, a signal box and a few railway cottages. All round was empty moorland—moorland with a fine outlook over the Kelvin Valley and the Campsie Fells. The E & G directors well knew that the way to make a railway pay was to have population at every station, so they set about cultivating a new town at Campsie Junction, announcing in the press and by poster that anybody who built a house there would be presented with a free first-class season ticket to Glasgow for at least five years. It was about this time that some of the older and once fashionable houses in Glasgow were getting past their prime and their owners, lured by the Edinburgh & Glasgow bait, made viewing excursions to Campsie Junction. Before long, the astute railway company had planted the nucleus of a sedate and attractive town round the hitherto isolated station.

The E & G had no intention of fostering a colony of huts and cottages. They wanted the cream of Glasgow's surplus population. To encourage the building of *big* houses the directors granted an additional year of free travel for every £100 spent on a house in excess of £1,000. The venture could not fail. The site was excellent, the streets of new villas spread, and the busy trains carried a much smaller proportion of non-revenue passengers than might have been suspected. Only householders had free seasons. Members of their families paid ordinary fares, and so did their friends when they came to visit them in their new homes. Ordinary freight rates were charged on the steady flow of foodstuffs and merchandise that came into the new town. When the company built a loading bank at Campsie Junction to handle the goods traffic they used stone blocks that had done service as sleepers on the nearby Monkland & Kirkintilloch Railway.

The E & G pampered the new town's inhabitants. They wanted to go to church on Sundays, so a church was made for them out of the station waiting room. When they wanted to travel to England they could have the London train stopped for them on giving ten minutes' warning at the station. There was one snag. Campsie Glen, down the branch, was a favourite spot for picnickers from Glasgow. All too often families bundled out of the trains at Campsie Junction only to find after the train had gone that they were at the wrong place. So Campsie Junction was renamed Lenzie. The settlement became a favourite dormitory for the Springburn locomotive superintendents; Dugald Drummond, Tom Wheatley and Matthew Holmes lived in Lenzie villas at one time or another.

The E & G took in hand another experiment in housing, this time nearer home, when in 1863 they built houses for their Cowlairs employees on the steep northern slope of Springburn Hill. They were constructed in a series of spectacular terraces, set one above the other on the steep face of the hill, in the Scottish baronial style with elegant turret staircases and crow-

stepped gables. A fine grey sandstone was used in their construction and the facings and other embellishments were in
red sandstone. The E & G houses became known as 'the Blocks'
and as workers' dwellings they had no equal. When they were
a hundred years old and scheduled as sub-standard they still
had an air of elegance and regality about them.

The Edinburgh & Glasgow was an enterprising and happy
railway. It was saddening, therefore, to see the company so
beset with difficulties in the sixties. Winchburgh had been
bad enough, but it had been a passing thorn in the flesh. The
very existence of the railway was threatened by the intrigues
of its powerful and covetous neighbours, the Caledonian and
the North British. The days of unbridled competition with
the Caledonian had given way to a 'joint purse', with the
Edinburgh & Glasgow and the Caledonian sharing the expenses of certain services. But the Caledonian directors used
the joint purse policy as an anæsthetic to lull the E & G while
they increased their own power and influence by pushing
their lines unobtrusively into the rich coalfields of Lanarkshire. There was bitter political warfare as the Caledonian
and North British jousted for control of the Edinburgh &
Glasgow. The Caledonian would have absorbed the E & G if
the government of the day had not cried 'monopoly' and pro-
hibited the deal. On the other hand the North British had
everything to gain by doing so, for with the inter-city line in
their hands their way to the west would be open. Again, the
North British were handicapped by the lack of a good workshop, and winning over the E & G would give them the plum
of Cowlairs. The Edinburgh & Glasgow boardroom was recon-
ciled to the fact that amalgamation must come sooner or later,
and the majority of shareholders favoured the North British.
But even at the eleventh hour the old 'Sabbath party' raised
its voice. A shareholder, the Rev James Meiklam, while con-
fessing that he knew little about railways, urged caution in
any approach to what he referred to contemptuously as 'this
North British'. In the reverend gentleman's view the North

British was the most notorious of all the Scottish railways in the running of Sunday trains. He was for a union of the North British and the Edinburgh & Glasgow only if the 'unbelieving husband should be sanctified by the believing wife'.

The 'wedding' took place in 1865, and another name came to Springburn. A *Railway Times* editorial summed up the matter neatly when it said, 'The North British in our judgement may well continue to be the legal name of the company; as such it would sufficiently represent its mission of being in continual competition with the Caledonian Railway.' The old order passed, and many were sorry to see it go. It was not long before the railwaymen of Springburn saw what their new masters were like. In October 1865 the North British management organised a *soirée* in the City Hall, then the largest indoor meeting place in Glasgow, and all E & G men within reach were invited to attend. A *soirée* should have been a social function. The North British used the occasion to put over what nowadays would be called a pep talk for the benefit of their newly acquired servants. The platform party was an imposing one. Hodgson of the North British was in the chair. On one side of him was Samuel Waite Johnston who had come to Cowlairs in 1864 and was the last independent locomotive superintendent of the Edinburgh & Glasgow Railway; on the other side was William Hurst, Johnston's counterpart from the North British works at Edinburgh. Hodgson made a speech, fantastic to modern ears, in which he told his listeners that he expected them to give their best for the glory and profit of the North British shareholders.

'We are all, from myself to the youngest clerk or porter present, alike servants of the united company, and it is our duty to do the best we can for the furtherance of its interests. I am satisfied that all present will, like myself, do their utmost for that purpose. The directors claim *no more* (my italics) from their servants than they are themselves ready to offer in its interests—their whole devotion, their whole time, their best talents and all their ability. They believe it to be their duty to work for the interests of the company as if it were their own. I believe that every man feels like myself that when promoting the company's interests he is doing that duty which he is called upon to do in this world.'

Hodgson went on to say that he had made a tour of the ceded territories and that he was of the opinion that the North British spirit could be whipped up among ex-E & G men. 'If you do your duty,' he concluded, 'the North British will pay as it ought to do to the shareholders.'

With that the chairman retired from the platform and the serfs were free to indulge in their merrymaking. That *soirée* speech was significant. In the years to come the North British management were to prove themselves remarkably inept at handling staff matters, even going as far as to interfere in the personal politics of their servants. In the winter of 1865, with the amalgamation only months old, employees of the former Monkland Railways, now in the North British net, were being referred to as 'remnants'. Remnant signalmen were put in North British boxes and given two hours to learn them. If they failed in their test at the end of that time they were unceremoniously sacked.

The brilliant victory that brought the North British into the heart of the Caledonian citadel got a swift Caledonian answer. In 1865 and 1866 there took place the great series of amalgamations that gave the Caledonian an unbroken, unified system stretching from Carlisle to Aberdeen. The Scottish Central and the Scottish North Eastern, which had already swallowed the Scottish Midland, lost their separate identities. Scores of engines were painted in Caledonian colours, hundreds of men were added to the Caledonian pay roll. With the Scottish North Eastern staff the Caledonian inherited a young engineman, John McIntosh, of whom we will hear again. St Rollox became the main works of a greatly enlarged railway company.

Meanwhile, changes were taking place at Hyde Park. After

he had built the factory and got it going Henry Dübs decided to part company with Neilson and build a locomotive works of his own. He picked a site at Little Govan (now Polmadie) on the south side of the Clyde, and there erected his Glasgow Locomotive Works. He took Sampson George Goodall-Copestake with him. Dübs had always considered Copestake as his protegé, and he knew what he was doing when he appointed him chief draughtsman. Copestake was an extremely competent man, like Robert Sinclair an English gentleman who had turned to locomotive engineering. He had gone from Repton to Sharp, Stewart's where he had come under the personal supervision of Charles Beyer. Dübs had met the youthful Copestake in those early days.

Walter Neilson was left with a fine new works, but with neither a manager nor a chief draughtsman. James Reid came back from Manchester to be managing partner at Hyde Park. Reid was an excellent replacement for Dübs, but good chief draughtsmen with locomotive experience were scarce. However, James Reid was only a matter of weeks back at Hyde Park when there arrived at the works on a casual visit the young locomotive superintendent of the Scinde Railway. Reid talked this young man into staying at Hyde Park, and thus recruited a remarkable personage who was to remain with the firm as chief draughtsman for 38 years. He was Edward Snowball. Snowball was born in 1830 in Northumberland among the first locomotives, and he stayed with locomotives all his life. He was apprenticed to Robert Stephenson when he was sixteen, and before his apprenticeship was finished Stephenson had made him chief draughtsman at his Newcastle works. Snowball was a perfectionist, with an eye for a beautiful locomotive. More than any other person he gave the Neilson engine its distinctive character. The Snowball touch was seen on engines all over the world.

The Springburn pattern was emerging. There was the Caledonian at St Rollox, the North British at Cowlairs, and between them was Neilson's Hyde Park. New houses, shops, schools and churches grew up. The old cottages vanished to give place to high tenements. No longer was there a country road linking two railway communities. Springburn was a single railway unit, albeit with a 'Caley end' and an 'NB end', for NB and Caley men tended to rent houses round their respective places of employment. Streets at the North British end then and later tended to have good North British names: Ratho Terrace, Eastfield Terrace, Craigendoran Terrace. And the local newspaper talked about *Caledonians* and *North Britons*. But Springburn had plenty of parkland and woods even then. When James Reid came back from Manchester he settled his family in Wellfield House, a stone mansion that stood on a wooded hillface not five minutes' walk away from the works, and took his guests out on shooting expeditions in the woods above the house.

production is best presented in tabular form:

Type	Dr. Wheels		Cyls	BP	Wt in WO		No built
	ft	in.	in.	p.s.i.	tons	cwt	
0—6—0	4	6	15 x 22	140	33	9	25
0—4—2	5	9	17 x 24	140	45	10	6
4—4—0	6	0	17 x 26	150	46	16	3
4—4—0	5	0	16 x 22	140	35	4	24

All were neat, efficient machines. The 5 ft 9 in. 0—4—2 tanks were intended for the coast trains and were given local names like *Helensburgh, Craigendoran* and *Roseneath*. In naming the last engine Drummond made a mistake that is common to this day. The hamlet and parish on the Gareloch is Rosneath —not Roseneath.

★　　　★　　　★

One day in 1881, 28 locomotive and operating men met in the canteen at Cowlairs to discuss the possibility of establishing a co-operative trading society in Springburn; by the time the meeting ended they had founded Cowlairs Co-operative Society. They selected as their emblem and seal the impression of a locomotive surrounded by a scroll bearing the name of the society. The engine is crudely drawn, but it is plainly a Wheatley 4—4—0 with slotted splashers and safety valve set far back towards the cab. Now, why in 1881 with plenty of new Drummond engines under their very noses, did the railwaymen choose a Wheatley? I have a theory about that. There was one engine above all others in the public eye that year, Wheatley's 4—4—0 No. 224. This was the engine that had gone down with the Tay Bridge on 27 December 1879, had been recovered and had spent part of 1880 in Cowlairs being refurbished. Somebody christened her 'The Diver', and she was known by that name until the end of her long career. I suggest that the 28 men had 'The Diver' very much in their minds when they selected the emblem for their Society.

Cowlairs Co-operative Society began trading with one small shop and one permanent employee. At first it was managed exclusively by North British men in their spare time, and it

Chapter 4

DRUMMOND DAYS

For many years there was published in Glasgow a weekly periodical, *The Bailie,* and the best-loved feature of that journal was its weekly biography of some well-known Glasgow citizen printed under the heading 'The Man You Know'. The subject of one of these essays was Dugald Drummond. The biographer said of him, 'When another series of Lives of the Engineers is compiled by some future Smiles, one of the more prominent figures of the volume will necessarily be Mr. Drummond.' Then the article got down to brass tacks and went on, 'Like most other people who have made their way in the world after an uphill battle, Mr. Drummond, if the truth be told, is somewhat impatient of control. He is, however, one of the friendliest of men. Sharp—or rather imperious ought to be the term—as may be his manner with those with whom he comes in contact, this sharpness, this imperiousness, covers a thoroughly genuine nature and a nature as honest, as transparent as the day.'

Drummond came to Springburn for the second time in 1875 and he left it in 1890. In fifteen years he revolutionised the locomotive departments of both the North British and the Caledonian Railways. Seventy years after he left Springburn a count of pre-grouping engines still in existence disclosed that (on a percentage basis) most were possessed by the North British and the Caledonian. Third on the list with pre-grouping engines was the London & South Western, a company that had known the Drummond touch. There could be no more eloquent tribute to the work of Dugald Drummond as a locomotive engineer. But before passing through the years with Drummond let us take a quick look at developments in Springburn in the decade that began with the amalgamations and ended with his arrival.

The 1865 amalgamations saw both St Rollox and Cowlairs in control of a hotch-potch of locomotives and rolling stock that had belonged to the small pre-grouping companies. Some of the items were odd indeed. The Monkland Railways were not quite sure how many locomotives they possessed. When the North British had a count of chimneys they found they had acquired 27 engines, one more than the Monkland Railways had on their books. They also found themselves with 2,244 Monkland wagons, 29 more than the Monkland thought they owned. The locomotive superintendents at St Rollox and Cowlairs were faced with an identical task, to scrap the hopeless ones, salvage the not-so-hopeless by rebuilding, and produce new designs to cope with the increasing traffic on the greatly enlarged systems.

The North British got off to a false start. The management decided to have *two* locomotive superintendents, S. W. Johnston at Cowlairs with the former Edinburgh & Glasgow and its appendages as his responsibility, and Hurst at St Margarets in charge of the former North British and its extensions into Fife and elsewhere. This impossible arrangement ended within two years, when Johnston went to the Eastern Counties Railway, and Cowlairs was made the workshop for most new construction and most heavy repairs, with Thomas Wheatley in command as sole locomotive superintendent. That the change led to serious confusion at first is evident from the following illuminating extract from a North British shareholder's letter of complaint dated 21 September 1867:

'The directors in their ignorance have ordered the locomotive superintendent to close a number of his repairing workshops, including those at Edinburgh, and given him instructions to send everything on to Glasgow which required anything like heavy repairs. Long trains of disabled carriages, broken down vans and dilapidated engines have accordingly occupied the line being brought up to the workshops in Glasgow only to have the doors closed against them in consequence of the wards in these hospitals being already chock full. The work of repair is not merely suspended in many cases, but trainloads of the disabled have, after blocking up once busy sidings in Glasgow, been sent back to perform the same obstructive office in Edinburgh. The unrepaired vehicles are gradually accumulating in all the useful sidings each apparently waiting its turn, as in a medical dispensary for the sick poor, to be called in and prescribed for.'

It was in 1867 that the North British distinguished itself by nearly wrecking the Royal Train at Cowlairs. The occasion was the unveiling of the Prince Albert statue in George Square, and Queen Victoria sent her son Prince Alfred to Glasgow to perform the ceremony. The train bringing him to the city was approaching Cowlairs West Junction under clear signals when a mineral train bound from Sighthill to Bowling cut across its path. It was reported at the time that the Royal Train was stopped with the engine's buffers less than a yard from the side of a coal wagon. The driver on that occasion was Jack Rennie, who later became a North British worthy. He had joined the Edinburgh & Glasgow in 1850 and, after spending 54 years on the footplate was made shed foreman at Helensburgh.

Rennie's fireman on that occasion was William Graham, the erstwhile printer's apprentice who had watched the Neilson engines passing through Glasgow. The locomotive had lured him to Springburn, and he had started as a cleaner on the Edinburgh & Glasgow in 1862. Graham entered Cowlairs in the middle of a wages dispute; the drivers were petitioning the company for a *reduction* of sixpence per day. Edinburgh & Glasgow drivers were paid the unusually high rate of 7s 6d, which made them liable for income tax. The reduction would have exempted them and increased their net earnings. Graham was a fireman by the time the North British took over, and he was the first fireman to run a Cowlairs engine right through to Berwick-on-Tweed and back in a day. He has left behind a vivid account of his first turn as a driver. 'The first run I had as a driver of a mineral train was pretty rough. The hail peeled the skin off my face and caused it to bleed. Through the medium of the press the drivers asked that cabs be put on the engines. They did not get the cabs just then, but they were supplied with overcoats.' He recalled that the regular footplate dress of North British drivers included leather gauntlets and helmets.

William Graham was a pioneer amateur photographer. He took railway pictures from Edinburgh & Glasgow days until the closing years of the North British. In 1891, after nearly twenty-five years as a driver, he became a professional photographer and achieved great distinction in Glasgow art circles for his many fine studies of Glasgow architecture. But he never forgot his first love, the railway. No Springburn living room was complete without a Graham print—the polished engine and the proud crew carefully posed in front of it. To this day some hang in Springburn homes. Fortunately, Graham's great friend, the Glasgow artist William Young, R.S.W., preserved many specimens of Graham's work in his scrap books and these have survived. Most of the prints have deteriorated physically and chemically, but a few of the best are included in this book.

At first Conner at St Rollox and Wheatley at Cowlairs relied on well-tried types of locomotive. Wheatley's first passenger engine (apart from rebuilds) appeared in 1870; it was a 2—4—0 with 6 ft 6 in. coupled wheels and 16 in. by 24 in. cylinders. The Caledonian equivalent of this machine was Conner's 2—4—0, first introduced in 1867 to supplement his eight-foot singles on main line express work. This engine had 7 ft driving wheels and 17 in. by 24 in. cylinders. In 1871 Wheatley gave St Rollox something to think about, and made

MEN OF SPRINGBURN. Top: *J. F. McIntosh (centre of picture)*
with Matthew Holmes on his left at a social function in St Rollox
wagon shop in 1897. Bottom: *Cowlairs craftsmen of the 1880s*

McINTOSH MASTERPIECES. Top left: *An '812' class at Glasgow Central in 1962*. Top right: *An '812' in stone on the abutment of a bridge in Belgium*. Bottom: *Dunalastair 1 class No. 727 at Lanark*

history, when he produced two bogie express engines. These were 224 and 264, the first British inside-cylinder inside-frame 4—4—0s. He followed these two years later with four more 4—4—0s. Some of the Cowlairs and St Rollox products of this period had a superficial resemblance, because both Conner's engines and the Wheatley bogies had slotted, paddle-box type splashers. Conner produced two series of 2—4—0 freight engines, but in this sphere too his work was eclipsed by Wheatley's enterprise. The Cowlairs superintendent turned out the first of his standard 0—6—0 goods in 1869 and by 1873 no fewer than 87 were in service on the North British. This engine, with 5 ft coupled wheels and 17 in. by 24 in. cylinders, was a winner from the start. It handled main line freight for many years and 22 of the class survived to be handed over to the LNER.

These were the highlights from the great mass of building and rebuilding that went on in the ten-year period that preceded the advent of Drummond. At the end of it, both St Rollox and Cowlairs were producing engines at a higher rate than they had ever achieved before. Wheatley had stepped up the annual production at Cowlairs from 6 to 40 engines. Both the North British and the Caledonian gave considerable orders to Neilson, and it was not unusual to see engines for both companies taking shape side by side on the floor of the erecting shop at Hyde Park. Orders from both went also to Henry Dübs. Dübs, who was to contribute many famous engines to home and overseas railways, proved himself a locomotive engineer of vision, and his Glasgow Locomotive Works very soon became Neilson's chief competitor. With the clay he excavated for the foundations for his works Dübs made the bricks with which the factory was built, each brick being stamped with a diamond trade mark that was to become the plate of the North British Locomotive Company in the last twenty years of its existence. Within twelve months of breaking ground he was steaming his first engine, and within a few years the Glasgow Locomotive Works was the second largest

111

G

establishment of its kind in Britain. A year before Wheatley produced his standard goods, Henry Dübs himself had designed and supplied to the North British an 0—6—0 goods engine that was in advance of its time. Two years later Dübs was advertising that he had the answer to the Fairlie locomotive, then enjoying much favourable publicity. He claimed that by taking two of his standard tanks and coupling them bunker to bunker with the patent Dübs—Copestake coupling, any railway management could make a Fairlie for themselves. The coupling, said Dübs, gave rigidity and flexibility at the same time. The crane engine was Dübs's invention, and orders for this useful device kept his factory busy.

Dugald Drummond came back to Cowlairs in 1875 as locomotive superintendent. Since his previous employment in the works in a minor capacity he had been following the star of William Stroudley. He had gone to Inverness as his foreman erector; then Stroudley took him to Brighton and made him works manager. Forming part of this itinerant entourage was Drummond's younger brother Peter, and he too came to Cowlairs. For the first time in his career—he was still only 35—Dugald Drummond had *power,* and every intention of using it. Cowlairs had improved greatly in Wheatley's time, yet motive power had only just kept pace with the demands of the operating department. Drummond was faced with a series of problems. For a start Cowlairs works were overdue to be re-equipped; much of the machinery had been there since Paton's day. The biggest operating problem was the finding of motive power for the new Edinburgh Waverley—London St Pancras service. The North British had never visualised their Waverley route as a great Anglo-Scottish trunk route. It had begun life as a branch line from Edinburgh to Hawick which eventually joined end-on with a branch line from Carlisle to Hawick. Up till now the North British had resigned themselves to accepting at Carlisle, for transport over the Waverley route, any crumbs that fell from the Caledonian table, for the Caledonian took all but a fraction of the through

112

traffic from Euston to Edinburgh. Who was to foresee that the Midland Railway would push a main line from the south over the Pennines and down into Carlisle, there to seek a partnership with the North British, a partnership that would operate an entirely new Anglo-Scottish route of their own? By 1875 the Midland—North British connexion was a reality. The branch line had become a main line, a tough one at that, and little better than branch line engines were available to work it. The best the North British could produce for the job were the Wheatley 4—4—0s. They managed, but with no margin to spare.

There were other problems too. The Wheatley standard goods engines had years of life in them yet, but goods trains were getting heavier and more powerful engines were needed. Again, the North British had thrown out innumerable branches, and Cowlairs had designed nothing to handle the traffic on them. Much has been written about the engines that Drummond built to solve North British problems, engines that made Drummond's name and began a tradition that will never die. Yet railway historians are apt to overlook the fact that it was not the engines alone that established Drummond as a great locomotive man; it was also the matter of brakes. The story is forgotten nowadays, so let us revive it.

The year 1875 was crucial in the history of railway brakes. Passenger trains were getting heavier and faster, and accidents more numerous and messier. Many would never have happened if the trains involved had been able to stop in time. In 1875 a Royal Commission on Railway Accidents was in session and in order to provide reliable data on brakes the Railway Companies Association organised the celebrated trials at Newark. Railway companies generally were not brake conscious, although that was no fault of the various purveyors of brake equipment whose salesmen laid siege to the offices of their locomotive superintendents. Drummond arrived at Cowlairs too late to do anything about the Newark trials, but Conner had already dispatched one of his seven-foot 2—4—0s and 15 four-wheeled Caledonian coaches to Newark to represent St Rollox. The train was equipped with the Caledonian's own Steel-McInnes air brake, John McInnes, joint inventor of the brake, being an inspector in the locomotive department.

As far as braking effect was concerned the Steel-McInnes brake stood up well to its competitors, but it fell down badly on its mechanical performance. The air in the reservoirs and train pipes was maintained at a pressure of 50 p.s.i., and the brakes were applied by relieving it. Wastage of air, which was stored in a large cylinder carried on the tender, was enormous. Again, the screws on the flexible pipes between the carriages were clumsy and the couplings took a long time to unfasten. The Conner 2—4—0 brought its train back to Springburn, and the Steel-McInnes brake was abandoned.

Drummond held his own brake trials in 1876, and in a way they were more important than those at Newark. He staged a day of competitive trials, but also ran twenty complete test trains in regular service for the better part of a year. The brakes that Drummond selected for testing were the Westinghouse Automatic and the Smith Vacuum, both American; he deemed no British brakes worthy of notice. It was characteristic that he summoned representatives of the brake companies and decreed that the trials should take place on his home ground. Not that the representatives were unwilling to come; too often their efforts to interest British railway companies in their wares had evoked no response, and now it seemed almost too good to be true that a major railway was seeking their presence. There were rich rewards to be had for the company whose brake was chosen. George Westinghouse considered the occasion sufficiently important to go to Cowlairs in person. The Smith Vacuum Brake Company sent their Mr Yeoman, who was not an engineer, but an American high-pressure salesman. One wonders what these Yankees at Drummond's court thought of their prospective Scottish client when they first encountered him in his Cowlairs den. We were to learn soon enough what Yeoman thought of him.

After negotiations Drummond agreed to fit ten engines, Nos. 4, 15, 22, 130, 136, 137, 282, 301, 467, 488, with Smith's apparatus and ten, Nos. 33, 53, 141, 151, 278, 321, 329, 434, 554, and 600, with Westinghouse's. The standard trains were made up of three first-class, one second-class and four third-class carriages and two brakes. In addition Drummond arranged for set trials to be conducted on 12 December 1876. The idea was that a Westinghouse engine would take a trial train from Edinburgh to Cowlairs and back. A vacuum engine would then set off on a similar run with an appropriate train. A committee of four engineers was appointed to travel with the test trains, the members being William Cowan, the locomotive superintendent of the Great North of Scotland, Barton Wright of the Lancashire & Yorkshire, Mr Haswell, chief assistant locomotive engineer of the North Eastern, and James Stirling of the Glasgow & South Western (this distinguished panel must have impressed the rival brake salesmen, for a good performance at Drummond's trials could well result in substantial orders from four railway companies). Drummond devised a primitive dynamometer car to be run with the test trains, which carried a speed indicator and a method of signalling to the footplate. The speed indicator was a Westinghouse invention, and in order to obviate any suggestion of fraud Drummond had it fitted and tested by one of his own assistants in the presence of Mr Yeoman, who expressed his complete satisfaction with the arrangement. Drummond's assistant was detailed to operate the machine during the test runs.

Invitations to attend the trials went out to a large number of railway people, and the first trial train, the Westinghouse, was well filled with interested passengers when it left Edinburgh. Twelve test stops were made on the way to Cowlairs on signals being given to the driver from the leading van, and eighteen stops were made on the return journey. The passengers were now due to transfer to the Vacuum train, for a repeat performance. Alas! the Vacuum train was a non-starter. To assist the vacuum ejector to create a vacuum rapidly a van with a pump was attached to the train, the pump being operated through gearing from the axle of the van. This vehicle, a GNR six-wheeler, was found to have a hot box and, anyway, the pump had failed.

A second trial was run later in December and this time the Vacuum train was dispatched first, although not until the brake blocks, which gave some initial trouble, had been adjusted. Two Great Northern pump vans were carried in addition to the prescribed test load, and the routine test stops were duly recorded by Drummond's assistant on George Westinghouse's machine. At the end of the day Drummond entertained his guests in Edinburgh, and in an after dinner speech he thanked his American visitors for their presence and assured them that he would test their respective brakes in daily service for at least six months. Yet the cloths were hardly off the festive board when the North British directors announced that they would begin *immediately* to fit all North British passenger stock with the Westinghouse brake.

Mr Yeoman was annoyed. On the face of it, it looked as if Dugald Drummond had double-crossed him. The affair might have ended there had not *Engineering,* which had been campaigning with scant success for the universal adoption of continuous brakes, printed a leader eulogising Drummond's decision. 'We confess that, having in view the extreme sluggishness that characterises the managements of railways in this country, we were unprepared for such a prompt action on the part of the North British, and it is therefore to the credit of Mr. Drummond and his directors that, having satisfied themselves that the automatic (Westinghouse) is not only thoroughly efficient, but the best brake at present known, they should have acted immediately upon this knowledge and adopted it for their line.' Not content with praising the Westinghouse brake, the article proceeded to lambast Smith's Vacuum, and any railway that was using it or thinking of using it, in terms that would not be acceptable in print nowadays. The Great Northern were warned that they were 'incurring a grave responsibility in selecting a notoriously imperfect means of controlling their trains'; the Midland, who were using the Westinghouse, but were experimenting with the Vacuum, were told that their experiments were 'unnecessary'.

When Mr Yeoman protested to *Engineering,* that journal commented, 'We presume that this gentleman considers that he has a grievance against us.' Yeoman stated publicly that during the North British trials Westinghouse had taken the readings himself on his own machine and he more than hinted that he had fiddled the figures. He further stated that the Westinghouse brake was well known to Midland drivers as a train-stopper—meaning that it leaked on inadvertently and trains stopped where they were not meant to stop. Westinghouse sent a solicitor's letter to his rival, and the Smith Vacuum Brake Company threatened proceedings against Westinghouse. Yet Dugald Drummond came out of the affair with clean hands. He tested the two brakes side by side for six months. A statement was issued from Cowlairs showing the comparative costs of the two systems, and details are set out below.

	Vacuum			Westinghouse		
	£	s.	d.	£	s.	d.
Material supplied by NBR	64	15	11	104	2	5
Cost of brake equipment	180	0	0	235	0	0
Labour	188	12	1	154	15	4
Total	433	8	0	493	17	9
Maintenance	8	5	4	5	12	3

No doubt Drummond's mind was made up even before he staged the trials. He had seen the Westinghouse at work on the Midland, and one of Wheatley's 4—4—0s was Westinghouse-fitted for working through Midland traffic over the Waverley route. The trials showed that the stopping value of the Westinghouse to Vacuum was in the ratio of 65 to 30. Tests on the North Eastern followed on the heels of the North

British trials and they produced a ratio in favour of the Westinghouse of 62 to 51. Trials held in Germany and Belgium at the same time yielded similar results.

The praise given to Drummond and the North British was well merited. The Caledonian were equally praiseworthy in equipping their trains with efficient continuous brakes, which was more than could be said for their august partner south of the Border. In this respect Springburn was far ahead of Crewe. In 1883 there occurred on the Caledonian at Lockerbie a serious accident to a West Coast express, the cause of which could be laid at the LNWR door. The *Railway Times* commented:

'The Caledonian Railway Company have adopted the Westinghouse continuous brake, and are rapidly bringing it into use all over their system, but as the L.N.W.R. do not approve of this particular form of brake, the absurd anomaly presents itself of the most important train upon a railway, which has adopted a good continuous brake, being run without this brake throughout the train, because another railway in connection with it belongs to a company which has not yet adopted any continuous brake fulfilling the requirements of the Board of Trade.'

Non-fitted passenger stock continued to be worked, mainly on branch lines, throughout the Drummond era on the North British. I like the story of what happened to a Kilsyth—Glasgow local at Bishopbriggs on 21 July 1887. The train consisted of eight coaches, of which only two had the benefit of continuous brakes. The driver got the Bishopbriggs down home against him, and made the usual brake application. He was mystified when he sailed as smooth as a curling stone past the home signal and crashed into the rear of another train. He was even more mystified when he discovered that that train too had failed to respond to a brake application and had collided with the train ahead of it. Meanwhile, a freight train that had preceded all three along the main line had stopped at Maryhill and was being inspected by its guard. He found that a 30-gallon cask had burst and thick oil oozing through a crack in the floor of the wagon was spreading a greasy film on the rail surfaces.

Railway operating was a hazardous trade in mid-Victorian times. Death and mutilation came the way of many a Springburn man. William Graham, the engine driver photographer, has left this hair-raising account of a shunting operation known as *jerrying*. This, according to Graham, was a

process of having a number of wagons travelling and being shunted to different lines at one time. The first and second guard and perhaps also the fireman would sit on the buffers of the different wagons which were destined for side lines. These wagons were not coupled, but the men sitting on the buffers kept a short space between the buffers by means of their hands and feet. The driver then uncoupled the engine and gave the train a start on a speed of say twelve miles an hour. The pointsman then shifted the points smartly between the moving wagons on which the men were sitting; further on perhaps the guard would jump off and shift a point in front of the moving wagons, and so on, the whole operation of several shuntings being done with the movement of the engine, and the various wagons running on to their different lines as desired. This was all right so long as everything went satisfactorily, but sometimes there would be a miss, and then mates were gathered round a limbless man or a mangled mass of flesh and bone.

The railwaymen themselves were keen to combat the fruits of these methods by learning first aid and organising ambulance teams. Incredibly, North British officials were bitterly opposed to any such move by the staff. In the end William Graham organised first-aid classes which he conducted in his off-duty hours. When the North British refused him the use of the waiting room at Cowlairs station he rented a two-roomed dwelling house in Springburn. When this proved too small for the number of men who turned up for the classes he hired a hall and ran the classes on Sundays. The men made their own stretchers and splints, bought their bandages and paid a Springburn doctor to lecture to them. They even collected £60 and bought a second-hand litter 'to promptly run our disabled brethren to the infirmary'. 'Foremen and station-masters,' lamented Graham, 'easily obtained information as to the members of the new classes, and had them booked for Sunday duty, and while this to a certain extent was a damper on the enthusiasm of some, it only proved a stimulus to others. Substitutes were procured for Sunday duty occasionally, and by dint of sacrificing here and there the movement still prospered.' Drummond, if he did not actively oppose the first-aiders, did nothing to help them. It was left to his successor to show appreciation of their efforts. 'When he (Matthew Holmes) gave us a donation of a sovereign,' wrote Graham, 'we felt very proud of the recognition.'

If the North British were indifferent to the men maimed in their service at least they had to make some arrangement for the removal from their property of the human debris that resulted from any accident. Reminiscing in the *Red Cross and Ambulance News*, William Graham wrote:

'One fine summer evening after a good day's work at Balloch, and having made out the daily report and washed my hands before going home, I was called back and told to take the first engine in steam and proceed immediately to Dalmuir. On the way I was to keep a sharp look out along the line for a man who had been run down by the 5.15 p.m. Helensburgh train from Glasgow, to pick him up and take him on to Dalmuir station. I could not get a fireman at the moment, but took with me the locomotive foreman's office boy who happened to be handy. Then attaching van and guard I set off anticipating that this preparation would suffice. I little dreamt of the work in store. Just before reaching Duntocher Road level crossing I saw the body of a man lying face downwards on the six feet space. His head was smashed and his legs practically mincemeat from the knees down. Under one arm lay the poor fellow's "piece", tied in a red handkerchief, while in his other hand was his tea can. There was no occasion for first aid. Sending the boy over to an adjacent farmhouse for some covering for the remains the guard and I made an attempt to improvise a stretcher. First we pulled up two stobs (posts) of the railway fence and getting two sides of a surfaceman's old bogie we placed these crosswise on the stobs. On this rough and ready hand-barrow we placed the corpse and had to gather the pieces of his lower limbs which were strewn over the line.' When Graham reached the level crossing where the body was to be transferred to a cart he found a hostile mob. 'Taking us for the men who had run down the victim,' he wrote, 'they pelted us with road metal by way of summary vengeance. No explanation was of any avail and we had to run literally for our lives, get on to the engine which was then bombarded, and putting on steam soon got out of harm's way.'

*　　　*　　　*

Drummond's first tender express engine for the North British was his fine single which appeared in 1876. It owed much to Stroudley. There were only two of the class and Neilson built them. With these engines Drummond introduced to Cowlairs the Brighton custom of giving engines the names of places they were built to serve, calling them *Glasgow* and *Berwick* to indicate the limits of their operating territory.

Drummond's *great* Cowlairs engine was his 476 class of bogie expresses for the Waverley route. There is a very fine model of 479, *Abbotsford*, in the Royal Scottish Museum in Edinburgh, painstakingly built on the generous scale of 1 : 6 by one of the Museum's own craftsmen in 1883 from drawings supplied by Drummond. It is a sectional model, the engine being split down the centre line to reveal the Drummond magic. If you want to see a Drummond boiler and Drummond motion actually working the Royal Scottish Museum is the place to go. *Abbotsford* is squeezed into a glass case along with a North British Atlantic built on a scale of 1 : 12. That is a mistake. Such is the place of the Drummond bogie in British locomotive engineering history that the model should be the central shrine in a Drummond Room. The Room would be softly lit and draped in black and a spotlight high in one corner would play on *Abbotsford* standing on a dais in the middle of the floor.

*   *   *

Carlisle Citadel station in 1878 was a railway shop window. The best trains of five main line companies converged on the Citadel, and the companies paraded the finest of their locomotive stock at its platforms. There was colour at Carlisle in the late afternoon, in the calm that preceded the arrival of the Midland and London & North Western trains from the south. One of James Stirling's big Glasgow & South Western bogies, maybe No. 107, would be waiting to take charge of the Glasgow portion of the Midland train. Not far away a Drummond 476 would be simmering, ready to make a dash for it up over Whitrope and Falla with the Edinburgh portion of the St Pancras express. And somewhere around would be two dear old Conner eight-footers preparing to replace the North Western engine on the West Coast train. The Caledonian had not moved with the times. George Brittain, who had taken over the St Rollox chair from Benjamin Conner, had produced a 4—4—0 in 1877, and hoped to put it in the Carlisle shop window along with the fine new bogie express engines fielded by his rivals. Alas! the first Caley bogie was a failure; it could not match the performance of the old Conner singles on the Carlisle road, and the eight-footers were kept on the principal expresses. The Midland train of the period would arrive in Carlisle more than likely with one of Johnston's new seven-foot 2—4—0s or one of the six-foot-six class built by Dübs in 1877. On the North Western train there would be one or perhaps two Precedents built any time since 1874. But in the imposing parade of new motive power no engine was more distinguished than Drummond's 476 class. Cowlairs had produced the showpiece of the Carlisle shop window.

122

The Drummond bogie was a big powerful engine in its day, solidly built of the best materials. The coupled wheels were 6 ft 6 in., the cylinders 18 in. by 26 in., the boiler pressure 150 p.s.i., and the weight of engine and tender in working order 75 tons 10 cwt.

Ten of the engines were given Waverley route names and distributed accordingly; two, destined for the trains to the north, were named *Montrose* and *Aberdeen*. The heaviest trains on the Waverley route remained the responsibility of these engines for twenty years.

While work on the last four of the 476 class was in progress at Cowlairs Drummond found himself with a strike on his hands. The building of so many new locomotives and the reconstruction of the works had depleted the North British coffers and the directors decided to rectify their shaky financial position by increasing the working hours at Cowlairs from 51 hours per week to 54 without a corresponding increase in pay. This proposal angered the men and, loyal though they were, they came out on strike. There was a recession in the private locomotive building trade at the time and Drummond recruited labour from among the 300 men who had been paid off by Dübs; but these soon yielded to the pickets and joined the strikers. Men were then brought from St Margarets to Cowlairs, but they too worked only for a few days before giving their support to the Springburn men. Drummond was determined to get his engines finished and in the end recruited anybody who had ever worked with iron. In so doing he earned himself a bad name in Springburn. Such was public feeling that the 'blacklegs' dared not show their faces in the district and for their own safety they slept in Cowlairs works for six weeks.

The outcome was that the regular workers accepted a piecework system which in effect gave the North British six days' work for the price of five.

During his stay at Cowlairs Drummond built (or had built by Neilson) 58 passenger tanks in four sizes. This feat of

says much for their business acumen that in a few years it became by far the largest trading organisation in Springburn. The success of the enterprise so alarmed an organisation called the Traders Protective Association that this body approached the North British management with the request that they dismiss from their service any employee who took part in the affairs of Cowlairs Co-operative Society. At that time there were six North British men on the Society's board, Michael Shields, a splicer on the Rope, John and Hugh Campbell, Andrew Cook, William Ross and Andrew Walker. All six received notices from the company to give up their association with the Society or relinquish their jobs with the railway. The ultimatum produced a wave of resentment in the district. The threatened six were honest men doing what they considered was a service to the community. The Springburn doctors and ministers and teachers, as well as the railwaymen, were conscious that a great wrong had been done and there was widespread support for the Springburn martyrs. One of the best-loved Springburn ministers led the fight against the railway. The North British very nearly had a major strike on their hands. In the end Mr William Maxwell (later Sir William Maxwell) of the Scottish Co-operative Wholesale Society met the general manager of the North British and as a result of their talks the dismissal notices were withdrawn.

Cowlairs Co-operative Society is still the biggest trading organisation in Springburn and railwaymen are still concerned in its management. The Society has never forgotten its railway origins. There is an engine on the Society's letterhead and on the cover of the periodical balance sheet issued to members. Until recently pastry bought at the Co-op was served in paper bags emblazoned with the engine *motif*. Milk arrives at Springburn homes in bottles with an engine design impressed on the glass. At Springburn Cross is the drinking fountain presented to the district by the Society at the time of their coming of age in 1902; it bears a commemorative plaque showing a Holmes 4—4—0 in bronze. The facade of the Society's head office exhibits a red sandstone carving of a Reid 0—6—0. And it is still possible to be a guest at a Springburn table and have tea poured from a white porcelain pot embellished with 'The Diver' in black.

Drummond did not have much to do to 'The Diver' when it was brought back to Cowlairs after its terrible adventure. In spite of the fact that it had dived not once but three times to the bottom of the Tay nothing as drastic as a complete rebuild was required. No. 224 had lost its chimney, and there was some distortion of the frame. It was the spring of 1880 before the first attempt was made to recover the engine. Divers found it partly embedded in the sand of the river bed, and by 7 April chains had been passed under it and all was ready for the lift by steam winches mounted on barges. The top of the boiler had just broken surface when one of the chains snapped and No. 224 went to the bottom again. It took the divers another two days to replace the chains. The second attempt at lifting was successful, and the barges moved cautiously towards the Fife shore with the 4—4—0, its wheels just clear of the water, slung between them. They had almost gained the beach when the chains parted and the engine took its third dive into the Tay. Two more days' work saw it safely beached near Tayport lighthouse. Before it was dispatched to Cowlairs it was photographed by a famous Dundee manufacturer of holiday view postcards. One of the resulting cards was still a steady seller in Dundee, along with the more traditional local views, sixty years after the disaster. The card had No. 224 as a centrepiece with several before-and-after views of the bridge arranged round it.

In 1885 No. 224 was the engine chosen when the North British decided to try out Nisbet's system of tandem compounding. New 20 in. cylinders were fitted under the smoke box and high pressure 13 in. cylinders were added immediately in front of and in line with them. The piston rods of the low pressure cylinders extended through the front covers to become the piston rods of the high pressure cylinders, steam

NORTH BRITISH SCENES. Top: *Cowlairs station during the widening of the platform at the turn of the century.* Bottom: *Sighthill goods station with St Rollox works in the background*

SPRINGBURN STATION. Top: *A Drummond 4—4—0 tank enter-*
ing the station in 1896 with an Outer Circle train. Bottom: *The station*
in 1963 with an electric train about to depart for Milngavie. On the left
are the derelict Atlas works and on the right Hyde Park

from which was then exhausted into the casing of the low pressure cylinders. The stroke of all four was 24 in. In its new form No. 224 ran on the Edinburgh and Glasgow expresses, and an account of its performance in a professional journal said that it gave increased power on reduced fuel consumption. The North British apparently did not consider the experiment a success, for the engine was soon restored to something like its original condition and 'The Diver' continued to do useful work for some thirty years. Observers took a morbid delight in watching for it. A shed visitor to Cowlairs in 1901 reported gleefully that both 224 and 602, the engine that headed the first train across the Forth Bridge, were on shed at the same time. It was commonly said that No. 224 was never allowed to cross the new Tay Bridge, but that was not true. 'The Diver' crossed on 29 December 1908 with the very train on which it had had that spot of trouble almost exactly 29 years before.

In 1925 the LNER scrapped an 0—4—4 tank that had been working on local services out of Edinburgh. She was one of the batch that Drummond had built as 0—4—2s in 1877. In those days she was No. 89, *Ladybank,* and in 1879 she was David Mitchell's regular engine at Dundee. By right No. 89 should have been 'The Diver', but on that fateful Sunday *Ladybank* was in need of repair, and Mitchell was given No. 224. It is an odd thing, but 224 had a similar escape from disaster earlier in 1879. On 17 May she should have been on the 4.15 express from Glasgow to Aberdeen, but her place was taken by 2—4—0 No. 427. The train collided with a light engine coming off the West of Fife mineral line at Whitemyre Junction, and the driver of 427 was killed.

Drummond's output of new engines built at Cowlairs never attained Wheatley's record of forty in a single year, partly because during Drummond's period in office the works were undergoing reconstruction, partly because Drummond had great faith in Neilson & Co. as locomotive builders. Drummond's singles *Glasgow* and *Berwick* had come from Hyde

Park. Neilson also built eight of his twelve 4—4—0 express engines, three of his express tanks and a score of the celebrated Jumbos—the powerful five-foot 0—6—0 freight engine he turned out in 1876.

Drummond must have got on well with James Reid. They were birds of a feather. Both were Ayrshiremen, although Reid was eighteen years Drummond's senior, and James Reid was decidedly Drummondesque. By the time Dugald Drummond got to know Hyde Park, Walter Neilson was no longer there. The story of the Neilson—Reid rift is not well documented. The two men must have been friendly enough at one time, for Reid named one of his sons Walter Montgomerie Neilson Reid. Contemporary accounts speak discreetly of Neilson relinquishing control of the firm to Reid. What is highly significant is that Walter Neilson cut himself off from the firm he had helped to found when he was little more than a schoolboy, and built a great new locomotive factory of his own in Springburn, an easy stone throw away from Hyde Park. For a quarter of a century James Reid was the sole proprietor of Hyde Park; he *was* Neilson and Company. The engines that were known the world over as Neilson engines were nothing of the sort. They were *Reid* engines. It was perhaps unfortunate for the reputation of this fine engineer that his name did not appear in the title of the firm until after his death. Neilson and Co. became Neilson, Reid and Co. in 1898 and existed as such for only five years before being swallowed up by the North British Locomotive Co. in 1903.

James Reid was Springburn's greatest citizen. Today the name of Dugald Drummond means nothing to the intelligent layman, but that of Reid lives on in Springburn. There is a Reid Hall; there is a Reidhouse Street. Children play on swings and roundabouts that James Reid put up for their grandfathers and grandmothers. Springburn lads and lassies do their courting among the tropical trees in a massive glasshouse, a gift of the Reid family long ago. And old James Reid himself in bronze and one and a half times life size watches everybody from his plinth in Springburn Park, a locomotive drawing clutched in his left hand. In an age when the wealthy Glasgow industrialists built their mansions in the Renfrewshire uplands or at the Clyde coast, Reid occupied a house almost in the shadow of his works. He worshipped in a Springburn church not five minutes' walk from the main gate of Hyde Park, and some of his workmen were elders in the same church. He was to be seen as often on the horse cars in Springburn Road as in his brougham.

In 1882 James Reid was President of the Institution of Engineers and Shipbuilders in Scotland (Walter Neilson had been an earlier President). The President's speech traditionally consisted of a review of papers read by members in the previous session and a brief survey of recent developments in engineering. Reid in his speech paid lip service to tradition, then contrived to deliver an address on the pernicious habit which some railways had acquired of building their own locomotives. Reid's theory was that the railways were simply common carriers depending on the manufacturing industries for the bulk of their freight traffic; therefore they were bound to encourage the manufacturing industries. He gave some grim examples, without being too specific, of railway companies that had built their own engines and had found the exercise unduly costly. An unspecified railway in the south of England, according to Reid, had spent £3,250 on a locomotive that Hyde Park could have turned out for £2,750. He criticised Crewe for building their own engines and neglecting to make public the cost of construction.

'It is sometimes argued in favour of their doing so,' said Reid, 'that the best workmanship and materials are ensured; but like many more arguments advanced in favour of this practice, it will not bear close examination by practical men well acquainted with the subject. The best workmanship and materials are more likely to be secured by the railway companies placing themselves in the hands of manufacturers of established reputation.

'Interchange of ideas and a knowledge of improvements are better obtained through the medium of private manufacturers who work for nearly every country in the world, than by any other known method; certainly very much better than if left to the individual and isolated research of each company's chief engineer, shut up very much in his own district and without proper means of communication with, or ascertaining what is being done in the world at large. The great stream of thought and development would be dammed up, or at least dwarfed into the merest rill, and the minds of those responsible for the production of the motive power on our railways would necessarily become cramped and wedded to their own ideas, and would lose that expansiveness and receptiveness so necessary to those who desire to do good service to engineering science.

'Further, it is evident in the presence of close competition manufacturers must necessarily have the strongest possible motives for improving design and simplifying detail, and for perfecting the methods and economising the cost of construction. As it is the business of their lives to do this, they are more likely to succeed than the man who in addition to undertaking to do all this, for behoof not of himself, be it understood, but of a large and wealthy company, has imposed upon him duties in connection with the working and maintenance of the rolling stock, duties which in themselves do, or at all events should, tax the energies of the best man in the country.

'True, the excellencies and deficiencies of the stock can only be proved in regular working practice under skilled supervision, and it may be argued that those who work the stock are better qualified to improve it than the manufacturers can be. But, notwithstanding the plausability of this argument improvement has, for the most part, taken rise in the private manufactory, mainly on account of the reasons already referred to.

'Furthermore, it is incontestable that the manufacturers can make a profit and at the same time supply engines at such prices as cannot be paralleled in the works of the railway companies, when every proper charge is included in the latter. Whenever the question has been fairly tried on its merits it has had to be admitted that the policies of companies manufacturing their own locomotive stock was unsound.'

Reid gave his address on 24 October 1882, and one of the members who listened to him was Matthew Holmes. It is not unlikely that Reid had Holmes very much in mind when he spoke, for Holmes had just stepped into the office of locomotive superintendent at Cowlairs, Dugald Drummond having just stepped out in a fit of high temper. The North British hierarchy were not easy to get on with. They had already lost one good locomotive superintendent, Wheatley, as a result of a quarrel, and it was inevitable that a man of Drummond's temperament would fall foul of them sooner or later. Drummond left his late employers a rebuilt Cowlairs and a remarkable stud of locomotives. The North British then had forty years of independent history ahead of it, but in all that time a succession of locomotive superintendents, with one fleeting exception, made no radical departures from the basic Drummond design.

The North British locomotive department must have been the envy of the Caledonian board room; and it must have been with glee that the Caledonian directors heard the news that the great Dugald Drummond was willing to accept the St Rollox chair. Here was drama indeed. For a man of Drummond's status and achievements the sudden transfer from Cowlairs to the great rival establishment of St Rollox was sensational. The task he faced at St Rollox was very like that which had faced him at Cowlairs seven years earlier. St Rollox works in 1882, like Cowlairs in 1875, were antiquated and needed to be rebuilt if the efficient conduct of the locomotive department was to be assured. Relatively few engines had been built there in recent years, Neilson and Dübs having contributed most of the new stock. What locomotives the Caledonian had were for the most part outside-cylinder Allan type. Only in the year before Drummond's accession had the Caledonian succeeded in producing a successful bogie, and even that was a light machine designed for working over the Oban road. The top trains were still being worked by Conner eight-footers and 7 ft 2 in. 2—4—0s. There was a chronic shortage of motive power of all kinds. When Drummond took over there was only one Caledonian engine to every $64\frac{1}{2}$ vehicles, the lowest engine-to-vehicles ratio of any British railway. The average was one locomotive to every 32 vehicles.

The provision of effective motive power was so urgent that Drummond put an intensive rebuilding programme in hand to meet immediate requirements. He converted Conner's old 6 ft 2 in. freight engines into passenger engines and put them on the principal expresses. He thought the eight-footers were 'all legs and wings', but he liked them well enough to rebuild them as they came through the shops. The Drummond look spread through the Caledonian system: fripperies like slotted splashers gave place to solid Drummond splashers; Sinclair's plain chimney, universal on the Caledonian, was replaced by the more ornate Drummond chimney. A chimney is to a locomotive what a hat is to a woman, and the new Drummond appendages took years off the life of the old Conner engines. The Caledonian became more like the North British every day.

The crying need on the Caledonian was for a modern bogie express engine to take over the working of the West Coast express traffic from the ancients then employed. Within two years of his appointment Drummond had just such an engine running into Carlisle to appear alongside his 476 class of the North British. The Caledonian bogie had the same cylinder dimensions and driving wheel diameter, and it did for the Caledonian precisely what the 476 did for the North British. Regrettably Drummond dropped the general practice of naming engines when he went to St Rollox, so enthusiasts at Carlisle were denied the satisfaction of seeing say *Annandale* meeting *Abbotsford* or *Symington* running into the Citadel alongside *St Boswells*.

Drummond produced a St Rollox version of his North British Jumbo, a design so successful that 244 of the class were eventually built. He repeated for the Caledonian, although not quite on the same scale, the marathon tank production he had achieved for the North British. For branch line services he built 24 small tanks very like his 5 ft engines for the North British. Once again he used the same cylinder dimensions, but his Caley tanks were 0—4—4s whereas the Cowlairs engines were 4—4—0s. There were two classes of six-coupled tank, a pair of 0—4—2 saddle tanks for working the Killin branch and sundry pugs. For the coast road from Glasgow to Greenock Drummond designed a 4—4—0 with 18 in. by 26 in. cylinders and 5 ft 9 in. driving wheels, of which twelve were built. On this class he employed his duplex whistle. There were two whistles, a small one and large one, both whistle valves being actuated by the same rod. Gentle pressure opened the first valve and produced a sound no louder than a guard's whistle; additional pressure produced a more stentorian note. Drivers were instructed to use the big whistle only when necessary. It was reported at the time that the object of the duplex whistle was 'to prevent horses being frightened in the stations'. The Greenock bogies, like all the Drummond engines, were robustly built of the finest materials. The specification mentioned frames of Siemens steel, and cast-steel wheel centres and axles made from 'selected extra best scrap'.

The Caledonian directors were so pleased with Drummond's work that shortly after the second anniversary of his appointment they increased his salary. Up to that time Drummond had continued to live at Norwood Villa in the North British residential town of Lenzie, but now he moved to an imposing city house at 186 Bath Street, Glasgow. At this time his brother Peter, who had followed him to St Rollox as works manager, lived in a plebeian tenement at 399 Parliamentary Road. He too moved shortly afterwards, but only to another working class tenement round the corner in Stirling Road. The Glasgow Directory perhaps tells us more about the character and outlook of the two brothers than pages of biography.

A correspondent of *The Ironmonger* who visited St Rollox in 1885 found the place in a state of organised confusion. Work on new locomotive construction and rebuilding was going on at full blast while new structures were actually rising over the heads of the workmen as they went about their jobs. 'Judging from such parts of the old buildings as yet remain untouched,' said the reporter, 'it is fair to assume that the remodelling has not been unnecessarily undertaken.' The visitor was surprised to find that the new buildings were painted 'a light Cambridge blue'. A Caledonian blue St Rollox! The man from *The Ironmonger* counted 31 boilers under construction, and thought there were a hundred loco- motives in the 600 ft long erecting shop. He was intrigued by a lathe that was big enough to take the driving wheel of a Conner single, and was shown a moulding machine made at St Rollox and worked by Westinghouse air that manufactured 250 axle box bushes a day. Then there was a frame slotter that could slot twelve frames in one operation—the first machine of its kind in the country. In addition to the new machinery there were old machines that had been remodelled by Dugald and Peter Drummond. The reporter also saw for himself the results of time and motion study introduced by Drummond. The factory was so arranged that cylinders were bored only 50 ft from where they were fitted, thus dispensing with a certain amount of labour.

Drummond found time to give thought to the comfort of Caledonian passengers. He introduced carriage lighting by the Pinsch oil system, and invented and applied his own sys- tem of carriage steam heating. Normally steam from the West- inghouse exhaust and from the engine exhaust was used, con- veyed by insulated pipes to a cylinder placed under one of the seats in each compartment. Each cylinder had a 'heating surface' of $8\frac{1}{4}$ sq ft and kept the temperature at 62 deg in the coldest weather.

*　　　*　　　*

The year 1886 was a colourful one in the story of Spring- burn, for in the summer the International Exhibition of Industry, Science and Art was held in Edinburgh, the first great exhibition ever to be staged in Scotland. A locomotive section was planned, and the Springburn designers set about producing something worthy of the occasion. Drummond had Dübs build a Caledonian bogie specially for the show, No. 124. Up at Cowlairs Matthew Holmes just had time to get the first of a fine new class of seven-foot 4—4—0s ready. By this time Walter Neilson had opened his brand new Clyde Locomotive

Works, just across the railway line from Hyde Park, to build and equip which no expense had been spared. Neilson had no lack of influential financial backers; everything in the place was new, the best that money could buy. David Jones of the Highland Railway had given the Clyde Locomotive Works their first order, for eight express passenger 4—4—0s, and Walter Neilson entered the first of the class for the Edinburgh show.

The engines had to be at the Exhibition grounds not later than 1 April, and up to 22 February James Reid had made no move to have Hyde Park represented at Edinburgh. On the following day an unknown copy clerk made this historic entry in the Hyde Park order book in his flowing, copperplate hand: 'One Bogie Express Passenger Engine and Tender to drawing and specification. Our offer of 22nd inst. and their acceptance of date. To be Exhibited at the Edinburgh International Exhibition where it must be delivered by April 1st 1886 without fail.' Neilson & Co.'s choice was a surprising one. When rivals were entering up-to-the-minute bogie express engines, James Reid elected to have his works represented by a type considered by many railways to be obsolete, and of which none had been seen in Scotland; a 4—2—2 with inside cylinders. Reid had only 66 days to build the engine. It was finished in time—superbly finished—and taken out into the yard and photographed with many of the men who built it.

The Edinburgh International Exhibition of 1886 was something of a disappointment to the Scots. Since it was Scotland's first venture into the exhibition field, they had expected Queen Victoria to come to Edinburgh for the occasion. But there were two exhibitions in England that summer, and the Queen chose to confer her patronage on one of the English shows, and sent Prince Albert Victor to officiate at Edinburgh. However, the railway enthusiast who visited the machinery hall was greeted with a rewarding sight. He could look at the Caledonian and North British entries and see at a glance what

Matthew Holmes had done with the basic Drummond design. He had not improved it æsthetically by giving it the stunted, rounded Stirling cab, for which his drivers could not have thanked him. He is reputed to have adopted it to save steel and labour costs. From the point of view of crew comfort the Holmes modification was a step back towards the old Wheatley bent-over face plate. At the same time Holmes had done away with engine names to save paint and painters' wages. Another difference between the Holmes engine and the Drummond engine was that in the Holmes engine the frames were visible above the front platform whereas Drummond cut the frames off flush with it. A glance underneath would also have shown the visitor that Holmes had replaced Drummond's deep sloping grate with a level grate.

The Caledonian entry represented all that was newest and best in Drummond design, although in one important respect No. 124 was different from her sister engines; she had Bryce-Douglas valve gear. Archibald Bryce-Douglas was in the engineering department of the Fairfield shipyard and his valve gear, which was reputed to give an improved distribution of steam, had been successfully applied to marine engines. This was its first application to a locomotive. Here is an intriguing thought. Dugald Drummond was born at Ardrossan in 1840 and, since his parents were God-fearing folk, they would present him at the parish kirk of Ardrossan for christening. The minister in those days was the Rev John Bryce, and in that same year 1840 his wife presented him with a son whom he called Archibald. In later years it was this same Archibald (who had inherited a minor estate and added Douglas to his name) who induced Dugald Drummond to try out his valve gear. It was not a success on 124, and it was soon replaced with link motion.

The Highland Railway engine, resplendent in light green, was eye-catching, and was the only outside-cylindered engine in the show. It had an Allan look about it. Poor Alexander Allan! That young Scottish engineer who had done such wonderful things at Crewe and subsequently wielded so much influence in locomotive design, deserved a better fate. By right he should have been one of the Springburn superintendents with a locomotive of his own at Edinburgh. But, after losing his job with the Scottish Central when that railway was absorbed in the Caledonian, he faded from the railway scene. When he died at Scarborough he was experimenting with a stabiliser for ships' hulls.

Neilson & Co.'s single must have been an enigma to the knowledgeable visitor to the Exhibition. It looked as Drummond as 124, yet the catalogue and the professional journals said it was Neilson. Both engines were blue. The visitor could half shut his eyes, imagine the big drivers replaced by coupled wheels, and see 124 in the Neilson engine. It was all very puzzling.

At the conclusion of the Exhibition Mr Bell and forty men of the North British had to get the engines back to their native element. Two hundred yards of sleepered track was laid down in Melville Drive. The Holmes engine was steamed, and it took in charge No. 124, two carriages and a second engine all coupled into one train, and proceeded to pull this cavalcade along Melville Drive. When the North British engine reached the end of the track, the length of rails was lifted and re-laid in front of the train. The process started at daybreak, and by the first afternoon the procession had reached the north west end of Brougham Place. There a halt was called, for Mr Bell was of the opinion that three engines and two coaches passing down busy Lothian Road would be more than the public would put up with. So the Holmes bogie was left simmering in an Edinburgh public thoroughfare until eleven o'clock that night when the journey was resumed. Two days later *The Scotsman* announced that 'the train was safely lodged in the Caledonian Railway goods yard'.

The coupled express engines went to their respective companies and earned their keep quietly for many years. But it was the odd one out, the Hyde Park single, that set the heather on fire. Everybody knows how, as Caledonian No. 123, Drummond put it on the West Coast expresses. Then in 1888 came the Race to Edinburgh, and the gallant little engine carried the Caledonian colours gloriously night after night over Beattock and Cobbinshaw and on to an exciting finish in Princes Street station. In a season of summer evenings No. 123 achieved immortality.

The publicity given to the Race to Edinburgh and to the performance of the Caledonian single raised many a professional eyebrow. The building of singles had all but ceased except on the Great Northern. The Midland Railway had stopped building them as far back as 1866; then between 1887 and 1888 three new classes of single appeared on their lines, for No. 123 helped to spark off a revival of the single as an express passenger type. Most contemporary accounts agree that 123's success would not have been possible without the new Holt sander. Slipping had been the bugbear of the single, and by all accounts the sander worked wonders. The Midland in an interesting trial had taken the rods off one of their coupled engines and fitted it with sanders. In trial runs over the Settle —Carlisle line the engine behaved just like a coupled engine; what it lost in adhesion was made up by the scientific application of sand to the rail.

Samuel Waite Johnston, speaking to the Institution of Mechanical Engineers, said, 'This class of engine (the single) is a great favourite with the drivers of express trains. I may mention that the steam sanding apparatus adopted within the last few years has been an indispensable factor in bringing these engines again into favour, inasmuch as this apparatus has rendered it possible for them to work satisfactorily on roads and with trains which they could not otherwise deal with in all weathers.' An echo of the single-with-sanders episode came from as far away as America. In 1887 the Hinckley Locomotive Works at Boston built an express single for the Boston & Maine, who intended to use it on their *Flying Yankee*. 'Experience in England,' commented the *Railroad*

Gazette of New York, 'goes to prove that the success of engines with a single pair of drivers depends entirely upon the character of the sand supplied.'

No. 123 had been doing great things with the West Coast expresses for more than three years when Sir William Acworth published his *Railways of Scotland* in 1890. In his book Acworth stated that Drummond designed No. 123. This claim brought a retort from Edward Snowball who wrote in a letter in *Engineering*: 'The general design and the whole of the detail drawings were made in Messrs Neilson's drawing office under the immediate supervision of the head of the firm, without any intervention on the part of the Caledonian locomotive superintendent.' What Snowball was saying here was that No. 123 was a hundred per cent James Reid! Snowball was Reid's chief draughtsman; he more than anyone was in a position to know who designed the engine. Yet it is difficult to reconcile Snowball's claim with the entry in the Hyde Park order book, with its phrase 'our offer—and their acceptance'. Whose acceptance? Again, in the famous photograph of No. 123 reputedly taken at Hyde Park *before* the engine was sent to Edinburgh the engine carries its Caledonian number. Presumably the Caledonian made an arrangement with Neilson's to purchase the engine *after* it was designed, but before it was built. The letter in *Engineering* sparked off a spate of replies, some of them angrily denouncing Snowball's claim. One writer named Stroudley as the true begetter of 123. Another declared that if the Caledonian had not taken 123 another British railway was ready and willing to buy it; this correspondent signed himself 'Cowlairs'. Neither Drummond nor anyone else in authority challenged Snowball's statement, and it certainly was not like Drummond to let someone else claim credit for work that he had done himself. A likely explanation is that James Reid and his staff designed the engine along currently popular lines in the expectation that it would be acceptable to one of the Springburn superintendents. It is remarkable that so much mystery should have surrounded so famous an engine when it was not yet four years old. One thing is certain; 123 was (and, happily, still is) a Springburn engine.

Business was brisk in the locomotive trade in the eighties. Railways at home and abroad were still extending, and demand was steady. Regularly throughout the decade the sidings at Hyde Park were lined with engines bearing the colours of a score of British companies, waiting dispatch to their customers. Engines for further afield were to be seen in steam on the work's sidings or on the Sighthill branch of the North British. One week it would be a big eight-coupled goods for the Southern Railway of Italy; another it would be an immaculate 4—4—0 compound on the Worsdell-Von Borries system for the Argentine Midland, or a Scott-Moncrieff tram engine. At that time Reid thought there might be a future in the compressed-air engine for short hauls. He built one and ran it with a load equivalent to 40 passengers for $8\frac{1}{2}$ hours up and down the Sighthill branch. The cost of the charging plant ruled out the vehicle as a commercial proposition. Big broad-gauge engines for India and elsewhere could not be taken to the docks by rail; they had to be taken through the streets of Glasgow to the Clyde. The local transport problem that Neilson and Co. thought they had eliminated by moving to Springburn was back with them again after only twenty years.

If Hyde Park's sidings were at times full to overflowing, the same could not be said of those at the great new Clyde Locomotive Works across the way. The Edinburgh Exhibition had proved a disappointment for Walter Neilson; the business he thought might have resulted from it did not materialise. The Clyde Locomotive Works were likely to attract orders mainly at the expense of Hyde Park and the Glasgow Locomotive Works, and the satisfied patrons of these concerns saw no reason for transferring their allegiance. Three years after it had opened the factory that had most of the ingredients needed for success—a famous name, moneyed backers, the best of machinery and the pick of staff—was only saved from disaster by the lucky chance that Sharp, Stewart of the Atlas Works, Manchester, were on the look-out for new premises. They bought the Clyde Locomotive Works at a third of what they had cost and added to the Springburn concern the one feature it had lacked, a long backlog of satisfied customers. The famous new owners, Sharp, Stewart and Co. Ltd, brought to Springburn with them the treasured name of their old works; the Clyde Locomotive Works became the Atlas Locomotive Works. James Reid now had on his doorstep not only a former employer, but a most formidable rival.

Meanwhile, at Cowlairs, Matthew Holmes was doing good work for the North British. He built six 0—4—4 passenger tanks differing little in design and dimensions from Drummond's '88' class. In 1888 he began producing his 18 in. six-coupled goods engines and in 1890 he turned out twelve new 6 ft 6 in. 4—4—0 express passenger engines to cope with the great increase in traffic that was certain to follow the opening of the Forth Bridge in March of that year.

To celebrate this opening another large-scale exhibition was planned to take place in Edinburgh that summer, and a railway enthusiast, Alfred Rosling Bennett, was put in charge of the railway section. Bennett set out to present the greatest railway show ever staged at a British exhibition. As his central theme he decided on three set pieces, each illustrating the locomotive work of an Anglo-Scottish partnership, East Coast, Midland and West Coast. It had long irked Holmes that his engines had played no part in the Race to Edinburgh for, by agreement with the North Eastern, the English company used their own locomotives to work the East Coast trains through from Newcastle to Edinburgh. Holmes, therefore, welcomed the chance to show off one of his new 4—4—0s in partnership with a Midland engine that Johnston had undertaken to send to Edinburgh. The East Coast companies provided a Great Northern eight-footer, No. 776, and the North Eastern a two-cylinder compound, No. 1521. The West Coast team turned out Webb's *Jeanie Deans* and Drummond's *Carbrook*. The

143

Caledonian engine was one of the newest of Drummond's bogies, with which Springburn anticipated Swindon by 14 years, for Drummond had produced, in 1889, a design with the Churchward features of high boiler pressure (200 lb.) and short direct ports enabling full regulator and short cut-off working. Bennett had a grand scheme for running *Jeanie Deans* non-stop from Euston to a point inside the Exhibition grounds where the locomotive, at the end of a world record non-stop run, would stop in front of a grandstand filled with admiring spectators. Webb was all in favour of this stunt, and was willing to run the engine with two tenders, there being no water troughs on the Scottish part of the course.

Even more daring was Bennett's plan to get an American engine over for the Exhibition. Letters were sent inviting seven leading American locomotive manufacturers to send samples of their work to Edinburgh. Drummond had already assured Bennett that he was agreeable to an American engine from the Exhibition being run with an American crew anywhere on the Caledonian between Carlisle and Aberdeen. Commenting on Bennett's offer, *Locomotive Engineer* of New York said:

'We hope some of our builders will take the matter up and build a winner which we think they easily could. Of course, there is no field open in Europe for the sale of American-built locomotives, but English, Scotch and German locomotives are largely sold in South America and other countries in competition with American locomotives, and to beat them on their own roads would be worth thousands of dollars to the winner in advertising alone. The thing now is that Cousin John has a chip on his shoulder and swelling around daring any Yankee locomotive builder to knock it off and whip him on his own ground. When a man thinks he can't be licked, the easiest way to argue with him is to do the licking. Nobody afraid of the English engine, is there?'

Whether anybody was afraid of the English (*sic*) engine was

144

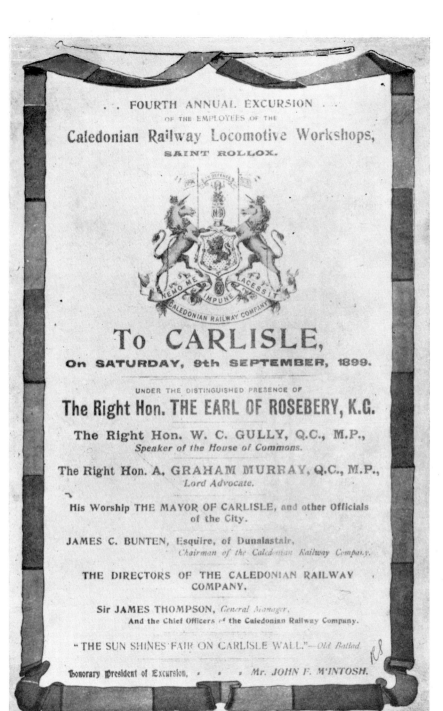

SOCIAL OCCASION. *The front cover of the brochure describing the great Caledonian excursion to Carlisle*

GLASGOW ENGINES EXHIBITED. Top: *Engines on view at the Glasgow International Exhibition of 1901.* Bottom: *A.W.G. class for India on view in George Sq., Glasgow, in Festival of Britain year 1951*

146

not reported; nevertheless, six of the challenged firms did not even trouble to answer the letter from Edinburgh. The one exception, Baldwins, asked for details of the Caledonian main line and the locomotive types and loads normally featured on it, and this data was forwarded. Baldwins were so certain that their engines had no hope of gaining a place in the British market that they were unwilling to risk money in sending a locomotive to Edinburgh. They agreed to send one only if the Exhibition authorities would pay the whole cost of transport both ways, undertaking to supply it at a rock bottom price so that it could more readily be sold in Britain, thus saving the cost of returning it to America. Bennett sounded several British locomotive superintendents on possible purchase, but none were interested, and the Exhibition organisers could not face the transport costs. Undaunted, Bennett set out to find a benevolent shipping company that would carry the engine for nothing; and he found one. The Anchor Line of Glasgow were willing. All seemed set for an exciting episode in Scottish locomotive history, but alas! at the last minute the Anchor Line found that there were no facilities at New York for loading locomotives and the project had to be abandoned. Scottish enthusiasts were spared the spectacle of a Baldwin heading the 'Tourist' out of Carlisle and wailing down the Clyde Valley in the dawn hours.

The 1890 Exhibition, if it did nothing else, revealed how uneasy were the Anglo-Scottish partnerships. The Caledonian would not agree to the grand entry of *Jeanie Deans* into the arena, so *Jeanie Deans* arrived unostentatiously. When the West Coast exhibit was set up *Jeanie Deans* was at the head of a London & North Western coach and Drummond's *Carbrook* was behind the coach, facing in the same direction as the North Western engine. Drummond was not the man to take kindly to the idea of his engine acting as banker to a North Western ensemble, and wanted *Carbrook* turned round so that it would appear to be pulling the coach. But Bennett could not make the change without ruining the symmetry of

147

K

his exhibit. The Midland board over-ruled Johnston and refused to send an engine to Edinburgh, and this meant that Matthew Holmes could not exhibit his 4—4—0. The all-English East Coast pair were got safely to the pavilion except that the Great Northern single arrived minus its cast iron chimney cap; somebody at Doncaster had forgotten about the low NB bridges. Worsdell wanted to run his compound on a special train over the newly-opened Forth Bridge, but the North British said NO to that. They were sensitive about North Eastern domination of their rails, and aware that the North Eastern had running powers to Perth!

Half way through the run of the Edinburgh Exhibition, Drummond handed his resignation to the Caledonian Railway, and the board accepted it with great regret. A few months earlier Sir Saul Samuel, the Agent-General for the Government of New South Wales, had been in London making a contract with certain business interests for the establishment of a large locomotive works in the colony. Dugald Drummond was appointed managing director of the Australasian Locomotive Engineering Company, and so, after fifteen glorious years, Springburn lost a remarkable man. He left behind him a rich legacy.

Chapter 5

THE DECADE OF THE DUNALASTAIR

The gay nineties opened on a grave note. Railway histories of the period are full of the glamour and the glitter of the great racing days, and there are endless descriptions of the epic performances of the engines and their drivers. I cannot recall that any of the writers mentioned that the Soutars, the Robinsons and the other great performers were paid six or seven shillings for each star appearance, and that their firemen were lucky to get 4s 6d. Four shillings and sixpence for shovelling coal from Carlisle to Perth! Nor have I seen it recorded that the signalmen who passed the trains safely on their way received as their reward 22s 6d per week or that their luckless booking boys were paid 5s for a week of 12-hour days; and no time off for meals. No. 123 sped over at least one level crossing that was manned for 17 hours of the day by a servant who was paid a wage of 10s per week. Yet in the very year when fourteen-year-old boys on the North British were being paid five-sixths of a penny per hour the general manager had his salary increased by £1,000 per year. Those are only some of the grim facts behind the glamour.

One January morning in the nineties a Cowlairs driver came off a shift to find a strong smell of gas permeating his home. The building in Cowlairs Road in which he lived was one of the first to be put up in the early days of the Edinburgh & Glasgow Railway, and it enclosed within its thick stone walls a warren of passages and small dwellings. On the ground floor was a long passage completely dark except for diffused

149

daylight that filtered through a grating on the floor of a similar passage above. Four doors opened off it, each giving access to what in Glasgow is known as a single-end; in other words, a one-roomed flat. Each measured 12 ft by 8 ft and housed a complete family, husband, wife and children. The only source of light was a small window with its sill four feet below street level. These rooms were not even cellars; they were cells. The engine driver and his family lived in one. In an adjoining cell lived a man named Castel with his wife and five children.

The engine driver investigating the source of the gas leak was alarmed to discover that nothing had been seen of the Castel family since the previous day. He sent for Castel's brother, who was employed by the North British making teak centres for carriage wheels, and then broke down the door. He found the entire Castel family—dead. The leak of gas had not occurred in the Castel home, which did not run to the luxury of gas lighting, but from a fractured pipe under the street. Castel was a decent hard-working man, and his pathetic little home was typical of some of the older houses in Springburn in the nineties. The room was tidily kept, and hung on a rope stretched across the room was the family wash which the reporter from the local paper described as 'wonderfully clean'. The walls were covered from floor to ceiling with bright pic-torial calendars, some of which were decorated with ever-greens showing that the Castels had made some attempt to brighten their home for the recently-past Christmas and New Year festivities. It was typical of the hypocrisy of the age that the Castels, unknown and ignored in their lifetime, were given a flamboyant funeral. Their remains were taken to St Rollox church and every minister in Springburn took part in the burial service. As was the custom of the time at important Springburn funerals, the railway trade was officially repre-sented. Chalmers from Cowlairs was one of the pall bearers. Thousands of people packed Sighthill cemetery for the inter-ment. 'We regret to add,' concluded a contemporary press report of the event, 'that in the crush a number of people got their pockets picked.' And that took place in the decade of the Dunalastair.

Long hours and low wages were accepted by the railway-men as their lot. After all, their brothers and cousins who worked in the grocers' and butchers' shops in Springburn Road were no better off. They served behind their counters from seven o'clock in the morning until midnight and ten-year-old errand boys were to be seen struggling up 'the Balgray' with their laden baskets after eleven o'clock on Saturday nights.

On the North British the locomotive men were required to work an aggregate of 144 hours in a fortnight. In practice the official aggregate was the *minimum* time worked. Overtime was called for as a matter of course. In 1890 the patience of the men was beginning to break. Locomotive production had not kept pace with new railway extensions and increasing traffic meant that engines and men were employed for more and more hours per shift. A contemporary journal estimated that, while the English companies owned on average two loco-motives per mile of track, the Scottish companies had only one. The event that triggered off the serious troubles of the nineties was the opening of the Forth Bridge. Edinburgh simply was not ready to deal with the big increase in traffic issuing from the bridge and long delays occurred to trains at the approaches to Waverley. Cowlairs men on the Carlisle goods and other trains bound for destinations east or south of Edinburgh bore the brunt of the chaos. It was not uncommon for them to take seven hours to get through Edinburgh. Professor James Mavor of Glasgow University conducted an investigation into the hours worked by railwaymen and the published results of his inquiries, had they come from a less distinguished source, would hardly have been credible. One crew on a freight run to Edinburgh worked the following hours on five *consecutive* days: $21\frac{1}{2}$, $21\frac{1}{2}$, 19, 19, 24. Another crew worked $17\frac{1}{2}$, $16\frac{1}{2}$, 18, 24, and 15 hours over a five-day period, and a driver averaged 17 hours per day *for a month*. Professor Mavor gave his conclusions in one stark sentence. 'One of three things must happen—the man must die, or he must find other employment, or he must combine with others to compel his employers to treat him better.' In the event, the men struck work.

The railwaymen of those days were fantastically loyal. In spite of their long shifts they would turn out an hour before booking on time to give their engines that extra shine. Such devotion to duty, such loyalty, was seldom appreciated or deserved by the railway managements. When the men's organisations called for a Scottish national strike, so ingrained was the tradition of self-discipline and loyalty that the response was half-hearted. But the men were at the end of their tether. After the first day 300 came out and by the fourth day the number had risen to 9,000. The Caledonian men came out in support of their North British colleagues, although they too had a grudge of their own. Because of the shortage of engines the Glasgow—Carlisle goods turns were being operated with six engines instead of twelve at each end, and the crews were required to do an 18-hour round trip. The Glasgow & South Western joined in too, but men on that system had relatively little cause for complaint.

Scotland had seen nothing like it before. Passenger and goods services, especially those in the Forth—Clyde valley and the Lanarkshire industrial belt, were seriously affected. Among the first trains to be cancelled were the 'Singer workmens', the great complex of trains that ran morning and night to convey some 6,000 men to and from the largest factory in Scotland, the Clydebank plant of the Singer Manufacturing Company. There was no practical alternative to rail transport in 1890 and the Singer factory, starved of both labour and coal, closed down. It was winter, and a severe winter at that, and because coal could not be moved into the city many citizens shivered at their empty hearths. A bleak Christmas was followed by a cheerless New Year. Many factories that closed for the holidays did not reopen, and thousands of men were thrown idle. Ocean-going ships that normally berthed in the Clyde took their trade to other ports because there were no bunkering facilities. The railway companies did what they could to beat the strike. Servants who had left railway employment in the past were re-engaged on a permanent basis. Professor Mavor stated that some of the English companies sent engines to Scotland to take over freight trains travelling to destinations south of the Border. He further stated that the owners of colliery engines were permitted to work coal trains from the pits to the consumer over the main lines, using their own engines and crews.

Far from being jubilant the Springburn men were apprehensive when they saw the ravages wrought by the strike weapon. Some wavered and went back to work. But most were encouraged by the massive public support they received, and it was significant that some of this support came from the propertied class and from some Members of Parliament. The strike leaders set up headquarters in the Albion Halls in College Street, Glasgow, and runners brought in reports from the various sheds and stations. The men organised concerts among themselves to pass the time between the arrival of the messages. ('Brother McMillan of Polmadie will now favour us with a rendition of "Annie Laurie."') The strike might have fizzled out quietly had it not been for the fact that the Caledonian made a monumental blunder. This was surprising, for the Caledonian were before their time in the field of staff relations. The company owned dwelling houses at Motherwell, whose tenants were on strike. The railway decided to evict the strikers and their families. News of the proposed evictions got around, and when the sheriff's officer arrived to carry them out he found the houses surrounded by 20,000 hostile people. The Caledonian, loathe to submit to mob rule, sought and obtained the help of the military, and the evictions were duly carried out. Because of this ill-considered action the company lost face with the public and suffered extensive damage to their property. A throng of indignant sympathisers stoned Motherwell passenger station and wrecked it, and a signal box was destroyed.

The news from Motherwell caused grave disquiet in Springburn, for some of the local strikers occupied North British houses. But the North British were shrewd enough not to invite the riot that Springburn evictions certainly would have initiated. Nevertheless, from that point onwards the morale of the strikers deteriorated. Men drifted back to work. When a rumour swept through Springburn that the Caledonian had posted a notice to the effect that all vacancies had been filled and no further applications for re-instatement could be considered, demoralised St Rollox strikers hurried to Cowlairs to apply for the jobs of North British men still on strike. In the end most of the men got their jobs back, and the companies made small concessions in conditions of service. But for many years the Springburn railwaymen were to talk about the '1890' men. These were the men who had joined the railway from outside during the strike. Bitterness was caused when these men were promoted over the heads of old servants. It was said that in the promotion tests there was one standard for the 1890 men and another more exacting standard for the ex-strikers; a man with long service could therefore find himself firing to an 1890 driver.

The malaise that afflicted the railway companies did not extend to the private builders. At a Hyde Park dinner held at that time James Reid's son, John, had this to say, 'Neilson and Company stand at the head of the trade in Great Britain, and has stood there for a great number of years. I think that, if you will permit me to say so, this is mainly due to the staff we possess.' The *Glasgow Herald*, after stating that the Glasgow locomotive houses had built 85 per cent of all new locomotives built in Britain in the previous year, elaborated on the theme. 'Possibly it may be on account of the good feeling which exists between the employers and employed that the locomotive trade has for years been free from sudden and unaccountable fluctuations. Employers have had faith in the good sense of their men, and could formulate their calculations with a reasonable certainty that they would not be upset by the action of their own at least. In this way trade has been fostered, grist brought to the mill, and to the great proportion of working men employed in the locomotive trade "hard times" is only a name, and has no practical significance to them.'

The private locomotive building industry was not to escape entirely from the hazards of industrial strife. By the end of the decade the private builders were strike-bound, and it was then that British railway companies were driven to seek engines in America. In Springburn the men of the public company, Sharp, Stewart and Co. Ltd, joined in the strike, but the workers in the family concern of Neilson, Reid and Co. would have nothing to do with it. When Hyde Park was invited to join the Federation of Engineering Employers, Hugh Reid declined on the grounds that there was no point in joining an organisation 'to fight for a freedom which we already possess'.

Dugald Drummond's place at St Rollox was taken by Hugh Smellie, who for twelve years had been locomotive superintendent of the Glasgow & South Western Railway. While Springburn had been busy producing the exhibition engines of 1886 Smellie in that same year had turned out at Kilmarnock an extremely fine 4—4—0 with 6 ft 9½ in. driving wheels and a boiler pressure of 150 p.s.i. Many observers watched with interest to see how Smellie would develop this design at St Rollox. They were never to know. Smellie died before he had got a Caledonian design on the drawing board, and John Lambie got his job. Lambie was the third successive Caledonian locomotive superintendent to have come from an Ayrshire coastal town. He was born in Saltcoats, Drummond in neighbouring Ardrossan, and Smellie in Ayr. Ayrshire was a nursery of railway talent. The Stirlings, James Reid and Bryce Douglas among others all came from the county of Robert Burns.

At Cowlairs, Matthew Holmes had a problem on his hands, for on 7 August 1894 the North British took on responsibility for one hundred miles of new railway, the West Highland. Never before had Cowlairs had to cope with anything like the West Highland, a line heavily graded yet lightly laid, passing through magnificent scenery with hardly a village, let alone a town, in all its length. Holmes had to design an engine powerful enough to master the stiff gradients with moderate loads yet light enough to be acceptable on the available roadbed. The result was the West Highland bogie, a 4—4—0 with 5 ft 7 in. wheels and 18 in. by 24 in. cylinders. Cowlairs had 12 of these engines ready for the opening of the line, together with several sets of coupé carriages of an entirely new design intended to give passengers an unrivalled view of the fine scenery on the route.

The West Highland problem was no sooner off his hands than Holmes was called upon to produce an engine for the Edinburgh—Aberdeen traffic. Since the opening of the Forth Bridge, and the wide publicity given to the East Coast's Bridges Route between King's Cross and Aberdeen, tension had been building up between East Coast and West Coast managements. For the first time the West Coast's 8 p.m. 'Tourist' from Euston to Aberdeen—in the season a most lucrative train—had a formidable challenger. An open declaration of war was not far off, and Cowlairs and St Rollox became munition factories for the manufacture of the necessary implements of war. Holmes produced a new 6 ft 6 in. express bogie with 150 p.s.i. boiler pressure. Down at St Rollox in that same year of 1894 Lambie turned out six new 4—4—0s. They were similar to the celebrated Drummond bogies, but with increased boiler pressure and a reduced heating surface. In the following summer, that of 1895, the battle began. Night after night the Holmes engines were racing against the Lambies on the last lap of the thrilling dash to Aberdeen. The deeds of Lambie's No. 17 at the hands of 'honest John Soutar' are legendary. No. 17 made Lambie's name, but he was never to know it. He died on the eve of battle. The man who directed the fortunes of the Caledonian locomotive department in the Race to Aberdeen, although not with his own tools, was John Farquharson McIntosh, whom we last saw as a young man on the Scottish North Eastern in 1866.

Springburn shed staff played no direct part in the 1895 races, though the shopmen at Cowlairs and St Rollox could take some credit for the performances of the locomotives. It was to Holmes and McIntosh that the directives came from the fevered meetings of the East Coast and West Coast chiefs, and it was Springburn men who tuned the engines to the peak of perfection for their exacting tasks. Holmes, we know, was prepared to run the East Coast train non-stop from Edinburgh to Aberdeen with the load cut to three vehicles.

The West Coast racecourse passed only seven miles to the north-east of Springburn. An enthusiast who had taken the trouble to go out to Garnqueen in the small hours of those summer mornings would have been rewarded with the sight of the West Coast flyer, fresh from performing wonders on Beattock, running over that three-quarter-mile stretch of wholly North British territory between Gartgill Junction and Garnqueen North Junction. And if he had been train watching in the early morning of 22 August he would have caught an unforgettable glimpse of Tom Robinson leaning from the cab of Drummond's No. 78, the engine blowing off impatiently as the driver eased her over the facing points. Once over Garnqueen North Junction and on to the main line to the north our observer would have heard the engine open up and go barking away into the dawn and to Perth where Soutar would be waiting with No. 17. One wonders what John McIntosh's thoughts were later that same morning when he got to his desk at St Rollox to learn that No. 78 and No. 17 had been outclassed in that night's racing by Matthew Holmes's No. 293 that had run the East Coast train from Edinburgh to Dundee in 59 minutes and No. 262 that had taken the train northwards from Dundee to reach Kinnaber Junction 14½ minutes ahead of Soutar. For McIntosh was turning over in his mind ideas for a locomotive that would make mincemeat of the North British performance.

The Bailie, the Glasgow magazine that had featured Dugald Drummond in its 'Man You Know' series, accorded the same honour to John Farquharson McIntosh. 'He is a man of massive and powerful physique and is in the very prime of life,' said the article. It did not mention that the new locomotive superintendent of the Caledonian Railway had only one hand; he had lost his right when he was a young engineman. McIntosh had joined the Scottish North Eastern as a boy of fourteen. By 1876 he was locomotive inspector for the northern division of the Caledonian. Then he was locomotive foreman successively at Aberdeen, Carstairs and Polmadie, and by 1891 had risen to be chief running inspector of the railway.

In explaining McIntosh's appointment to the staff at St Rollox Sir James King said, 'Instead of going outside for a man with great fame and perhaps a reputation which would not be borne out by experience when he came to the works, we took one of ourselves, and I am sure we have no reason to regret the choice.' *The Bailie* concluded its sketch of the new man at St Rollox by saying: 'Great things are hoped for from Mr McIntosh as Caledonian Locomotive Superintendent and possessing as he does the warm support of his workmen and the sympathetic good will of his directors there is every likelihood that the hope will be fully and completely realised.' It was. The issue of *The Bailie* containing these notes was dated 27 May 1896. On the previous day the press had been taken on a tour of St Rollox and there they had been shown the Dunalastair.

The Dunalastairs had been running on local and express trains since the end of January that year, and had attracted a lot of attention. A news item in the *Railway Herald* of 22 February 1896 said: 'The last few mornings there was a large assembly at Beattock and other stations on the main line of the Caledonian Railway to see the Dunalastair, the first of the new type of engine being put out by the company. The Dunalastair was attached to the first passenger train from Glasgow to Carlisle last Saturday. It is reported to be proving a splendid locomotive and practically is making a royal progress on the journeys.' As well it might, for here was an engine that was a milepost in British locomotive history. Basically the Dunalastair was Drummond, but McIntosh had given his engine a much bigger boiler than had been seen on an express locomotive up to that time. The drivers who took out the first Dunalastairs found they had an engine that produced steam like magic and ran faster with heavier loads than they had ever known. The big boiler made the Dunalastair look powerful; and it was powerful.

Charles Rous-Marten came up to Carlisle to have a look at the new engine. Rous-Marten was a New Zealand journalist who in his country had developed a technique for describing locomotive performance, and had subsequently made a name for himself in the then voluminous railway press. By 1896, to borrow the slogan of our most august railway periodical, he was 'read wherever there were railways'. For a locomotive superintendent to have a new engine given the Rous-Marten accolade was akin to an author having a new book praised in a top-of-the-page review in *The Observer*.

Rous-Marten arrived in Carlisle by the 'Tourist', and shortly before two o'clock in the morning he saw his first Dunalastair back on to that famous train. It was a case of love at first sight. Rous-Marten had ridden the race trains of the previous year and no doubt he was rubbing his hands at the prospect of a resumption of the battle in 1896. With the Dunalastairs at his command McIntosh would have welcomed a spell of racing, for the Caledonian was in an impregnable position. Unhappily, the 'Tourist' had a nasty spill at Preston that summer and the resulting press campaign against excessive railway speeds put paid to any idea the companies may have had of staging another Race to Aberdeen. Rous-Marten need not have worried. The Dunalastairs in ordinary service gave him plenty to write about. In 1896 the Dunalastair ran almost to the timings of 1895, but with double the 1895 loads. 'I am forced to the conclusion,' wrote Rous-Marten, 'that they surpass in merit any that have ever come under my personal notice. They embody in a high degree all the points of merit specified—speed, weight, pulling and gradient climbing.' In no time he was at 130 Springburn Road ensconced with McIntosh. They must have made an incongruous pair, the elegant colonial in top hat and tails and the rough and ready but kindly, humorous Scot. Rous-Marten was given facilities for viewing the work of the Dunalastairs at close quarters and it is to some extent on the published results of his observations that their reputation rests.

Cowlairs was never quite the same after the advent of the Dunalastairs, for the North British always seemed to be a step behind the Caledonian. What St Rollox did today Cowlairs did tomorrow. There was nothing the matter with Matthew Holmes's engines except that he lacked the facilities for showing them off. The North British had no 'Tourist' on which their engines could show their paces. Of the 'Tourist' Rous-Marten wrote: 'The particular train which made the reputation alike of the Caledonian Railway, of the Dunalastairs, and of Mr. McIntosh the designer of the latter was the 1.54 a.m. ex-Carlisle, perhaps on the whole *the* most remarkable one that ever ran anywhere. A large order! Yes, I admit that, but I maintain it.' There was something exciting and romantic about Carlisle Citadel station in that second hour of the day when the 'Tourist' came in from London behind the bramble-black English engine, and the shining blue Caledonian engine backed in to take its place for the long haul over the hills to Perth.

No similar scene was enacted on the East Coast route. For some thirty years North Eastern engines had run the expresses from Newcastle to the Tweed and on over North British metals into Edinburgh. At one time the $124\frac{1}{2}$-mile run from

Newcastle to Edinburgh had been the longest non-stop in the world, but the North British had been denied any part in it. There was no middle-of-the-night frontier scene at Berwick. The East Coast equivalent of the 'Tourist' came scudding up through Northumberland, steadied momentarily for the crossing of the Royal Border Bridge, then slipped through Berwick in the dark. Yet Berwick was the perfect frontier station. It seemed only natural that an express from London should stop at Berwick and that the English engine should be replaced by one typically Scottish for the journey onwards to Scotland's capital.

The North British decided to end this affront to their dignity from 14 January 1897. They gave notice to the North Eastern that from that date all northbound trains would stop at Berwick and that North British engines would take charge of them on North British metals. The North Eastern went to the House of Lords over the matter, and were told that their agreement with the North British was not a legal right. So the North Eastern took their complaint to the Railway Commissioners, the basis being that the Berwick engine change would result in a deterioration of the service to the public. But by that time the East Coast trains were stopping at Berwick, and the North British were masters in their own house.

The North British undertook to get the down trains into Edinburgh on time in spite of the Berwick stop. This called for extremely smart station work at Berwick, and footplate work of a very high order on the $57\frac{1}{2}$-mile run from Berwick to Edinburgh. The North British were in a good position to accept the challenge, for there seldom had been a time when Cowlairs could offer so many new, or almost new, powerful express engines. Among the locomotives allocated to the new duties were 633, 634, 639 and 640 of the 6 ft 6 in. 1890-91 class and 595, 596, 598, 603 of the 7 ft engines of 1886. Some old Drummonds, among them 477, 479 and 486, were enlisted as helpers. The North British well knew that any default in time-keeping on their part would result in the Railway Com-

missioners handing the traffic back to the North Eastern, so
an all-out effort was made not only to keep to the timetable,
but to improve on it. All the night expresses were double-
headed. As soon as the North Eastern engine had hooked off
at Berwick the North British engines—often a Holmes and a
Drummond—backed in; and off they shot in a wild scamper
along the tops of the toothed cliffs, over Cockburnspath and
finally helter-skelter down to Dunbar and on to the Capital.
There were exciting dawn runs for the night travellers on the
East Coast route in the summer of 1897. What a thrill it was
to soar in through Longniddry and Prestonpans in the high
seventies with the first light of the sun coming in over the
North Sea and lighting the Salisbury Crags. And the excitement lasted right to the platform ends at the Waverley station.
Once the trains had coursed through Portobello the engines
had to tackle the last $1\frac{1}{4}$ miles of 1 in 78 from St Margarets up
through the Calton Tunnel and into the station. Was there
ever a more exciting approach to a main line station or a more
dramatic finish to a long express run? One of the sights of
Edinburgh in recent years was that of an A4 bursting from
the top end of the Calton tunnel with exhaust still thundering
only a few coach lengths from journey's end.

Rous-Marten came north to join in the fun. For a season he
rode up and down, on or behind a variety of engines and his
records give a vivid picture of happenings on the line that
summer. On a typical night one North Eastern engine
brought the express up to Berwick from Newcastle in $73\frac{3}{4}$
minutes, and two North British engines ran from Berwick to
Edinburgh in $57\frac{3}{4}$ minutes. Writing of the double-heading on
the North British, Rous-Marten rather naively said, 'The
second engine was merely a reserve of extra power to be used
in case of need.' He was of the opinion that Mr Holmes's
engines 'ran very smoothly at 80 miles an hour'. There was
one glorious run from Berwick to Edinburgh completed in
57 min 49 sec, in spite of a 15 m.p.h. speed restriction through
Dunbar, with a thrilling sprint home from East Linton, $23\frac{1}{2}$

New Clyde Coast Train de Luxe at Gourock

31 Glasgow to Coatbridge. 8 miles.

1906. Corridor Train passing over Beattock Summit

CALEDONIAN POST CARDS. Top: *A Drummond 'coast bogie' with three twelve-wheeled coaches at Gourock.* Bottom: *A typical publicity postcard issued by the Caledonian in the 1906 period*

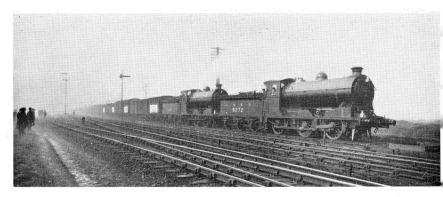

ENGINES OF W. P. REID. Top: *Two J37 class on a whisky special.*
Middle: *Scott class No. 498 'Father Ambrose', the engine on which
Driver Deuchar was fatally injured.* Bottom: *The restored Glen class
No. 256 'Glen Douglas' piloting a J37 on Cowlairs Incline with a
railway enthusiasts' special on 1 June 1963*

miles in 22 min 1 sec. The last three miles, including the $1\frac{1}{4}$ miles at 1 in 78, were run in 3 minutes. On another occasion an up express, the 11.15 ex-Waverley with a 213-ton load, arrived at Berwick in 58 min 49 sec. The first $29\frac{1}{4}$ miles to Dunbar were covered in 28 min 58 sec, and only $6\frac{1}{2}$ minutes were required for the $4\frac{3}{4}$ miles of 1 in 96 up Cockburnspath. The day trains, the *Flying Scotsman* and the afternoon diner, were usually worked by one engine. These trains were much heavier than the night trains, and they had easier bookings. The *Flying Scotsman* was allowed 77 minutes for the down and 72 minutes for the up journey. These allowances must have been on the generous side for Rous-Marten found that the down *Scotsman* ran into Waverley $7\frac{1}{2}$ minutes early in spite of a $3\frac{1}{2}$-minute stand at St Margarets at the foot of the 1 in 78. The load on that occasion was 234 tons and the engine was of the 633 class, although the narrator does not specify which one. On another trip with an engine of the same class the up diner arrived at Berwick 10 minutes early. It was great sport while it lasted, but double-heading is an expensive exercise and probably no one was more relieved than the North British when the Railway Commissioners decided that the North Eastern were to take over the through traffic. There had been no prestige to be gained in doing with two engines what the Caledonian were doing easily with one.

Meanwhile, one example from the many recorded by Rous-Marten will suffice to show what the Dunalastairs were doing with the 'Tourist'. Armstrong, with No. 733, left Carlisle with equal to 16 weighing 161 tons. He passed Beattock, $39\frac{3}{4}$ miles, in 37 min 50 sec, and then covered the 10 miles to the Summit in 15 min 43 sec. The speed up the last 6 miles of 1 in 75 never fell below 36 m.p.h. 'Just fancy that,' said Rous-Marten. 'Why, some railways think that good with such a load even up 1 in 200.' The 50 miles from Carlisle to the Summit were run in 53 min 33 sec. Then followed a hair-raising dash down the Clyde Valley with the stop watch recording 42 seconds over several miles: 85.7 m.p.h. The $23\frac{3}{4}$

L

miles from the Summit to Carstairs were reeled off in 19 min 13 sec, the whole journey from Carlisle to Stirling, $117\frac{3}{4}$ miles, being completed start to stop in 116 min 53 sec. Perth, $150\frac{3}{4}$ miles from Carlisle, was reached in 151 min 37 sec. David Fenwick took over at Perth with No. 726 and ran up to Forfar, $32\frac{1}{2}$ miles, in 30 min 51 sec. The last $57\frac{1}{4}$ miles to Aberdeen were covered in $58\frac{1}{2}$ minutes. 'Seeing that a 6 feet 6 inch wheel can do this sort of thing, what more could be done with a wheel 7 feet, 8 feet or 9 feet in diameter?' asked Rous-Marten.

In 1898 Holmes produced the Cowlairs answer to the Dunalastair, the 729 class of 4—4—0. The Dunalastair had $18\frac{1}{4}$ in. by 26 in. cylinders, and so had the 729s. Both had 6 ft 6 in. coupled wheels. The Dunalastair weighed $47\frac{1}{2}$ tons, the 729 $47\frac{3}{4}$ tons. Dunalastair had a total heating surface of 1,403 sq ft and a grate area of $20\frac{1}{2}$ sq ft. The 729 had 1,350 sq in. of heating surface and a grate area of 20 sq ft. Boiler pressures were 160 p.s.i. for the Dunalastair and 175 for the 729. Rous-Marten has written that when he called at Cowlairs to view the 729s, Holmes confessed to him, 'They are just Dunalastairs.' One would have thought that an interesting ploy for the railway observer of the day would have been a detailed comparative study of the performance of the Holmes 'Dunalastair', and that of the genuine St Rollox article, but this study Rous-Marten refused to make; or at least make public. In reply to a letter that had appeared in one of the journals to which he contributed he wrote: 'My correspondent is desirous to have my opinion and experiences of Mr. Holmes's 729 class of North British express engine. These I shall give with pleasure. But I must absolutely decline, as I always have done and do, to be led into any comparison between these engines and the Caledonian Dunalastairs.' Rous-Marten gave no reason for his refusal other than Dogberry's dictum that 'comparisons are odorous'. Rous-Marten's work bristled with mysterious statements or statements that are half complete. On one occasion he wrote: 'During the last month of the last century (December 1900) I once more attained on a British railway the exceptional speed of 87.9 miles an hour. But wild horses shall not drag from me the information as to what engine did it and on what line it was done. Some day I may reveal the fearful secret. But not yet.' On another occasion, on the Caledonian, he stated that he had recorded the second highest speed he had ever encountered on a British railway, but he neither mentioned the actual speed nor the conditions under which it had been achieved. Even more intriguing was his disclosure that he had heard from the lips of McIntosh himself that the record time for the journey from Carlisle to Beattock Summit was made in 1896 by a Conner 7 ft 2 in. 2—4—0 hauling one coach. Beyond stating that the engine took 36 minutes to pass Beattock and 47 minutes to the Summit he offered no information on this notable feat. Mr Rous-Marten's exercises in melodrama may have intrigued his Victorian readers; they irritate Elizabethan researchers. If there is an Elysian Fields Railway Society, Rous-Marten must be hard-pressed answering questions from recently-joined members.

By the time Holmes had his 729 class at work, McIntosh had produced another 15 Dunalastairs more powerful than the first batch. These had cylinders 19 in. by 26 in.; the boiler pressure was stepped up to 175 lb. and the heating surface increased to 1,500 sq ft. The engine's range was increased by the provision of a large tender on two four-wheeled bogies with a water capacity of 4,125 gall. and space for $4\frac{1}{2}$ tons of coal. In the first Dunalastair the engine steps were so placed that they obscured the second wheel of the bogie. In Dunalastair II these steps were placed between the bogie and the leading pair of driving wheels, a small change in detail that enhanced the engine's appearance.

The new engines were no sooner out of St Rollox than Rous-Marten was in Glasgow to see for himself what they could do. Driver Andrew Dunn was testing the engines and Rous-Marten found him with No. 766, the first of the class, on the 2 p.m. 'Corridor' at the Central Station. A large crowd of sightseers had assembled at the platform end to watch the departure. 'The engine was absolutely mobbed by admiring spectators,' wrote Rous-Marten. It was a rough day with a strong persistent side wind as the 'Corridor' pulled out with a 330-ton load, but No. 766 soon had the train climbing through Uddingston at 60 m.p.h. Speed dropped to 30 m.p.h. on the succeeding long stretch of 1 in 100 and Carstairs was passed one minute late in 47 minutes. A signal check at Symington cost the train a minute and a half, but 766 topped Beattock in 80 minutes from Glasgow still going at 31 m.p.h. The 50 miles from the Summit to Carlisle were run in 50 min 55 sec with speeds touching 73, 74 and 75 m.p.h. In the last few miles Dunn, aware that he was gaining on booked time, took matters easy. Even so, he brought his train to a stand in the Citadel station with three minutes to spare.

Rous-Marten returned to Glasgow with the down 'Corridor' on the same day; same engine, same driver. The load was somewhat lighter—276 tons—but the storm of the morning had worsened and greasy rails were an added hazard. No. 766 got away to a flying start and the first four miles to Rockcliffe were run in six minutes. Lockerbie, $25\frac{3}{4}$ miles, was passed in 30 min 28 sec. Then at Murthat, after the engine had put 36 miles behind it in 40 minutes, came a bit of bad luck; adverse signals brought No. 766 almost to a dead stand. Dunn had meant to tackle Beattock without assistance, but he had assumed a high speed run at the bank. Checked at the foot, he took the precaution of stopping for a banker. Minutes were lost while the banker was attached, but once he was over the top Dunn sailed down to Strawfrank Junction, $23\frac{1}{2}$ miles in 20 min 49 sec, touching speeds of 78, 79 and 80 m.p.h. Notwithstanding a five-minute delay at Strawfrank the Dunalastair had the 'Corridor' home right on time.

Rous-Marten's next experiment with a Dunalastair was of a different order. This time Dunn had No. 767 on the 4.13 Glasgow Central—Gourock boat train. This was the famous residential express that was booked to run the 26¼ miles to Gourock with passengers for the Caledonian Steam Packet Co.'s boats in an exciting 35 minutes; exciting, for the route for a good part of the way was through congested built-up areas fraught with curves and facing points; exciting because the 4.13 was running in competition with the corresponding Glasgow & South Western train on a roughly parallel course from Glasgow St Enoch to Greenock, Princes Pier. True, the gilt was partly off the gingerbread when Rous-Marten made this run, for the Caledonian and the South West had reached an agreement about not cutting their published overall times on these expeditions to the coast. Dunn observed the letter of the law and at the same time gave his guest a run for his money by taking it easy from Glasgow to Paisley and then opening out on the mostly flat, straight stretch between Paisley and Port Glasgow. The load was 200 tons, and at one point on the journey Dunn had 767 clocking 76.3 miles an hour. He pulled up in Gourock in 31 min 44 sec.

The Dunalastair II's big tender was to lead to the death in unusually dramatic circumstances of Driver David Fenwick of Perth, the same Fenwick who had been in charge of No. 726 when Rous-Marten made his memorable trip with the 'Tourist' in 1896. The date was 1 June 1898 and the occasion the journey south of Queen Victoria after an early summer visit to Balmoral. To power the Royal Train out of Aberdeen the Caledonian provided their latest passenger locomotives No. 779 and No. 780. These last two of the Dunalastair IIs were almost brand-new out of St Rollox. No. 780, Fenwick's, was the train engine and No. 779 was piloting. McIntosh and his second in command at St Rollox, Tom Macdonald, were present and when the train left Aberdeen Macdonald was on the footplate of No. 779, and McIntosh was in the coach reserved for senior railway officials. The Royal Train must have made a grand spectacle that day as it swept out through Ferryhill and rounded the Bay of Nigg, the new, immaculate Dunalastairs sending their thunder into the air.

All went well for the first five miles. Just after the train had passed Cove Bay station No. 780 began emitting a series of pop whistles and when Tom Macdonald looked back from the footplate of No. 779 he saw an agitated fireman obviously signalling that he was in need of assistance. Macdonald scrambled over the tender of No. 779 as the train swung along the cliff tops with the sea far below. Then he dropped on to the front end of No. 780 and worked his way along to the cab. There was only the fireman on the footplate; of David Fenwick there was no trace. According to the fireman Fenwick had climbed on to the tender, apparently to adjust the communication cord, while he himself had been attending to his fire, and when he turned round Fenwick had disappeared. If the train had been an ordinary express Macdonald would have stopped it at the next box. But he had to think twice about delaying the Royal Train. He took over the regulator for the 80-odd mile trip to Perth. One can imagine the feelings of the men on the footplate of No. 780. What for them should have been a proud occasion was turned into a nightmare.

While the Royal Train was steaming south grievous news was received at Perth. The stationmaster at Cove Bay sent a telegram to say that immediately after the passage of the train through the station he had found on the line a driver's cap with half a human head in it. There was no trace of a body. The officials at Perth had no illusions about the unpleasantness that would attend the impending arrival of the Royal Train. There was only one place where poor Fenwick's body could be, and that was on the tender of No. 780. The train was due to be received with all the pomp and splendour that such occasions demanded, and it would arrive with a dead man, grossly mutilated, on the engine. Only senior officials were told about the accident. When the train drew alongside Perth platform a mere handful of the assembled dignitaries knew of 780's grim burden. Both engines were quickly uncoupled and run straight on shed with Fenwick's body still on the tender. The Queen was not told about the accident until the Royal Train had resumed its journey. She sent a letter of condolence to Mrs Fenwick, and when the driver was buried at Perth three days later a personal wreath from the Queen was among the family wreaths that covered the grave. Fenwick was a tall man, and the Dunalastair's unusually big tender was heaped high with coal at the start of the journey. The driver had struck his head on the overbridge at Cove Bay station.

*　　*　　*

The interesting tale of the Belgian Dunalastairs really began with an order that Sharp Stewart completed for the Holland Railway in 1890. The Dutch engines were big, handsome 4—4—0s with inside cylinders and frames, very British in appearance, and finished to Sharp Stewart's highest standard. They were painted a rich chocolate brown and the framing and wheels were red; they had polished brass domes and double brass beading round the driving wheel splashers. These were the first bogie engines to appear in Holland and the first British bogie engines on the Continent; they created a sensation, not only in Holland but in Belgium and Germany too, for the Dutch put the engines to work on the international trains that ran into both countries. It was said that German railway officials made special trips to the frontier station of Oberhausen to see the Springburn engines. Their smart appearance and brisk performance resulted in repeat orders being given to the Atlas works. Because of a change in Dutch railway politics subsequent batches appeared in olive green livery lined with black and vermilion. The wheels were dark red with vermilion lining; each spoke carried a fine vermilion line that bifurcated at the boss and tyre.

These beauties advertised Springburn wares with such success that a delegation from the Belgian railway administration turned up in Springburn shopping for a 4—4—0 inside-cylinder, inside-frame engine for *their* international trains. They knew precisely what they wanted—a Dunalastair. The Belgians brought with them a supply of Belgian coal and a request to McIntosh that they be allowed to burn it in a Dunalastair on a series of test runs. McIntosh, with the blessing of the Caledonian, obliged and the result was that Neilson got an order for five Dunalastair IIs in March 1898. McIntosh undertook to act as consulting engineer for the Belgians while the engines were under construction.

One day toward the middle of October the locomotive superintendent of the Caledonian Railway went up to Hyde Park attired in his black hat and morning coat to be photographed standing all by himself beside the first of his Belgian Dunalastairs. McIntosh was very proud of this engine. It was Caledonian pure and simple even to the glorious blue livery. The number 2414 was carried on the tender, which was otherwise bare, except for a scroll on either side of the number and the builder's plate was on the splasher. Any alterations to the original design were superficial. There was right-hand drive, the hand lamp positions were changed to suit Belgian practice, and steam reversing gear and the quick-acting type of Westinghouse brake were added. No. 2414 was steamed on 21 October 1898. During the following week wheels and rods were dismantled and the engine was shipped as deck cargo on one of the small vessels that plied between the Clyde and Antwerp, where it duly arrived without as much as a scratch on its paintwork.

On 11 November the engine, running its trials on the Brussels—Ghent express service, averaged 53 m.p.h. including stops and completed the journey in two minutes less than the previous best time. A more elaborate trial was arranged with a train made up to simulate an international express, and on the successful completion of these trials No. 2414 and her four sister engines were put to work regularly on the international trains. The Dunalastairs revolutionised them. Previously the Belgian sector had been run in two phases, Schaerbeck to Jemelle, and Jemelle to Arlon with an engine change at Jemelle. Two engines had been used on each phase and 3 hr 10 min had been allowed for the overall journey. One Dunalastair now completed the whole journey, which included 9 miles of 1 in 62, in 2 hr 52 min. In other words, one Dunalastair did the work of four of the old Belgian engines. A proud little paragraph in a Scottish contemporary publication read: 'While each nationality in Europe possesses its own distinctive type of locomotive, a notable exception is Belgium whose Government are superseding with all possible dispatch the cumbrous and antiquated engines which have so long done duty on the State lines with exact copies of the five Improved Dunalastairs designed for them by Mr. McIntosh.'

The Springburn 4—4—0s influenced locomotive design in Belgium and Holland for many years. When the Belgian Minister of Railways was presented with an official report on the Dunalastairs, special reference was made to the excellence of their workmanship. It was decided to order a further 40 and put them in charge of all the international and *de luxe* trains, and Neilson offered to build them for £3,000 apiece. That would have been a welcome and well-deserved order for Springburn, but there was an outcry in Belgium about so much money going out of the country and the order went to Belgian builders at a price £340 more per engine than Neilson's. At the same time 10 McIntosh six-coupled goods engines were put in hand at a price, so we are told, of 1.88 francs per kilogramme.

Following the success of the initial batch of 4—4—0s in Holland, an order was placed with Sharp, Stewart for a typical British 0—6—0 design. Then, in the year that Belgium got its Dunalastairs, Holland took 25 4—4—2 inside-cylinder passenger tanks from Sharp, Stewart for local and intermediate services. They were the first tank engines to be put on Dutch metals for nearly a quarter of a century, and they gave such a good account of themselves that a further 30 were built in Holland.

To listen to some tales it would appear that everybody except McIntosh had a hand in designing the Dunalastairs. Robert Urie, who was works manager at St Rollox, has been

173

credited with suggesting the big boiler. A writer in *Railway Age* (New York) claimed that the McIntosh design was a copy of an American design. 'The English (*sic*) builder,' complained the writer, 'has followed American lines pretty closely in designing all that is important in the engine.' Considering the clean lines and graceful symmetry of the Dunalastair, and the repulsive ugliness of the typical American engine of the period, the claim was ludicrous. *Railway World* of London answered the American critic. 'It is rather a pity,' said a leading article, 'for the credit of the latter (American) engines that they do not resemble more closely so excellent a model as the new Caledonian engine. Little attempt to reconcile shapliness of outline and general harmony of proportions seems to be made by American locomotive builders, although it cannot be much more difficult to make a handsome engine than an unsightly, top-heavy mountain of metal with all its working parts exposed.' The Dunalastair owed its handsome appearance to an Edinburgh solicitor—or so he claimed. Norman Doran Macdonald, writing with breathtaking pomposity in *The Locomotive* at the safe distance of fifty years after the event, referred to the time that McIntosh 'let me help him in the development of the Dunalastair class—and especially in their architectural looks'. This was the same Macdonald who talked Worsdell into appointing him guide to an official North Eastern delegation to America, even although he himself had never set foot in the place.

I have an uncle who still has in his possession a personal reference that McIntosh gave him when he resigned his job as office junior in the office of the St Rollox locomotive superintendent to take up an appointment at Cowlairs. 'What was McIntosh like as a man?' I asked my uncle. 'Och, he was a cheery old chap,' I was told. 'He always signed his letters with his left hand, and he didn't make too good a job of it. He had a claw arrangement on his right arm that he stuck a knife into when he had a meal.' (It would not be too surprising to learn that this device was McIntosh designed and made at St

Rollox.) The triumvirate in those days was McIntosh, Tom Macdonald and Tom Porteous, the chief clerk. My uncle recalls seeing drivers and firemen coming up to the office to be tested for promotion or reprimanded for some misdemeanour. The footplatemen came to the office to collect their premium cards; these were issued to men who had had an accident-free year, and were worth from £3 to £5 in cash. Thursday night was a busy night for the office juniors. On Thursdays Tom Macdonald got out the diagrams for the week-end engine workings. They were completed about tea time and the originals were given to the boys who had the job of making copies on a messy, old-fashioned duplicator. The copies were eventually sealed in two bulky envelopes which the boys took down to Buchanan Street station by train; one was delivered to the stationmaster; the other to the stationmaster at the Central. In those pre-typewriter days handwriting was important and Porteous insisted on a high standard of calligraphy from his staff. The junior who was judged the best writer had the privilege of inscribing J. F. McIntosh's personal cards. My uncle's father was a foreman at Cowlairs. He told me that he remembered Matthew Holmes coming to the house on the occasion of his mother's funeral. The fact that the locomotive superintendent of the North British Railway attended the funeral of his foreman's wife tells us quite a lot about Holmes as a man. 'A perfect old gentleman,' was my uncle's verdict of him.

McIntosh had been on the footplate, and no one knew better than he did that the British locomotive man had one defect; he knew far too little about the mechanism of his engine, for unlike his counterpart in some European countries he was given no mechanical training. To remedy this defect and enable his drivers to give first aid in cases of locomotive failure on the road, McIntosh introduced Mutual Improvement classes at St Rollox. They were held outside normal working hours and attendance was voluntary. McIntosh attached considerable importance to them and he either took the classes himself or delegated the job to Macdonald or another senior officer. Theoretical and practical lectures were given by experts in their particular field, and the 'mutual improvers' were taken on shed visits and given practical problems to solve. Here is McIntosh speaking to a class at St Rollox: 'I believe there is no branch of industry, skilled and unskilled, in which a wider field opens up to the engineering mind, than that of the engine driver. He has golden opportunities of husbanding a valuable store of practical information regarding the working of his engine.' During a typical exercise a freight engine that had just come off a trip was announced as having a broken valve spindle, and the class instructor called for two volunteers to put the engine in a condition to move with one side out of action, using only the tools available on the engine. Driver Anderson and Fireman Baxter described their remedy for the disabled engine; they put the plan into action and steamed the engine from the goods yard to the shed. Driver Morrison and Fireman Appleyard had the job of restoring the engine to full working order. McIntosh had great faith in his classes, which had ninety pupils at one time, and is on record as saying that they resulted in a substantial improvement in the quality of candidate who came up for examination. It was not long before the Cowlairs men were asking Holmes to start mutual improvement classes for them!

By the middle nineties Springburn was a bustling suburb of Glasgow with a population of 27,000. The railway permeated the place. The working day began when the works horns howled over the tenement roofs at 5.30 in the morning. That was the first horn. By the time the second horn blew at 5.53 virtually thousands of workmen were tramping along the streets towards one or other of the four great railway establishments. At 6 o'clock the long horn blew for three minutes. The stragglers streamed in through the gates shouting their names and a timekeeper put a chalk mark against them on a large blackboard. Anybody who failed to get past the timekeeper before the long horn ceased was quartered; that is, he lost a quarter of an hour's wages. At 9 o'clock the breakfast horn warned the Springburn housewives to pour the porridge from the bubbling pots in readiness for arrival of their menfolk. Those were the days when the Springburn shopman had done before breakfast what his modern counterpart would consider a good day's work. The smiths, slogging at their anvils in the summer heat, kept beside them a pail filled with cold water into which oatmeal was stirred When they began to lose too much sweat they quenched their thirsts with copious draughts of this fluid. There was a mid-day break for dinner, and the working day finished at 5.30.

Springburn was vital and alive then. Its people *did* things. There were concerts galore. Organ recitals in the churches drew big attendances. The umbrella-type bandstand in Springburn Park, a gift of the Reid family, was a favourite rendezvous for the railwaymen and their families on Sunday afternoons and fine summer evenings. The best bands of the British army played to the delight of Springburn audiences. There was a band from France once, its players in bright blue uniforms, and there was a memorable occasion when a concert orchestra all the way from Berlin played in broad daylight and in the open air in full evening dress. There were adult night classes in the schools on all manner of subjects, and lectures in plenty. One wonders what signalman James Gibson had to say when he talked to the Caledonian Railway Debating Society·on 'Philosophy of Life'. On Saturday afternoons there were football matches between teams drawn from rival railway establishments, or for railwaymen in search of peace and quiet there was the Caledonian Railway Reading and Recreation Room.

Meetings of railways and social clubs were occasionally entertained with demonstrations of the new cinematograph. Audiences watched in wonder five-minute dramas with titles like *Napoleon at Moscow* and *Wellington at Waterloo.* The early cinematograph operators often made their own films, and since they were always on the look-out for subjects that moved they took pictures of locomotives and trains. One enterprising operator made films on the Caledonian which went the rounds of Caledonian audiences. There was one showing trains at Merchiston and other stations, of which a contemporary film critic wrote: 'The general scamper of the passengers who left the trains represented a scene of astonishing animation.' The same commentator mentioned that the audience was in 'a fever of excitement' during the performance. One can imagine the fever of excitement that would result if this old film had miraculously survived and could have been shown to audiences of present-day enthusiasts.

The great entertainment of the nineties and after was the *soirée*. *Soirée* was a word much used in Springburn in those days. All the churches had their *soirées*. There was the Sighthill Shunters' Soirée and the Cowlairs Painters' Soirée. But the big event of the year was the Caledonian Railway Soirée. The *soirée* was an entertainment for all the family, a kind of indoor picnic plus a concert. I never attended a Caledonian *soirée*, but I remember as a boy looking forward for weeks to the church *soirée*. On those occasions a merry audience filled a large hall. They sat on long wooden forms, and the back of the form in front had a hinged flap that could be raised and secured by brackets to support cups and plates. During the evening some careless or mischievous urchin was sure to knock away a bracket and a flap would collapse with a bang, sending tea and ham sandwiches cascading over the floor.

The Caledonian *soirée* was a grand affair. It usually took place in the City Hall and was always graced by members of the Caledonian hierarchy who gave every appearance of enjoying themselves. An elaborately printed programme was issued in advance, and was eagerly scanned by would-be participants (in 1895 there was a picture of Drummond's No. 78 of racing fame on the cover). The routine seldom varied; an official speech, good things to eat, and a concert. There would be a rollicking evening of singing, piping and fiddling, and

178

the comedian could be depended upon to crack an anti-North British joke. It was not unknown for the distinguished guest to tilt at the rival railway. At the 1896 *soirée*—that year called the Saint Rollox Employees Festival—Sir James King gave the address (McIntosh was in the chair) and said: 'Our keenest competitor has, of course, been the North British Railway Company, the other great Scottish line, and in the amicable contest for traffic during the past year we have been running a neck and neck race. It has ended, I am happy to say, by the Caledonian being at the top. (Cheers.) It was a very narrow shave. About £1,800,000 has been drawn by each and the difference is only the comparatively small sum of £9,000.' Joseph Goodfellow was at the 1896 *soirée*. It is a pity that Robert Sinclair could not have been there with him, for it was he who had organised the very first Caledonian *soirée* away back in the Greenock days of 1850. The Caledonian had 108 engines then; in 1896 they could muster 736 engines. On the night of the 1896 *soirée* Sinclair was old and ill and living quietly in retirement far away in Florence. When he died two years later Mr C. Du Riche Preller, writing in one of the professional journals, gave this picture of Sinclair in his last days: 'He lived,' wrote Preller, 'chiefly for and in his beautiful and extensive library, ever fresh in intellect and active in body, although well advanced in years. Sincerely beloved and respected by all who served under him professionally he was equally so by all who knew him in his private life, or like myself, in his placid, cultural retirement where few were aware that the Mr. Sinclair of refined literary tastes was Sinclair the engineer of the Caledonian and Great Eastern Railway fame.'

The railway élite of Springburn went through the nineties opening bazaars, laying foundation stones, attending weddings and funerals. In 1892 James Reid made his four sons, Hugh, Walter, Andrew and John, partners with him in Neilson and Co. In 1893 James Reid died, and Springburn mourned. Shops were closed and blinds were drawn on the tenement windows on the day of his funeral, and on the following Sunday eulogies were read from pulpits. When John Reid was married a fleet of horse buses was sent to Hyde Park to collect the entire office staff and transport them to the reception at the Grand Hotel. The list of guests reads like a page from the membership record of the Institution of Locomotive Engineers. During the nineties there was a campaign to stage a great Springburn Railway Exhibition. It failed, as did a campaign to erect statues to the two men above all others who had brought fame and fortune to Springburn, George Stephenson and James Watt. But the local citizenry subscribed readily for a statue of James Reid.

★   ★   ★

McIntosh, always looking at problems from the engineman's angle, produced his gauge-glass protector. Matthew Holmes was approached by 'a retired Stirling gentleman' with an idea for sheeting wagons. Hitherto tarpaulins had been roped over the wagons and a great deal of wastage resulted when crates and other sharp-edged loads cut them, or when pools of rainwater collected and rotted the fabric. The new device consisted of two uprights, one at each end of the wagon, supporting a wooden bar which in effect formed a girder above the centre line of the vehicle, over which the tarpaulin was draped tent-fashion and secured at the sides of the vehicle. Rain water ran off the tarpaulin, which at the same time was suspended free of objects likely to cause damage. The contraption was hinged, and the bar could be folded down flush with the sides of the wagon to allow unimpeded loading. Down at St Rollox, Mr A. T. Grafton produced a self-adjusting sandpipe nozzle. The invention proved very useful on the Oban road and on other curving routes where the cant of the rail caused sand delivered from a fixed pipe to fall on the edge of the rail. Grafton's nozzle insured that the sand was delivered to the centre.

★   ★   ★

The Springburn of the nineties was fortunate in having a

180

LNER DAYS. Top: *Eastfield shed in 1930.* Bottom: *Ex-NBR Atlantic 'The Lord Provost' about to leave Queen Street with an Edinburgh express in 1935*

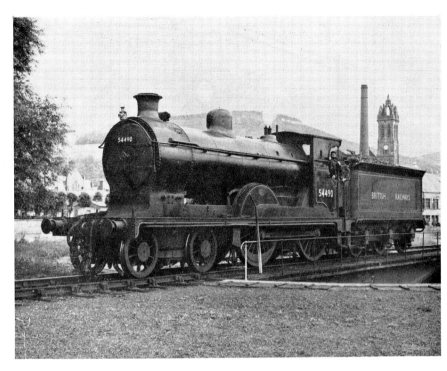

THE CALEDONIAN 4—4—0. Top: *The final Caledonian 4—4—0 design. A Pickersgill 4—4—0 at Peebles in 1948.* Bottom: *The most famous of them all. The first of the Dunalastair class 1 ending its days on a Gourock—Glasgow stopping train in the early thirties*

lively, well-written local newspaper, the *St Rollox and Spring-burn Express*. The *Express* published not only general news, but local, national and even international railway news. This was commendably accurate; it had to be, for every reader was a knowledgeable critic.

One Monday morning the Editor of the *Express* was glancing over his *Glasgow Herald* when two items of railway news caught his attention. One concerned the introduction of a new type of compressed-air drill at Cowlairs, and the other described a new passenger carriage that had just been built at St Rollox. From his knowledge of local railway matters the Editor was aware that these 'innovations' had first appeared three years previously, so he cut the paragraphs from the newspaper, handed them to one of his reporters, and sent him to seek audiences with Matthew Holmes and John McIntosh. The reporter went first to Cowlairs. The story of the interview was told in the next issue of the *Express*:

'Will you be so kind,' asked the reporter, handing Mr. Holmes the *Herald* cutting, 'to state the age of that?'

Mr Holmes laughed, and glanced over the paragraphs. He was surprised, he said, and he looked it. 'Why,' he added, 'we have had these tools in operation for nearly three years. New improvements!' And he laughed again. 'When we have anything worth communicating to the press,' he concluded, 'we are willing to give it when desired, but these paragraphs which appear in the Glasgow papers from time to time are not only inaccurate as a rule, but annoying.'

With this highly satisfactory statement safely in his notebook the *Express* reporter took the tram down to St Rollox. There he explained his business to Porteous, and presently John F. McIntosh had the appropriate cutting on his desk. 'To say that the eminent superintendent was annoyed,' wrote the reporter, 'was to put it mildly. He authorised the writer to explain that the paragraph was some three years old, and had in whole or part appeared in the newspaper columns of the time.' The next issue of the *Express* contained the bold

M

headline: ''The Herald Caught Napping. Messrs McIntosh and Holmes Interviewed.' The text under the headline in part read: 'On several occasions lately we have been instrumental in nailing canards of an exceptionally spicy nature, and today two counterfeits are added to the list. Having had experience of the city papers' engineering experts and firmly believing that the foregoing was merely a repetition of ancient history we deemed it advisable to make inquiries.'

*   *   *

As early as 4.45 on the morning of 9 September 1899 the electric cars were moving up and down Springburn Road. It was a Saturday; in those days Saturday was a working day, but not that Saturday. Springburn had never known a day like it. By half past three the tenement windows were yellow with gaslight and in scores of kitchens porridge pots were simmering on the hobs. By half past four Springburn was athrob with activity. Whole families, merry and excited and dressed in their Sunday best, emerged from the tenement closes and pattered down Springburn Road in the first light. Springburn was going to *England*. Few families enjoyed a real holiday then, and a day outing was an event in most households. And England seemed so exciting and far away.

All roads led to St Rollox that morning. Special electric cars, one every two minutes, climbed up from the city and deposited their passengers at the station. It was not only in Springburn that people were rising early. Everybody on the Caledonian who mattered was up with the larks that morning —the chairman himself, James C. Bunten of Dunalastair, J. F. McIntosh, the Honorary President of the Excursion, a covey of directors, even shareholders—and all were heading for St Rollox. In far away Newcastle, Lord Rosebery, the Chief Excursionist, was still abed after his previous night's political speech in the city, but soon he would be astir and ready to cross to Carlisle to greet the greatest Scottish foray into England since the Forty Five. He must have had a quiet smile to himself when he realised the significance of the date;

184

it was the anniversary of Flodden.

I first heard of the great Caley trip quite literally at my mother's knee. My mother had been *there*. Even in' the twenties, a quarter of a century later, the trip came up in conversations. Of course in that exciting September of 1899 it was not the *Caley trip*; it was the Fourth Annual Excursion of the Employees of the Caledonian Railway Locomotive Works, Saint Rollox. In practice anybody who had a friend at St Rollox who was willing to get him a ticket was eligible to join the excursion. And the return fare to Carlisle, to *England*, was one shilling. During the week that preceded the great excursion ticket-holders were issued with a souvenir programme, a lavish production with the cover printed in Caledonian blue and bordered with the Committee's colours of rose and primrose. The amazingly-varied contents included operating instructions for the special trains, an illustrated guide to Carlisle, a portrait gallery of the distinguished guests, and complete details of all entertainments arranged in Carlisle for the visitors, not forgetting the programmes to be presented at two organ recitals. 'The Committee believe,' said the introduction, 'that a most enjoyable holiday will be spent in "Merrie Carlisle" and that this trip will be a record one in every respect.' Everyone was promised a day of real pleasure and happiness. Of the Chief Excursionist the souvenir programme had this to say. 'The honour that Lord Rosebery is conferring on the Railway World by attending this Excursion is thoroughly appreciated by all the Railway Employees in the United Kingdom, and is another proof of the great interest which His Lordship takes in everything that pertains to the wellbeing and the brightening of the lives and the homes of the working classes.'

Two hundred and fifty carriages, many of them the latest lavatory carriages, were made up into fourteen trains and McIntosh detailed fourteen (out of his thirty) Dunalastair I's and II's to work them. And that on a *Saturday*. Each engine carried a disc bearing the train number in front of the chimney. The first departure was at 5.10 a.m., the train arriving in Carlisle fifteen minutes before train No. 14 left St Rollox. To minimise confusion in handling the huge crowds, the trains were dispatched alternately from St Rollox station and from the Cattle Bank adjoining it. The latter was reserved for employees of the turning, fitting, wagon, wagon paint, copper shops and sawmill and families from Dawsholm shed, while trains from St Rollox were for employees from the boiler, carriage, erecting, smith, paint and trimming shops, the foundries and Polmadie shed. An operating note said, 'On the Going Journey Trains No. 1, 4, 7 and 10 will stop at Beattock; Nos. 2, 5, 8 and 11 at the Summit; and Nos. 3, 6, 9 and 12 at Strawfrank Junction for Examination of Carriages. On the Return Journey all the trains will stop at Beattock Station for Examination of Carriages and Collection of Tickets.'

One by one the Dunalastairs, all spit and polish, pulled out with their trains of 16, 17 and 18 coaches. It must have been a sight to see them starting up with their great loads on the rising gradient. The trains wound in procession up the Clyde Valley, over the Summit and across the Border with the 15,000 excursionists to arrive in Carlisle at intervals of ten minutes. All ran to time except the last, which was delayed by a freight train.

In Springburn it was a day of idle shops and empty streets, but it was different in Carlisle. Not since Prince Charlie's visit had Carlisle seen anything like it. The Mayor had instructed the townsfolk to decorate their houses and shops and 'Welcome to the St Rollox Visitors' signs hung out everywhere. The Carlisle eating houses were serving breakfasts by eight o'clock; tea or coffee with a choice of meats and all the bread and butter you wanted for a shilling. The invasion built up steadily as train after train rolled in and by mid-morning Springburn was in possession of Merrie Carlisle—and merrie was the word. Before the last train had arrived the band of the Glasgow Highlanders was dispensing the harmonies of Balfe in the public park, and in a hall not far away the Geisha

Boys (brought specially from Scarborough for the occasion) were giving the first of three performances. Elsewhere the Springburn visitors danced the polka, the lancers and quadrilles or in a quieter mood listened to the Glasgow Male Voice Quartette. Said the souvenir programme:

'Come and trip it as you go
On the light fantastic toe.'

And they did.

All too soon the merry morning was over and Carlisle settled down to providing a main meal for the multitude. Staff work by the committee had established that the combined catering facilities would produce 3,000 meals at one sitting. 'It is specially requested,' noted the Programme, 'that parties will leave as soon as possible after they have been served so that everyone may be supplied with as little delay as is necessary.' The Queen's Hotel supplied a cold lunch for 9d and at the Red Lion soup, joint and sweet cost 1s 6d. Lord Rosebery was feted at the County Hotel with his fellow excursionists, the Right Hon. W. C. Gully, Q.C., M.P., Speaker of the House of Commons, the Lord Advocate and the stars of the Caledonian galaxy.

The afternoon began quietly with two organ recitals, one given in the Cathedral by Dr Ford, the other in the Presbyterian Church in Fisher Street by Ewart John Rae. A modern sociologist might marvel at the taste displayed by late nineteenth century railwaymen; Dr Ford played Mendelssohn's *No 1 Organ Concerto* while Mr Rae played the same composer's *No 2 Organ Concerto*. But what impelled Dr Ford to include Chopin's *Funeral March* in his programme?

The procession of officials left the County Hotel for the public park soon after lunch. Their route had been advertised in advance and the streets were lined with crowds so dense that the carriages were caught up in the press of people for many minutes. At the park Sir James Thompson, general manager of the Caledonian, introduced Lord Rosebery to the excursionists. They cheered and threw their hats into the air, and among them were the caps that Anderson the hatter had made specially for the excursion, with portraits of McIntosh, J. C. Bunten and Lord Rosebery in the lining. Anderson had advertised them as 'Caledonian Railway Excursion Caps' at first but later he changed the description to 'Rosebery Caps'. The committee had sent two caps to Lord Rosebery but he had sent them back, so the local paper said, on the grounds that they were too small!

Rosebery began by apologising for making a speech on such an occasion. 'That is what we came for,' shouted someone in the crowd. There were allusions to early, less friendly Scottish visits to Carlisle. 'I give you a guess,' said Rosebery. 'What is this the anniversary of?' 'Bannockburn!' shouted a voice. 'No, not Bannockburn,' replied Rosebery, 'Flodden! Well, you cannot spend that grievous anniversary better than by spending it on English ground close to the Border.' In the numerous speeches that followed the excellent machines that had brought the excursionists to Carlisle received due praise. 'Puffing Billy has given place to the Dunalastair,' said one speaker. 'There is no department on the railway of more importance than that in which the locomotives are constructed. The Dunalastair is recognised as the finest engine in the world, and great honour is therefore due to Mr. McIntosh the designer.' In his reply to this compliment McIntosh said: 'The desire of everybody in the locomotive department is not only to make the Caledonian Railway equal to any other, but if possible, better.' That, surely, was a diplomatic utterance concocted specially for delivery on English soil. Every Caley man knew, and no one better than McIntosh, that the Caledonian Railway had *no* equal.

There was more dancing and singing and music in the evening, but by four o'clock the first of the excursionists were tramping back to the station. The return trains had to thread their way through the normal Saturday evening main line traffic and therefore their departure was spread over a $5\frac{1}{2}$-hour period. By 10 o'clock the last train had left Carlisle and by one o'clock on Sunday morning all the excursionists were safely back in Springburn. It had been a memorable day.

In the following week the Caledonian issued statistics about the excursion. In spite of the shilling return fare the trip had been run at a profit. The trains were a better paying proposition than the West Coast expresses on the same route. Revenue on the regular passenger trains between Glasgow and Carlisle was given as 2s 5d per mile, while the excursion trains had produced 4s 1d per mile. Each engine used 1 ton 12 cwt of coal, which was 35 lb. per mile or 2.2 lb. per passenger. The rolling stock used on the occasion was worth upwards of £200,000. *Engineering,* mindful that the country was on the eve of war, saw in the excursion the pattern for mass movement of troops. It considered the demonstration satisfactory and reassuring. A few days after the excursion the Chief Constable of Carlisle wrote to St Rollox in the following terms: 'Your people behaved themselves in a most admirable manner, and I am pleased to say that no person was arrested by the Police during the day.' But somebody (an NB man no doubt) was churlish enough to inform the *St Rollox and Springburn Express* that 88 Caley men were locked up, drunk and incapable, in the station waiting room at Carlisle, and dispatched to Glasgow on the Sunday morning.

That Lord Rosebery, then at the height of his political fame, and the Speaker of the House of Commons were patrons of the excursion was a clear indication that the Caledonian Railway was a power in the land. The prestige that the excursion brought to St Rollox was not lost on the other place, and nobody was surprised when Matthew Holmes announced that a grand North British excursion would take place two weeks after the Caledonian outing, on Friday 21 September. Like the Caledonian, the North British were in a position to take their patrons across the Border and still stay on their own territory. Berwick-on-Tweed was the chosen destination. In due course a committee from Cowlairs waited on the Mayor of Berwick and let it be known that a civic welcome would be appreciated. Holmes organised ten trains of his newest carriages and earmarked ten of his latest 4—4—0s for the excursion. The committee turned out a souvenir programme on the lines of the Caledonian. A railway periodical commented: 'The management of the latter company's (the Caledonian) excursion cannot feel otherwise than highly flattered that all their arrangements were so faithfully copied by the North British even to the programme.'

And so it came about that for the second time in a fortnight Springburn invaded England in force. The ten trains carried 7,000 people away from Springburn between 5.10 and 6.15 on a morning of torrential rain. It was a poor spectacle compared with the Caledonian pageant. There were no big names from outside, and few from inside the industry. The chairman and directors were invited, but regretted that they could not attend. Berwick was pleased enough to welcome the visitors, but somebody commented wryly that the only places that were decorated were the tea rooms and the public houses that hoped to capture the custom of the excursionists. The official dinner, under the chairmanship of Matthew Holmes, took place at the King's Arms Hotel, but Holmes's staff dined at the Hen and Chicken Hotel. It is recorded that during the course of the afternoon the diners at the Hen and Chicken sent this telegram to the King's Arms. 'To Mr. Holmes, Chairman. Members of the Locomotive Staff toast enthusiastically Success to the North British Railway Company, and health to you and yours.' And back came the telegraphed reply, 'We've received and read to meeting assembled, who received same with much enthusiasm. We reciprocate your good wishes.' During the afternoon two excursionists fell off the castle ramparts and were killed. And in the following week a Berwick man expressed himself as follows in a letter to a newspaper. 'The Cowlairs trip is over, and most people must be glad of it. The streets were disagreeable and crowded all day and when at night the rain came on it made one miserable to see the wretched plight of the poor souls. To them we would much rather say "good-bye" as au revoir.'

*   *   *

In the closing years of the nineties the Dunalastairs heaped fame on their designer. 'No living engineer has done more for the cause of railway progress,' said Rous-Marten, writing about McIntosh. It was the Dunalastair that put a 60 m.p.h. start-to-stop timing into Bradshaw for the first time. It was the Dunalastair that earned for the Caledonian main line between Forfar and Perth the reputation of being the fastest stretch of railway line in Britain. When enumerating the best British runs of 1899 Rous-Marten said: 'One run on the Caledonian at 59 miles an hour; two on the same line at over 56; three on the same line over 55. Those are in Scotland. In England proper we have not a single run at 60 or 59, or 58 or 57 or 56 miles an hour. No, not one!'

At the end of the century Rous-Marten set out to see what No. 123 was doing. He found the engine that had been the toast of the country not ten years before working a humdrum semi-fast train over the much-vaunted fastest stretch of line in Britain. The famous single went out with the 9.45 a.m. from Perth to Aberdeen, returning from Aberdeen at 5.25; there were six intermediate stops. On Rous-Marten's visit No. 123 with a 112-ton load ran the $32\frac{1}{2}$ miles from Perth to Forfar in 33 min 32 sec. On the return trip the Forfar—Perth lap (booked time 40 minutes) was run in 31 minutes with a maximum speed of 82 m.p.h. The engine was ex-works and was running under test conditions. On an ordinary working day with no Rous-Marten on board such fireworks would not have been forthcoming. Notwithstanding the fine show put on for his benefit Rous-Marten wrote that No. 123 was 'running steadily on a falling gradient—going downhill in fact'.

It was on that occasion that Rous-Marten called on McIntosh to try to induce him to preserve a single. Preservation was in the air. Several English companies had planned to preserve famous locomotives from the past, and there were three possible candidates on the Caledonian. There was No. 1, a well tank built in 1881 from bits and pieces of two old Greenock well tanks and now functioning on officers' specials. There was No. 123, the darling of the 1888 races. But the engine that Rous-Marten had specially in mind was the last surviving Conner eight-footer. 'I pleaded as hard with my friend Mr. J. F. McIntosh,' he wrote, 'as if I had been begging for the life of a friend.' Rous-Marten departed from Springburn with the impression that the Conner was safe, but his back was scarcely turned when McIntosh tossed the engine on the scrapheap and used its boiler as a stationary boiler. The little well tank was scrapped in 1902 and it was No. 123 that survived to keep alive the memory of Caledonian deeds in the nineteenth century.

In June 1899 McIntosh took time off from St Rollox to go on a jaunt on the London & North Western. The Engineering Conference of the Institution of Civil Engineers took place that month in London and on the 8th Webb invited the delegates to ride with him to Crewe and inspect his premises. He also asked the locomotive superintendents of the major British railways to come along. The special show train was made up of thirteen brand new family saloons which, with a dynamometer car at the head end, gave a load of 410 tons 5 cwt. The locomotive was the four-cylinder compound No. 1903, *Iron Duke*. Together in one of the saloons were Webb, George Whale, McIntosh, Worsdell, Churchward, James Stirling, and others. It was said that as the train climbed away from Euston many of the distinguished engineers looked discreetly backwards to find out the nature of the banking assistance. There was none. Webb's compound was lifting the fourteen vehicles up the Camden bank unaided, and making a good job of it.

Webb had set out to impress his guests with the success of compounding. There must have been some interesting conversations on that journey. What had Webb and McIntosh to say to each other? If Webb did not actually say, 'Now try your damned Dunalastair on this lot,' the sentiment perhaps passed through his mind. The Euston—Crewe demonstration run was marred by severe slacks between Blisworth and Stafford, but in spite of that No. 1903 did the trip in 3 hr 10 min. At Crewe, Webb had an assortment of new engines fresh from the paint shop on parade. In his address to the delegates he asked them to observe that the North Western was not short of locomotive power (a dig at the Midland who were importing American engines) and that Crewe had achieved power without reaching finality as far as the loading gauge was concerned.

*   *   *

The nineties began with a boom in the private locomotive building industry, the middle years saw depression and then, towards the end of the decade, prosperity returned. The slack years gave Neilson's an opportunity to demonstrate how quickly they could fulfil an order. On 26 September 1894 Hyde Park accepted an order for twelve engines from the Nippon Railway Company, undertaking to produce the locomotives from drawing board to track inside three months, and agreeing to pay a penalty of £100 per engine for every week they fell behind their delivery dates. In ordinary times Neilson's would not have accepted such conditions, but with the prevailing slackness they were able to throw a large part of their resources into the building of the Japanese engines. While the drawing office was busy on design, materials and components were ordered from all over England and Scotland. The date specified for the completion of the first four engines was 15 January 1895; the first was actually finished and photographed on 30 November 1894. It had been built in 65 days, beating by one day the record set up with No. 123. The first four engines were aboard ship by 15 December, and all twelve were complete by the end of the eighty-fourth day.

In 1894 there came from the Atlas Works the most powerful locomotive so far seen on a British main line. It was also the first 4—6—0 to run on British rails: the famous 'Jones' goods. Sharp, Stewart turned out fifteen of these striking engines. No. 103, the first of the class, is with us yet, restored to the condition in which it emerged from the Atlas works to start its journey to the Highland Railway headquarters at Inverness. Also preserved is another David Jones design on which Sharp, Stewart were at work the year after the appearance of the celebrated 4—6—0, the 0—4—4 tank *Dunrobin,* the private engine built for the Duke of Sutherland, with 4 ft 6 in. coupled wheels and 13 in. by 18 in. cylinders. Its special feature was a large, spacious cab equipped with a cushioned bench. The duke was very fond of taking his guests out for a spin on his engine, and many a famous royal personage sat on that bench and watched Archie Rhind, engine driver to the Sutherland household for fifty years, at work. Royal footplate riders had their names inscribed on a panel carried on the engine.

McIntosh turned out a Dunalastair III with the same cylinders as its illustrious forerunners, but with increased heating surface and boiler pressure and a longer and deeper firebox than its predecessors. To cope with the rapidly increasing freight and mineral traffic he also built an 0—6—0 goods engine round the Dunalastair I boiler. This was his famous 'Dunalastair goods', an extremely useful engine with 5 ft coupled wheels and $18\frac{1}{2}$ in. by 26 in. cylinders. Also, with the Caledonian's expanding freight traffic in mind, he designed and built at St Rollox a 50-ton bogie wagon having a timber body on a steel frame, and three doors on each side for rapid unloading. One of the professional journals in describing it assured readers that in spite of its American size and appearance it *had* been built at St Rollox.

Its background is interesting. In the nineties the steelworks of Lanarkshire and Ayrshire were booming and the Caledonian were doing increasing business in the haulage of iron ore. Normally the ore ships sailed up the Clyde into the heart of Glasgow to discharge their cargoes direct into Caledonian wagons. About this time ore ships were held up, sometimes for days, because of wagon shortage at the congested Clyde quays. Some shippers therefore directed them to Ardrossan where the Glasgow & South Western as well as the Caledonian had a finger in the pie.

The Sou' West were in an excellent position to feed the Ayrshire steelworks from Ardrossan and so the Caledonian were spurred on to produce a big wagon to counter this threat to their traffic. The 50-ton wagon was labelled 'iron ore' but was put on general service on occasion, and contemporary photographs show it loaded with crates and packing cases.

Traders were invited to St Rollox to view the new wagon, and prospective users were sent a letter:

'The Caledonian Railway Company have just inaugurated a novel departure in railway practice in the form of a huge truck, having the enormous carrying capacity of 50 tons. The new vehicle runs on two four-wheel bogies, has steel underframe, three doors on each side, concave journals and measures in length over the ends of the buffers 38 feet 4 inches. It is so constructed as to glide easily round any curve in the system, is sufficiently pliable to negotiate any siding, and a feature has been made of rendering the journals readibly accessible for examination and attention. It has been designed specially for the conveyance of iron ore in which material the Company have a very extensive traffic, and which is at present carried in wagons holding from seven to eight tons. The new truck, while accommodating a load equal to seven ordinary wagons, will weigh only about half their tare, and twenty such trucks will be able to empty a ship carrying a thousand tons of ore, the effect of such being a welcome acceleration of dispatch in handling this commodity and also a considerable reduction in deadweight—two very vital points in railway economy.' But only one 50-ton wagon was built.

The decade of the Dunalastair ended on a note of high optimism. The Hyde Park and Atlas erecting shops were full, order books were bulging, and prosperity lay ahead for Cowlairs and St Rollox.

Chapter 6

TWENTIETH CENTURY EXCITEMENTS

The Glasgow locomotive builders celebrated the arrival of the new century by exhibiting at the Glasgow International Exhibition of 1901 their twentieth century express passenger locomotives. Sharp, Stewart's entry was a Wainwright Class 'D' 4—4—0 for the South Eastern Railway. In dark green livery, its beautiful curves accentuated by elaborate lining, its polished brass dome and copper chimney cap gleaming, the 'D' was reminiscent in perfection of turn-out of the 4—4—0 that had delighted the Dutch a decade earlier. The Neilson exhibit was a 4—4—0 for the Midland, the work of Samuel Waite Johnston who had been at Cowlairs 35 years previously. This engine had its driving wheels raised slightly off the rails and periodically set in motion by means of compressed air for the entertainment of visitors. The third, which Dübs had built specially for the show, had a Springburn look. It was a fine 4—4—0 in green with the wheel bosses and tyres burnished bright; in the previous two years they had built 30 of the class for its designer, the locomotive engineer of the London & South Western Railway—one Dugald Drummond. The engine was a 'T9'.

Dugald Drummond's Australian venture had come to nothing, so he stayed in Glasgow and founded the Glasgow Railway Engineering Works. The factory was in Helen Street, Govan. It is not clear what Drummond hoped to achieve with this venture. He could not have had any illusion of doing in Govan what James Reid had done in Springburn. The example of Walter Neilson's disastrous failure was only three years away, and Drummond, with no private building experience, could not have hoped to succeed where Neilson, with all his wealth and knowledge, had failed. Drummond concentrated upon producing small industrial locomotives, rail cars and railway accessories. He invented, patented and tried to market various railway devices. He imagined that with his reputation as a railway engineer his old associates would be willing to buy his wares, but he found there was a world of difference between being a buyer of railway equipment and a seller. Anyway, Dugald was not the man to be happy fiddling with gasworks engines and rail cars. When the chair of the locomotive superintendent of the LSWR fell vacant in 1895 Drummond left his sons to look after the Glasgow works—which they did for thirty years—and had himself enthroned at Nine Elms. The Drummond influence spread through the South West; and nearly seventy years later it has not been entirely eliminated.

What did the English drivers think of Drummond and his engines? In an age when railwaymen came close to genuflecting before Dugald the Great it was refreshing to find men who ventured to criticise him. Rank and file railwaymen were liberal contributors to the correspondence columns of the popular railway press in those days, and these were sometimes used to ventilate personal grievances. A writer in the *Railway Herald* who rashly gave his address as Nine Elms, but otherwise hid behind a pen name, wrote of Drummond's '292' design:

'The numbers commence lower than those of the preceding express engines, the '577' and '677' classes, and I am sorry to say they are correspondingly low in efficiency and quality. It is nothing uncommon to see the gauge glass filled with one solid mass of sand or chalk which defies removal except by breaking the glass.'

Another disgruntled writer who signed himself 'Onlooker', but whose material suggested that he was far from being an onlooker, seemed intent on settling an old score with Drummond.

'We have the experience here of the want of continuity of handrails on Dugald Drummond engines. I say it is nothing but a perversion of common sense by the superintendent. The late Ben Conner, in the end of the fifties, designed his outside cylinder engines with continuity of handrails, comfortable cabs with the windows to open with a hinge, which is very convenient for air or to clean the glass in time of a snowstorm. But in the middle of the '80s Mr. Drummond comes on the scene and all is changed. All new engines, and any that he rebuilt, got short handrails and fixed windows; he changed all the regulators and injectors and many a poor fellow was suspended and his work made miserable, not so much through the fault of the injector as the way they were fitted on to the old engines.'

Dugald was criticised not only for his handrails and cab windows; his engine steps and 'steamboat buzzer' also roused the English ire. Another criticism was Drummond's narrow boiler tubes which, so it was said, could not be picked out when they became 'blinded' because they were obscured by the brick arch. Another complaint was that the brake brackets were of cast iron and fractured too readily in derailments. Even if the authors of these complaints lived their full allotted span they have vanished now from human ken. But Drummond's engines are with us yet.

At the time Sharp, Stewart built the Wainwright 'D' class for the Glasgow Exhibition they had on order fifteen 'R1' 0—4—4 tanks for the South Eastern. An extraordinary mistake made by an Atlas man working on those engines had fascinating repercussions. During the assembly of the Westinghouse brake gear a leading hand noticed a screw orifice in the equalising chamber. Since no such orifice was shown in the drawing the leading hand decided, without consulting anybody, that it would have to be closed by a plug, and since Westinghouse had not sent the requisite plugs the Springburn fitter had them made and fitted in all fifteen engines of the class. There were two methods of operating the pattern of Westinghouse brake supplied for those engines. By moving the brake handle between stops 3 and 4 a gradual application of the brake was obtained, and that was the method officially advocated on the South Eastern. A rapid application could be obtained by moving the brake handle between stops 4 and 5, but the company frowned on the use of this method except in emergency. What the Sharp, Stewart fitter did when he screwed the plugs into the exhaust passage of the equalising chamber was to make the brake entirely inoperative when used between stops 3 and 4. It worked perfectly when used with the handle between 4 and 5, for a rapid application caused a separate orifice to open.

The finished engines were tested at Springburn, were found to be mechanically satisfactory in every respect and were duly dispatched to Ashford. Experienced drivers put them through a series of routine tests, including brake tests, before they were allocated to sheds. No. 698 was sent to Battersea where it was again inspected, this time by Mr Eaton, the company's instructor in the use and maintenance of the Westinghouse brake. Eaton found the plug inserted at Springburn, and was aware of the effect it would have on the brake. Nevertheless, when he found similar plugs, all expertly machined and fitted, on the other fourteen engines he concluded that the plug was a modification of the brake design of which Westinghouse had neglected to inform him. The tanks went into traffic, and for two weeks nothing happened —proving that South Eastern drivers were ignoring official instructions, and using the brake only between stops 4 and 5.

On 23 November 1900 the 9.25 a.m. Sevenoaks—Victoria passenger train arrived at Aynsford Junction, and Driver Ward coupled on 'R1' class No. 698 to double-head the train for the remainder of the journey. As driver of the leading engine Ward had control of the brakes. On the approach of the train to Swanley Junction he made two brake applications and for some reason best known to himself he made them with the handle between 3 and 4. Nothing happened. What flashed through Ward's mind was that Russell on the train engine had failed to put his brake valve in the neutral position. Too late Ward made an emergency application, but by then No. 698 was off the road at the catch points.

The Swanley accident had the distinction of being the subject of two reports. Major J. W. Pringle in his initial report put the blame for the accident on Ward, whom he said had been inattentive to his duties and had approached Swanley at too high a speed. The inspecting officer had found the plug in the brake system, but he failed to realise its significance. It was when the Westinghouse company denied all knowledge of the plug that the storm broke. The inquiry was reopened and a second report issued three months after the first brought to light the true story of the 'R1s'.

★   ★   ★

In June 1901 Willie Brown, a Springburn driver, was killed instantly on the Caledonian main line at Ecclefechan when his head struck an overbridge. He had been up on the tender checking the water level. At the subsequent fatal accident inquiry at Dumfries the presiding officer said that it seemed ridiculous that a driver should have to climb over the tender to check water, and he exhorted the Caledonian to find a device that would indicate the water level to an observer on the footplate. Ironically, McIntosh had already produced one and was fitting it on his new 0—8—0 freight engine then under construction at St Rollox. No. 600 came out for its trial spin a month after Brown's death.

The '600' class were the first 0—8—0s to work in Scotland. They had an exceptionally long boiler and wheelbase, and presented an unusual appearance in that the axle centres were irregularly spaced to allow the deep firebox to be fitted. The wheels were 4 ft 6 in. in diameter, the cylinders were 21 in. by 26 in., and the boiler was pressed to 175 p.s.i. These engines were built to haul trains of the newest 30-ton all-

200

metal iron ore wagons, the Caledonian's second venture into high-capacity wagon production. So much was this wagon before its time that Sir James Thompson in an address to Caledonian shareholders revealed that there was not a single port or iron or steel work on the system capable of dealing effectively with it, nor were there more than six collieries on the Caledonian able to accommodate it. Nevertheless, Sir James hoped that the company's customers would adapt their plant to take advantage of the new wagons. That they did so was shown by the fact that over 400 of the 30-tonners were built, and a '600' could take 30 of them at a time—loaded.

The '600s' were not the first 0—8—0 freight engines with unequally-spaced wheels to be built in Springburn. Some twenty-five years earlier Neilson had turned out just such an engine for the Great Indian Peninsula Railway to haul trains up the steeply-graded Ghats section. It was a saddle tank on the lines of Neilson's patent of the 1850s. A peculiar feature was that the lever of the Ramsbottom safety valve pointed towards the chimney instead of the footplate, to defeat the efforts of Indian drivers who were not above tampering with the lever to produce an extra ten pounds of pressure when they found themselves making heavy weather of it on the hills.

By 1902 the Caledonian main and branch lines were furnished with modern, efficient engines for all purposes; with one exception. The Callendar and Oban passenger trains were still being hauled by the small 4—4—0s that had been built by George Brittain twenty years earlier, although all had been rebuilt at St Rollox during the previous four years. None of the new bogies could be put on the Oban road because of their heavy axle loads, and much expensive double-heading was resorted to during the tourist season. McIntosh designed a neat little 4—6—0 for the Oban road, his '55' class. It was a bold step, for 4—6—0s were far from plentiful on British railways at the turn of the century. Certainly McIntosh had the example of the Jones goods on the Highland, but that was

201

primarily a freight engine. The '55s' had 19 in. by 26 in. cylinders, 5 ft coupled wheels and a boiler pressure of 175 p.s.i. Nine were built at St Rollox, and did all that their designer expected of them.

It was not only on the Oban road that loads were increasing. The North Western were now handing over prodigious trains at Carlisle and even a Dunalastair could not take them on to Edinburgh and Glasgow single handed. Beattock was a grim barrier. (An LNWR driver who rode north from Carlisle on the footplate is reputed to have said, 'If you have any more like this I'm going home.') McIntosh therefore produced the largest and heaviest engine in Britain. It is not easy to convey now the sensation that Caledonian Nos. 49 and 50 created in railway circles in 1903. With their enormously long boilers pressed to 200 p.s.i., their 6 ft 6 in. coupled wheels and tractive effort of 24,990, nothing like them had been seen before. One was put to haul the 2 p.m. 'Corridor' from Glasgow to Carlisle and back to Glasgow. The down train left the Citadel station at an hour when the burghers of Carlisle were out for their evening stroll, and a surprising number of them found their way to the station. Rous-Marten found a policeman keeping the crowds away from No. 49. 'A whacking whopper! Mr McIntosh has gone *three* better!' was his verdict. There was no turntable big enough for the new engines, and engine and tender had to be turned separately at Carlisle, a demoralising sight for any North Western man who witnessed it. Soon there were comments in the railway journals about West Coast trains arriving from the South with two engines and departing for the north with one. A writer complained that 'The train was drawn by *two* powerful engines has become a stock phrase without which no inspired paragraph of a London and North Western performance is ever complete.' In the summer of 1903 McIntosh was presented with a wonderful opportunity to show off his new engine. A special train was arranged to convey delegates to the International Telegraph Conference from London to Glasgow and the LNWR and the CR went out of their way to impress their special passengers. The North Western provided a train of ten dining cars and two brake vans, and *Commonwealth* and *Charles H. Mason* took this load to Carlisle non-stop. What a slap in the eye it would have been to the North Western if the Caledonian had taken the train out of Carlisle with one engine! It is said that McIntosh gave serious thought to putting No. 49 on the train. But even No. 49 could not have got that load up Beattock without a banker, so McIntosh settled for two Dunalastairs and a non-stop run from Carlisle to Glasgow.

The year of the big Caledonian six-coupled engines was one of change for Springburn, for the intensive service of local passenger trains linking Springburn's three stations with the various Glasgow stations finally collapsed. In 1897, the year before the electric cars, the public timetables contained four separate services linking Springburn with the city. Between Cowlairs and Queen Street there were 47 daily advertised down trains and 25 up trains (the down trains, it will be recalled, stopped for the attachment of the Cowlairs Incline brakes). Between St Rollox and Buchanan Street there were 26 down trains and 14 up trains. Springburn station, well situated in the centre of the district, offered a train every hour of the day from 7.1 a.m. to 10.1 p.m. to Queen Street Low Level, and in addition 29 Glasgow & South Western trains left Springburn for St Enoch. The disintegration of this complex service followed immediately on the introduction of the electric tram. The Glasgow & South Western withdrew their trains from Springburn in 1902, and the North British service to Queen Street Low Level was curtailed. A little-used, skeleton passenger service was maintained on this route until 1960 when it was replaced by an excellent half-hourly service of electric Blue Trains. Trains were still advertised to stop at St Rollox, but after 1903 they were little patronised. Commenting in 1903 the *Evening Times* of Glasgow said: 'Perhaps when the people have no alternative but overcrowded cars they will long for the comfort of the roomy compartments in the train.'

Matthew Holmes died in 1903, without seeing his last engine fully at work. Like its predecessors it was a 4—4—0 (the '317' class) but bigger and more powerful than anything that had appeared on the North British hitherto. It weighed 52 tons, had the usual 6 ft 6 in. coupled wheels and 19 in. by 26 in. cylinders, and a steel boiler pressed to 200 p.s.i. By the time the engine had got into its stride Matthew Holmes had made his last, sad journey along the main line from Lenzie to Haymarket and thence the short distance to Dalry Road cemetery where he was buried—with Caledonian chimneys peeping over the graveyard wall. The *St Rollox and Springburn Express* accorded him not just an obituary notice, but a leading article. It said in part:

'By the passing away of Mr. Matthew Holmes, Glasgow, and particularly Springburn, is the poorer. Of a quiet and unobtrusive nature Mr. Holmes was a gentleman every inch. He did much good work in his sixty odd years and he always did it without placing a trumpet to his mouth. To the humblest workman he was always accessible and a patient hearing was always afforded whether the complaint was groundless or the reverse. Men in his position do not always act so. The imperious tyrant had no part in the life of Matthew Holmes who was beloved by the men under him, and no better compliment perhaps can be paid an overseer than that in the discharge of a sacred trust he evinced humanity of the kindest pattern. In every sense of the term he left the railway world better than he found it. He is another example of those captains of industry who have risen from the ranks, and to the last was an example of affability and kindness of heart.'

Holmes was succeeded by William Paton Reid, his outdoor assistant. Not related to the Reids of Hyde Park, he was a descendant of that William Paton who had first occupied the chair of Superintendent of Locomotives at Cowlairs.

THE RIVALS.

Cartoon neatly expressing the rivalry between British and American builders at the turn of the century

The most profound of the 1903 changes took place among the private builders. In spite of the bounding prosperity that ushered in the twentieth century the shadow of Baldwin's was beginning to loom over the Springburn builders. If Sharp, Stewart and Neilson, Reid were pleased with their production figures, Baldwin had even more reason to be pleased with theirs. Here is the growth of Baldwin output:

Year	Engines Produced	Year	Engines Produced
1894	313	1899	901
1895	401	1900	1,217
1896	547	1901	1,375
1897	501	1902	1,533
1898	752		

In five years Baldwin's had tripled their production. Few American railways could afford the luxury of a McIntosh or a Drummond turning out individual designs in dribs and drabs. They bought off the peg from the builders. Baldwin's built locomotives by the mile and cut them off in sizes to suit all requirements. As long as this colossal production was absorbed by a voracious, expanding home railway system there was no threat to the British builders. But the very firm which in 1890 had not considered it worth while to send an engine to a Scottish exhibition, by 1900 was pushing its wares with vigour in all the traditional British markets. Baldwin's took to producing at intervals a lavish brochure full of useful data, *Record of Recent Construction,* which they circulated to railway managements round the world. American consuls were told to furnish details of local construction and their reports were made available to American locomotive manufacturers. No one was more active than the American consul in Glasgow, Bret Harte. He reported that Neilson, Reid were producing 200 locomotives a year with 2,500 men, at a time when Baldwin's was producing 300 locomotives with 1,400 men.

British observers poured scorn on American engines. Rous-Marten saw some specimens of Baldwin's work at the 1900 Paris Exhibition and thought they were something made by the village blacksmith. Neilson and Sharp, Stewart used to wine and dine their customers when they came to Springburn to collect their newest engines. These were occasions for speechmaking, and railwaymen from overseas who told the tale of American engines falling to bits almost as soon as they were off the boat were sure of an appreciative audience. The *St Rollox and Springburn Express* scoured the professional journals for matter critical of the performance of American locomotives, and reprinted it for Springburn consumption. The Midland's lukewarm reception of its American engines was given full prominence. *Engineering* was reported as saying: 'The Japanese railways with few exceptions have discarded American locomotives in favour of those of British manufacture.' But a few weeks later the same journal was reporting a repeat order for 18 Baldwin locomotives. The scoffing critics should have listened to the echo of Walter Neilson's voice coming to them from half a century ago—'We may look to our friends across the Atlantic with the expectation of learning something from them even in railway engineering.'

Wishful thinking could not hide the fact that American locomotives were making inroads into traditional British markets. Overseas locomotive superintendents who hitherto had bought Springburn engines without question, now succumbed to American salesmanship. Some organised comparative trials between British engines and their American counterparts. The Egyptians arranged a direct test between a Baldwin freight engine and a similar Neilson-built engine. Each had the same sized driving wheels and cylinders, but the American engine had a boiler pressure of 160 p.s.i. against 140 for the Scottish. The test trains were run over 130 miles between Cairo and Gabbari with 60 wagons weighing 443 tons for the Baldwin and 555 tons for the Neilson. According to the *Egyptian Gazette,* 'the British engines did their work with ease, the American engines with difficulty. The trials of the ten American engines are not yet completed, but so far the preliminary runs have demonstrated results more accentuated in favour of the British engines.' On the other hand Neilson's lost an order for 20 dock tanks for the Commissioners for the Port of Calcutta to Baldwin's. Neilson's price was £1,549 each, Baldwin's £1,378. It was in Springburn's most valuable market, India, that Baldwin's made their most spectacular gains, and it was over the allocation of Indian orders that a memorable row blew up. Mr J. C. Baird, the Member of Parliament for Glasgow Central, acutely aware of the threat of foreign competition to the city's locomotive industry, accused Lord George Hamilton, the Secretary of State for India, of giving British locomotive builders a raw deal by handing out Indian orders indiscriminately to American and German builders. The Secretary of State in a stuffy letter replied that the British locomotive manufacturers had themselves to blame for not turning out the right engine at the right price. Hugh Reid was provoked into calling together representatives from Sharp, Stewarts and Dübs, and the result was the Glasgow builders' historic letter to *The Times*:

Sir,

We have read with interest your article dealing with Lord George Hamilton's letter to Mr. Baird on the subject of competition of American and German locomotive builders for locomotive engines for India and we—the Locomotive builders of Glasgow—wish to submit jointly the following considerations.

First, as to American competition.

The American engine is designed with the view of reducing as much as possible the amount of labour in the course of its construction, and substituting machine work instead, and it is therefore a cheaper engine to build in works which are equipped for its construction than the British engine is in works constructed for the construction of the British engine.

With the commencement of American competition for Indian locomotives some three or four years ago all engines ordered for India were of the British type modified, of course, to suit local and climatic conditions, and British builders were asked to build these types only. When the American builders began to compete they were allowed to offer their own type of engine, except in the case of some details which did not affect the general construction of the engine. In case of the broad gauge engines, for instance, all have been supplied with outside cylinders and without crank axles, whereas with very few exceptions the Indian engines made in this country have inside cylinders and crank axles, the latter being the most expensive part of the engine per ton.

It follows, therefore, as far as design is concerned, the Americans were allowed to supply a cheaper engine than British builders.

As to materials employed in the construction, the British builders are compelled to obtain certain materials from two or three makers whose products have been found to give the most satisfactory results in working, but which are not unnaturally costly. Were the American builders in all cases restricted to the same makers?

As to workmanship, we have reason to believe that the American engines supplied to this country were very far below the standard of workmanship obtained in the best locomotive works in Britain, and we have before us official infomation from India which goes far to show that the same was the case in the Indian engines.

You, Sir, treat the matter, rightly we believe, as one of national importance, and we suggest that Lord George Hamilton should send a small commission to India to inquire into the results with the American engines there, and also that the English railway companies who have American engines working on their systems—say the Midland, the Great Northern and the Great Central Railways—should be allowed to allow the same commission to inquire as to the results obtained on the railways.

As to German competition, as the two orders recently sent to Germany are the first that have been given for locomotives it has yet to be proved that 'Germany can serve her (India) better than England in the matter of locomotives'. For ourselves we frequently get and are at the present time getting orders for engines for foreign countries such as Holland, Sweden, Spain, etc. in competition with German makers for railways whose directors have learned that what is cheaper in the first cost is not always cheaper in the long run.

It would be interesting to know what makes of material are to be accepted in the case of the German engines. We can buy German tyres, axles, etc. much cheaper than we can get them in this country, but so far we have not desired and have not been invited to use these materials in the construction of engines for India.

It does not appear to be known that since the East Indian Railway and the Assam—Bengal Railway sent their orders to Hanover, two other Indian railway companies have placed orders for 25 and 6 engines respectively with home manufacturers preferring to pay a higher price and to wait longer for what they personally believe will ultimately prove to be the cheapest source of supply.

The present difficulty has been caused by the simple fact that we are filled with orders sent to us from all parts of the world by companies who know our work and who in forecasting their needs prefer to wait for us, rather than go elsewhere, while obviously they do not regard our prices as prohibitive.

With regards to the future, if the Indian railways are prepared to accept the cheapest engine offered without regard to quality of material and workmanship then the capacity of the existing establishment is quite ample to satisfy demand. On the other hand if it is proved that the British engine though not the cheapest in the first cost is the most economical in working and maintenance and the Indian railways are prepared to restrict themselves to British manufacturers in future we are prepared to take such steps as may be necessary to meet any future demand.

We are, Sir,

Your obedient servants,

Neilson, Reid and Co.

Dübs and Co.

Sharp, Stewart and Co. Ltd.

(J. F. Robinson, Managing Director).

The Glasgow builders were too smug in assuming that their Indian customers would hold their orders back until it suited Glasgow to deal with them. The Indian railways went where they could get engines quickly and at a reasonable price. The insinuation that American engines were built of inferior materials was answered by the large handsome 2—8—2 tanks built in America for the 5 ft 6 in. gauge Mushkaf—Bolan Railway in the North West frontier area. To all intents and purposes these were British engines built in America. They *looked* British. Only the best Yorkshire iron was used; the tyres, axles and crankpins were of Taylor's steel; the boiler mountings were British and the engine was equipped with the vacuum brake. The Mushkaf—Bolan tank proved that the Americans could build a British-type engine.

Meanwhile, the locomotive superintendent of the Oudh & Rohilkhund Railway was reporting in writing on ten Baldwin's he had acquired:

'Those ten engines have been working passenger trains, running at 30-35 miles an hour, and goods trains running at 20 miles an hour, chiefly the former, and they have done their work well. They steam capitally, are remarkably good starters; they get away from a station with 55 loaded vehicles equal to about 1,300 tons with the greatest ease. They are higher in coal consumption than our new class B (British). They are easily repaired, but repairs will have to be kept up as if not they will go to pieces sooner than our other engines would. They do not, as far as I can see, cost more in repairs than other engines, and I am very satisfied with them.'

210

If they were to meet the American threat the Glasgow builders had to do something more drastic than write a letter to *The Times*. In the autumn of 1903 Neilson, Reid, Dübs and Sharp, Stewart amalgamated to form the largest locomotive manufacturing concern outside America. The new firm decided upon the grand title, The British Locomotive Company Ltd, but found that a small engineering business which had never built a locomotive was trading under that name. So they became the North British Locomotive Company with headquarters in Springburn. With a North British Locomotive Company and a North British Railway Company, both headed by a Reid, functioning within half a mile of each other a certain amount of confusion was inevitable, but not locally. Springburn folks never referred to the North British Locomotive Company as anything other than 'the Combine'.

The story has a curious tailpiece. A London firm of consultants, H. T. Van Laun and Company, claimed that they had engineered the formation of the North British Locomotive Co., and demanded from the former constituent companies payments totalling £34,207, $2\frac{1}{2}$ per cent commission on the estimated purchase prices of the businesses. In the lawsuit that ensued it was admitted that as early as 1899 this firm had sought to arrange an amalgamation between the Glasgow builders and an unspecified English builder. The Judge accepted that the constituents of the North British Locomotive Co. had instructed Van Laun to prepare such a plan, but since no formal contract had been signed the claim failed.

The success of American locomotives in India led to the English Engineering Standards committee preparing, after consultation with British builders and consulting engineers, a series of standard designs to meet the requirements of Indian broad and metre-gauge systems, with which builders hoped to cut costs and speed deliveries. During 1903 three standard metre-gauge types were designed, a 4—6—0 express, a 4—6—0 mixed traffic and a 4—8—0 freight. One of the first orders for a standard engine went to Hyde Park, for four mixed-traffic engines for the Dibru—Sadiya Railway.

After the turmoil of 1903 the two following years were tranquil. The old Cowlairs engine shed that had stood at the north end of the works since 1842 was at long last closed in 1904 and the new one opened at Eastfield, half a mile further out on the main line. The old shed housed 26 engines; Eastfield provided accommodation for 84 engines in 14 roads and controlled 106 engines distributed in various sub-sheds. In 1905 a civil landmark was reached when Springburn was provided with a large, handsome Public Hall.

High up on the facade was a sandstone carving of a Grecian goddess holding in her hands—a locomotive. Hugh Reid and Andrew Carnegie between them equipped the hall with a 2,796-pipe grand organ, and Herbert Walton played the opening recital.

Nineteen hundred and six was a great year for Springburn. That was the year of *Cardean,* and the North British Atlantics and the Battle of the Block Trains. McIntosh turned out *Cardean* as CR No. 903 and the Caledonian proceeded to sell it to the public in the way that airlines half a century later were to sell Viscounts and Comets and Tridents. This bigger-than-ever 4—6—0 was put on the 'Corridor', and the faithful flocked to the stations; it is doubtful if any engine anywhere ever had such a large and devoted following. *Cardean* appeared on postcards and bookmarks. The Caledonian advertising department put on sale for only 2s 6d a remarkable gauge 'O' model designed by Henry Greenly and marketed by Bassett-Lowke, of which thousands were sold. It was 17 in. long, painted in Caledonian blue and correctly lined out. A robust clockwork motor provided the motive power. The model was designed to run on a smooth table top or floor, but the wheels were flanged and it could be adapted to run on gauge 'O' track. A West Coast 12-wheeled composite coach 16 in. long was offered at the same time for 1s 6d.

It is interesting to compare the Caledonian engines with contemporary 4—6—0s on a basis of length of boiler barrels:

212

Railway	Year	Class	Length of Boiler Barrel	
			ft	in.
Caledonian	1906	903	17	7
Caledonian	1903	49	17	4½
North Eastern	1901	2111	15	10½
LNWR	1903	1400	15	6
G & SW	1903	381	15	5
Great Central	1902	1067	15	
Great Western	1902	98	14	10
Highland	1900	140	14	4½
LSWR	1905	330	13	9

By 1906 not only the Caledonian, but the Glasgow & South Western and the Highland were handling their principal passenger trains with 4—6—0s, though the North British was still a 4—4—0 line. W. P. Reid, with the Caledonian turning out large, eye-catching 4—6—0s, had to produce a really big North British design, not merely for prestige, but because it was urgently needed for the ever-increasing loads and faster timings on the Waverley route and the Aberdeen road. It is said that the Cowlairs superintendent had a close look at the North Eastern and Great Central Atlantics and then took his problem to the Reids at Hyde Park. This was the period when the De Glehn Atlantics were attracting a lot of attention. McIntosh had already designed one for the Caledonian, although he never built it, and the NBL were very enthusiastic about the De Glehn. Almost exactly at the time when Reid was discussing his proposed new engine with the Hyde Park design staff, the NBL were doing their best to induce their excellent Indian customer, the Bengal Nagpur Railway, to try a De Glehn compound Atlantic. When the BNR questioned the wisdom of ordering such engines Hyde Park offered to build two on approval. If they failed to come up to the makers' expectations the NBL would take them back, and the venture would cost the railway company nothing. The De Glehns were built, delivered and tested in express passenger service, and were so successful that the BNR ordered a further batch of thirteen. One of their good features was that they could make much longer non-stop runs without taking water than the simple engines they replaced. In 1929 the BNR ordered and Hyde Park built eighteen huge De Glehn Pacific compounds. When these engines went into service in 1930 the two original compounds were still at work. The first had run 739,988 miles; a new firebox had been fitted after 611,000 miles and the copper tube plate had been renewed after 575,209 miles. The NBL had not erred in their assessment of these engines.

Now, if the Hyde Park Reids had such faith in the De Glehn Atlantics in 1906, it is more than likely that a compound Atlantic was suggested to W. P. Reid as worthy of consideration. But Reid did not share the NBL's views on compounding. In 1905, when he must have been giving serious thought to his new engine, Reid attended a meeting of the Institution of Engineers and Shipbuilders in Scotland when John Riekie gave a talk on the compounding of locomotive engines. Reid took part in the following discussion, saying that he believed that several systems of compounding, including the De Glehn system, were not as good as they were claimed to be. He listed back pressure, extra friction and excessive upkeep of bearing parts as among the disadvantages. He considered that the compound locomotive had no advantage over the simple except on non-stop runs of over one hundred miles, and the North British had no such runs. It was known, too, that Walter Chalmers, Reid's chief draughtsman, held strong views about compounding. At a Hyde Park dinner he was reported as saying: 'So far as I can judge the compound engine is not likely to become the engine of the future, as the first cost and upkeep are so much in excess of that of the simple engine.' It was not surprising that when Reid's long-awaited big engine at last appeared it was *not* a compound. Anyway, railway politics were such that the North British could not risk an experiment. They needed a safe, reliable performer to match against the Caledonian big engines.

The Reid Atlantics were unlike anything that had appeared or was to appear on the North British. With their big boilers and Belpaire fireboxes, squat chimneys and flattened domes they gave a tremendous impression of power. They were like crouching tigers preparing for a spring. They were masculine engines whereas even the biggest Caledonian 4—6—0s were graceful ladies. The big cab with side-windows in pairs was new to the North British. Outside cylinders (20 in. by 28 in.) had not been seen on an NBR passenger engine since pre-Drummond days. With the Atlantics Reid revived the happy Drummond practice of naming the engines after the localities in which they were to work. He gave East Coast names to the engines allocated to the Aberdeen run (*Aberdonian, Dundonian, Bon Accord, Thane of Fife, Auld Reekie* and *Dunedin*) and Border names to the Waverley route engines (*Midlothian, Waverley, Liddesdale, Hazeldean, Abbotsford, Tweeddale* and *Borderer*). *St Mungo*, the fourteenth engine, apparently was meant to visit the city of its birth from time to time. All were built at Hyde Park.

A great deal of drivel has been written about the North British Atlantics. Railway writers keep harking back to that solitary, inadequate trial run over Shap when the Atlantic was said to have gobbled coal, and trot out piffling runs they have made themselves in the remote past when the Atlantics were supposed to have performed with scant distinction. In Springburn, among the men who built, ran and serviced the Atlantics, we got an entirely different impression of the engines. The drivers *loved* them. If they were heavy on coal the firemen made no fuss. If you were an Atlantic driver you were *somebody*. Even to set foot on one was a privilege accorded only to the few. Pride in them extended to the shopmen. In Cowlairs there was a separate 'Atlantic section' where only the best tradesmen were employed. Atlantic men are thin on the ground nowadays, but if you encounter one sitting on a bench in Springburn Park puffing at his pipe, and you veer the conversation round to the Atlantics he will look wistful and say: 'Ah! the Atlantic! Now *that* was an engine.' It is significant that of the five identifiable engines that are commemorated visually one way or another in Springburn all are North British and two are Atlantics.

Up to 1905 both the Caledonian and the North British attracted public attention with spectacular locomotives and fast services, but neither company had made a sustained attempt to win passengers by the obvious method of providing superior accommodation. When the Caledonian and North British engines were receiving adulation in the public and the railway press, the passengers who travelled behind them often had to put up with appalling conditions. The dirty railway carriage constantly recurred in the correspondence columns of the daily papers. The Public Health Act of 1899 had given local sanitary inspectors the right to inspect and if necessary condemn public conveyances plying through or within their districts, and railway carriages came within the meaning of the Act. The Medical Officer for Dundee had some blistering comments to make on coaching stock passing through the city, and a local paper echoed his sentiments thus: 'There are few railway cushions capable of sustaining the test of even a playful tap from a walking stick. The stick leaves a print of itself. The proper colour of the fabric blazes forth over a limited space, and the traveller has unparalleled opportunities of studying the dance of motes in the sunbeam.' About this time Irvine Kempt, general superintendent of the Caledonian, issued a directive to all members of the operating staff complaining about unpunctuality of trains, overcrowding, dirty carriages, and loss or damage to passengers' baggage, and urging everybody to take steps to remedy matters.

The third-class passenger who walked up the platform at Buchanan Street to take his seat in the 10 a.m. Grampian Express for Aberdeen on 10 April 1905 must have had the breath taken away from him. Standing at the platform were four of the biggest railway carriages that ever graced Scottish rails, shining in freshly-varnished cream and purple lake. On

216

opening the third-class compartment door he might have thought that he had stumbled on a very superior type of first-class compartment. Reassured by the '3' on the door, he would have stepped on to a layer of thick cork linoleum. Above him the high arched roof of the carriage was panelled in white-enamelled Lincrusta; the woodwork was of polished mahogany and the seats were upholstered in pale blue decorated with a floral pattern in black and orange, and were springier than anything he had previously encountered on a train. A panoramic plan of Glasgow was exhibited on one of the wall panels. The window blinds were enclosed within bronze covers, and could be lowered and fixed in any desired position. Condensation on the window, that used to run down the passenger's sleeve, was carried away in sloping grooves let into the woodwork.

A peep into one of the first-class compartments at the other end of the corridor revealed a scene of opulence: Cashmere floor rug, polished walnut panelling, seats covered with brown moquette and trimmed with silk vellum lace, gilt blind covers, white and gold roof panelling, and real Morocco leather padding on the insides of the doors. Once the train moved away the traveller found his coach gliding along with a quietness and smoothness not before experienced on any railway journey, thanks to the layer of felt with which the double floors, sides and roof of the vehicle were padded, and to the carefully-sprung six-wheeled bogies on which it was carried. At one stage of his journey our passenger would encounter what looked like a tiled lavatory at one end of the coach. What did it matter if it was only zinc panelling painted to look like tiles?

Such was the splendour of the Caledonian, St Rollox-built block train of 1905. These huge coaches were 68 ft 6 in. long over the buffers and 64 ft 10 in. over the headstocks; with a width of 9 ft at the waist and a height of 12 ft 1 in from rails to roof they just about filled the loading gauge. They established a new standard of service on the north route. The four

Glasgow coaches were joined at Perth by two similar coaches off the 9.25 ex-Princes Street, and the combined train went on to Aberdeen. The Edinburgh portion was a positive threat to the North British Edinburgh—Aberdeen service. The North British could beat the Caledonian in time over their Bridges Route, but their coaches could not match in comfort what the Caledonian had to offer. Designs for a North British block train were put in hand at Cowlairs forthwith. The North British found themselves short of labour for the job, and borrowed skilled men from the LB & SCR, one of whom stayed in Springburn, and became well known as a trombonist in the Springburn Band. Work on the new stock went on night and day, to the delight of the craftsmen and the annoyance of the foremen who were not paid extra wages for the extra hours worked. When the job was done Reid took the foremen and their wives to Montrose in the brand new stock and entertained them in a local hotel. It was not until 1906 that the North British block trains entered into full competition with the Caledonian for the Aberdeen traffic. Unlike its Caledonian counterpart the North British coach was a four-wheeled bogie, but nearly 11 ft shorter and 6 in. narrower than its St Rollox rival. With its high elliptical roof, steam heating and electric light it was a big advance on the typical flat-roofed matchbox type North British vehicle of the period with its austere seating, gas lighting and warming pans.

For many years there was a steady if modest traffic in prisoners being transported between Glasgow and the long-service prison at Peterhead on the Great North of Scotland Railway and the Caledonian and North British competed for this specialised traffic by providing railway prison vans. The North British van was a six-wheeler with heavily barred windows, the interior containing a number of individual cells and a central compartment for the warders. The Caledonian seemed to do their prisoners rather better than the NBR. A paragraph about the Caledonian vehicle in the *North British Daily Mail* said: 'In keeping with the philanthropic and humanising tendencies of the age a prison car lately built at the works (St Rollox) is fitted with gas and provided with heating apparatus for providing hot coffee for the notorious voyagers.'

At the time that the Grampian corridor coaches were built several similar vehicles without corridors were turned out for short distance services. These massive coaches each had eleven compartments and seating accommodation for 132 passengers. It was quite a sight to see a rush hour train of the big carriages coming into the Central station. As the train eased into the platform dozens of doors swung open and while the train was still in motion passengers poured in a torrent on to the platform. I travelled extensively on the Caledonian suburban twelve-wheelers, though not on Caledonian metals. One afternoon in February 1941 I was deposited from a Southern Electric on to the platform at Liss in Hampshire, after a 27-hour journey from Crieff in Perthshire that had been spiced with snowblocks in Westmorland and sundry bombings in Middlesex. I crossed over to the station platform of the Longmoor Military Railway and there I found a three-coach train headed by an 0—6—0 tank lately off the Great Eastern Railway. It was the middle of the three coaches that halted me in my tracks. It was dusk by then and there were no lights of any kind either inside or outside the train, but there was something unmistakably Caledonian about that shadowy outline. It was indeed one of the famous non-corridor Grampians, having changed not at all since I had last seen it on its native heath, except that the LMS maroon had given place to LMR dark green. I found a seat, and in the flicker of somebody's cigarette lighter saw that the famous panel pictures of Scottish beauty spots were still in place. And so our train set off on the climbing, curving track to Longmoor Downs, a stately Caledonian coach sandwiched between two relics from a first-war Great Western ambulance train, the lot pulled by a Stratford 0—6—0.

There were four of the Caledonian twelve-wheelers on the

Longmoor Military Railway. They arrived still in LMS livery, and were painted in LMR colours at the Royal Engineers' workshops. They were peculiar vehicles to put on the LMR, with its sharp curves, anything but robust military track, doubtful clearances and inexperienced and often genuinely amateur operating staff. An early attempt to run a train made up of two Caledonian coaches ended in fiasco when the vehicles buffer-locked on a curve. Thereafter it was decreed that Caledonian coaches might only be coupled to Great Western stock. One morning the carriage shunters forgot the instruction and sent out a train with two Caledonian coaches coupled next to each other. The mistake was discovered when the set got to Longmoor Downs and a shunting operation was initiated to put matters right. Unfortunately, during this operation the Westinghouse leaked off on one of the detached coaches, and it started down the gradient leading to Longmoor Yard. The line crossed a public highway on an unprotected crossing, and the great juggernaut of a coach lumbered across the road. Fortunately the yardmaster at Longmoor Yard managed to beat the runaway to a ground frame and divert it into a long loop where it collided harmlessly with a rake of old wagons used for shunting exercises. The twelve-wheelers were referred to in LMR operating instructions as 'the Caledonian coaches'. McIntosh could never have guessed, when he turned out these classic vehicles, that they would finish their days bumping through the Hampshire woods behind an Adams 0—4—2 or a North Staffordshire passenger tank.

On 17 April 1908 a Caledonian engine failed at Larkfield due to the fracturing of a crank axle after running 147,574 miles. On 2 February 1909 there was a similar failure for the same reason at Merchiston. Both axles had broken at the sharp angle between the journal and the wheel seat. For a period in between those two dates—from 26 August until 21 October—No. 903, *Cardean,* was in St Rollox undergoing heavy repairs. During the course of these repairs the engine was stripped down to the wheels, and the wheels were turned and inspected. There was no sign of any flaw in any exposed surface, but the wheels were not removed from their axles, and the wheel seats, therefore, could not be inspected.

No. 903's crank axle was similar to that which had failed, and to that which was to fail later. On one end was stamped the figure '99', indicating that the wheel had been pressed on the axle at a pressure of 99 tons or 11.64 tons per in. of diameter. Further, the wheels were keyed to the axle by pins 6 in. long by 1 in. in diameter driven in from the face of the wheel. Manufacturer's markings on the other side of the axle indicated that it was No. 1,174 supplied by John Spencer and Sons Ltd, of Newburn Street Works, Newcastle, that the metal used was of a particular quality, and that the axle had a breaking load of 31.94 tons per sq. in. Before the manufacture of the axle had begun a Caledonian engineer had visited the Newcastle works and tested a sample of the metal to be used, and a further sample was sent to St Rollox for additional tests. All tests proved satisfactory. The crank axle for *Cardean* was made and delivered with the guarantee that Spencer would replace it if it failed before it had run 200,000 miles.

Cardean was outshopped at the end of October and took up its traditional duties on the 2 p.m. 'Corridor'. The winter passed without incident. Then shortly after 9 o'clock on the evening of 2 April 1909 No. 903 breasted Beattock with the down 'Corridor', shed the banker and started on the swift descent of the Clyde valley. By the time Crawford slipped rapidly past, crank axle No. 1,174 had run 145,388 miles, and it had one more mile of life left in it. With the speed mounting into the sixties *Cardean* gave a sudden ferocious lurch that snapped the coupling between engine and tender. The driver and fireman were dismayed to see tender and train drift back into the darkness while *Cardean*, tenderless, ran on. When the engine eventually stopped a quick inspection showed that it was still on the rails all wheels except one. The left hand leading driver was missing, the coupling rod broken, the frame bent and the brake gear and reversing rod destroyed. Of the train there was no sign.

Passengers in the train became aware that something was amiss when there was an uncomfortably rapid application of the brakes. In the brief space of 250 yards the speed of the 'Corridor' was reduced from something above 60 m.p.h. to zero. In the process of this rapid deceleration the train split in two between the fourth and fifth coaches and when the severed portions came to rest there was a gap of twenty yards between them. Some of the vehicles ran off the rails to the left and were guided to a more or less gentle stop by the soft earth embankment, while others were derailed to the right and blocked the up line.

The *Cardean* incident had all the making of a major disaster—a heavy express travelling downhill at high speed, derailed, and part of the wreckage thrown on to the up line over which a freight train was due to pass within minutes. The night was dark and the nearest signal box was a mile away. There was no disaster because all the railwaymen involved did the right thing that night and did it promptly. The leading guard of the 'Corridor', when he went forward to investigate, was surprised to find a tender but no engine or crew at the head end. He placed detonators on the up line at the regulation distances from the obstruction and took up post with his lamp ready to stop any approaching train.

Meanwhile, an up goods was standing at Abington, the first station to the north, ready to proceed. Harry Browning the signalman held it, for the 'Corridor' had been ten minutes in section and there was no sign of it. Browning was apprehensive. A less intelligent signalman might have let the goods go with possibly disastrous consequences. At 9.55 the fireman of the 'Corridor' reached Abington on foot, and reported the obstruction. Investigation revealed that *Cardean's* crank axle had broken. There was damage to the track where the fracture took place which continued for about 300 yards. The missing driving wheel was found leaning against the boundary fence, having run like a child's hoop up the shallow bank and struck the fence, partly destroying it.

The Caledonian's most publicised locomotive had failed, and the company's prestige train had escaped disaster by a hairsbreadth. There was consternation at St Rollox. McIntosh organised a series of intensive tests of the metal from which the crank axle was made. Chemical tests were carried out in the laboratories of the Steel Company of Scotland with borings sent from St Rollox. The Glasgow & West of Scotland Technical College conducted microscopic examinations of metal fragments. Reports from the various sources were collated and by 28 April McIntosh knew what had happened. When samples of the metal were tested to destruction the resulting fracture was seen to be brittle. The chemical tests showed that the metal had a high carbon content and there was present foreign matter likely to create weak spots that would give way under stress. A fascinating series of microphotographs actually revealed the brittle structure of the metal, a condition resulting from over-heating or incomplete mechanical treatment. The report concluded: 'The axle has been made of inferior metal which had been left in an overheated condition and suffered from fatigue in use.'

When the summary of railway accident statistics for 1909 was published the Board of Trade congratulated the British railways on the reduction in the number of accidents due to axle failures. There had been 101 such failures during the year, and of these 46 had been failures of crank axles.

*　　　*　　　*

The improved facilities offered by the new Eastfield shed together with a recent extension to Queen Street station, where the goods station was removed and two passenger platforms added, put the North British in a better position than hitherto to handle their increasing traffic. But there remained the obstacle of Cowlairs Incline and the Rope. In 1908 Reid conducted a series of tests using Holmes 0—6—0 tanks as

223

bankers, including examination of the tunnel roof for the possible effects of blast. The North British directors were chicken-hearted about working the Incline with adhesion, but Reid insisted that adhesion was not only safe but necessary if the traffic originating at Queen Street was to be handled effectively. At long last Reid won the day, and the great Neilson beam engine ceased to function in 1909. The Incline brakes were left to rot in the shunting neck at the top of the Incline for some years before they were scrapped. One was sent to Galashiels where it was used as a brake van on local trip trains. It was known locally as 'the sanatorium brake'.

Printed regulations were issued to the staff on the working of the Incline by adhesion, and Reid instructed his shed foremen to see that every man knew and understood the regulations. 'Engine drivers, firemen and guards,' said the key sentence in the rules, 'must give their undivided attention to its working.' Drivers of incoming trains had to have their speed down to 10 m.p.h. at Cowlairs West Junction, 815 yards from the top of the Incline. Drivers of trains not stopping at Cowlairs were told to regard Cowlairs as a terminal station. On passing the platform they had to reduce speed to 3 miles an hour, and if they did not have full pressure in the Westinghouse train pipes they were required to stop. If all signals on the Incline were not showing clear the drivers had to hold their speed down to 3 m.p.h. during the descent, and in no event was the time taken from Cowlairs to Queen Street to be less than 5 minutes.

During the forenoon of Saturday 12 August 1911 the artist G. Fiddes Watt was engaged in the Glasgow City Chambers painting a portrait of Sir Archibald McInnes Shaw, the Lord Provost. When the sitting was over Lord Provost Shaw walked across to Queen Street station to see his artist off on the 2.10 express to Edinburgh. The train duly departed from platform No. 2. At that time platform No. 3 was empty, and the signal at the tunnel mouth indicated that it was about to receive the 1.5 express from Edinburgh, due at 2.10, but running a few minutes late. As the Lord Provost crossed the narrow, crowded circulating area behind the buffer stops he was hailed by a railway detective of his acquaintance, and the two men stopped for a chat. The station was thronged with a typical summer Saturday afternoon crowd, and the refreshment room opposite the buffer stops was well patronised.

Suddenly a sustained roar echoed to the station roof. The 1.5 from Edinburgh had burst out of the tunnel and was coursing down platform No. 3 towards the buffer stops at an unseemly speed. There were shouts and exhortations from the station staff; the crowds in the circulating area parted like the waters of the Red Sea. Seconds later there was a resounding clatter as 4—4—0 No. 575 demolished the buffer stops and, without its tender, leaped up on to the circulating area almost at the Lord Provost's feet. The driving wheels crunched into the concrete pavement and churned up the soil beneath. There was a second crash as buffer beam and smokebox door burst through the refreshment room wall. When the engine came to rest the buffers were touching one of the tables. Crockery was upset, and patrons overturned some tables in their panic to leave, but nobody was hurt. The chimney was pressed hard against the outside wall of the refreshment room. The bogie had been torn off and could be seen under the footplate. The driving wheels were sunk deep into the platform, and steam and water from broken pipes added an infernal touch to the scene.

At first sight the accident looked very bad, but the station staff were relieved to find that only seven passengers had been injured, none seriously. The fact that the engine jumped up on to the circulating area gave the train an extra forty or fifty yards in which to stop, and the braking effect of the broken concrete and underlying soil prevented No. 575 from lumbering into the crowded refreshment room. The coaches, except for the leading pair, were undamaged and in fact worked back to Edinburgh on the 3.10. No. 575 was an embarrassment to the North British for the rest of the day. The engine stretched from the refreshment room to the buffer stops, forming a barrier which divided the station in two. Once the fire had been drawn the engine was discreetly sheeted, but passengers who bought tickets at the main booking office had to go outside the station and walk round by West George Street and Queen Street to reach trains departing from platform No. 4 and upwards. No. 575 was removed early on Sunday morning.

How did the train contrive to get out of control on the Incline? The story began with the departure from Waverley. Normally, the train was made up of ten coaches, but because of the additional traffic offered on that busy Saturday afternoon two coaches were added, making the weight 277 tons, 11 tons over the permitted load for the class of engine used. No. 575 was one of the six built by Matthew Holmes in 1884 —his first passenger design—and had only recently emerged from Cowlairs rebuilt by Reid. Forrester, the driver that day, had his work cut out to keep time with his heavy load. The train made its booked stop at Haymarket, and ran non-stop from there to Queen Street. Forrester had dropped several minutes by the time he got to Cowlairs, and that may have induced him to go past Cowlairs platform at 25 m.p.h. instead of the regulation 3 m.p.h. According to the driver's own story he brought his speed down to 4 m.p.h. at Cowlairs station box and that left him with 60 lb. of air in the train pipes. He dropped down the tunnel cautiously, but when he tried to make a brake application at the first ventilating shaft—961 ft from the buffers—he could get no result. He used the sanders and put the engine into reverse, but there was no appreciable drop in speed. J. McLachlan, a carriage examiner, was waiting at the top end of platform No. 3 to check the stock of the incoming train. When No. 575 flashed past him he saw either the driver or the fireman screwing down the handbrake. He watched the carriage wheels as they passed, and saw that there were no brakes on other than the guard's brake. Yet when he examined the train immediately after the crash the brake

226

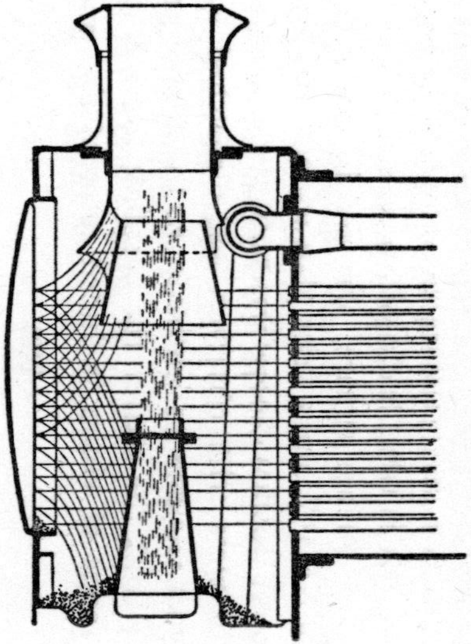

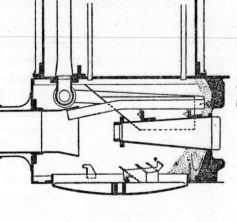
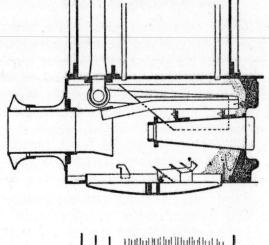

Fig. 3.
Path of Sparks, Smoke-box Clean.

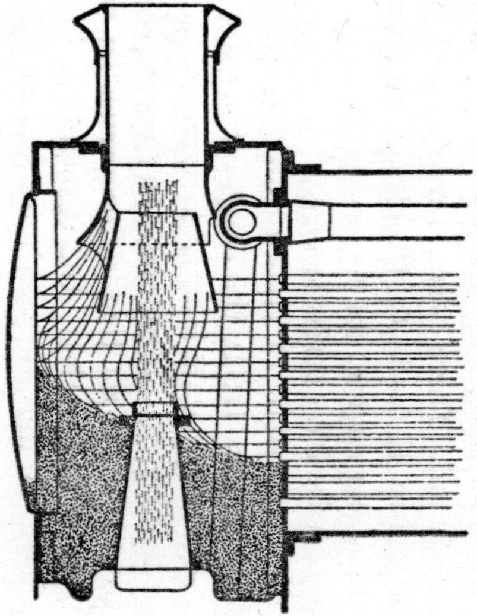

Fig. 4.
Path of Sparks, Running Condition.

Fig. 8.
Path of Sparks, with Arrester and with Ejector Pipe.

Three diagrams showing operation of spark arrester on Caledonian Railway No. 147

blocks were tight on every wheel. The Westinghouse gear was stripped from No. 575, reassembled on another engine and tested. It functioned perfectly. Forrester had to shoulder the blame for having approached Cowlairs at excessive speed and of letting his train get the better of him on the Incline.

* * *

St Rollox continued to do things in a big way. In his nineteen years with the Caledonian, McIntosh turned out six 4—6—0 designs—three of them in the one year 1906—which comprised a total of only 42 engines. Over the same period McIntosh completed 65 Dunalastairs in four classes. In addition he produced 22 superheated 4—4—0s, No. 139 built at St Rollox in 1910 being the first high degree superheated engine in Scotland. There were, therefore, 87 McIntosh 4—4—0s as against 42 4—6—0s. In spite of the glamour that surrounded the big engine, the 4—4—0 remained the backbone of the Caledonian express service.

One of the Dunalastair IV class featured in an interesting series of tests held to decide the design of a spark arrester. The steam engine by nature is an arsonist and in the opening years of the century the Caledonian were paying out £2,000 a year in compensation for lineside properties set on fire by sparks from their locomotives. And that did not include the cost of damage to the company's own property. Various attempts at spark arresting had been made, but the chief obstacle to a successful design was ignorance of what exactly happened inside a locomotive smokebox. The only way to find out was to look inside the smokebox *while the engine was at work*; and that is what McIntosh proposed to do.

A hole, four inches square, was cut in the side of the smokebox of No. 147, and a thick glass window was fitted over the aperture. A wooden canopy was built at the front end and No. 147, complete with observer, was dispatched with the 6.10 p.m. from Glasgow to Kinbuck. As the engine pounded up Kinbuck Bank the man at the peephole had a fascinating view. His range of vision included most of the smokebox

228

interior and the lower portion of the chimney. What he saw surprised him. The jet of exhaust steam from the blast pipe entered the chimney in a parallel column. Red hot cinders coming out of the tubes at terrific velocity passed through the exhaust jet in a horizontal path—even sparks passing a quarter of an inch above the orifice were not deflected—to impinge on the smokebox door. Small cinders were blown out of the chimney, but large pieces fell to the bottom of the smokebox and formed a drift against the door. The observer noted that there was little emission of sparks at first, but as the drift of cinders against the door increased a fountain of red embers erupted from the chimney above him. After 13 miles of climbing the cinder drift was half way up the smokebox with the high part of the drift on the door. The exhaust pipe was buried up to the nozzle. The cinders from the tubes now raced up the face of the drift and passed at once out of the chimney. Later examination of the engine revealed that of the 80 cu. ft of the smokebox 18 cu. ft were filled with cinders.

The problem, then, was to produce a device that would prevent as far as possible the formation of a cinder bank. A V-shaped plate was fitted between the exhaust pipe and the tube plate, the angle of the plate pointing towards the tube plate. Above the V-plate was erected a baffle plate to prevent sparks from escaping from the upper tubes. Inside the angle of the V-plate a 3 in. vertical pipe ran from just inside the chimney to the floor of the smokebox. The idea was to induce a draught on the floor.

With this apparatus in place No. 147 was again dispatched on the 6.10. (On these occasions the engine took the train to Kinbuck after which it ran forward light to Perth. It then took over the 9.40 Perth to Coatbridge, and worked back light to St Rollox where the staff were waiting to examine the data collected on the trip.) What the observer at the peephole now saw was this. The cinders were directed downwards to the front bottom corners of the smokebox where they formed cinder banks as before. But fresh cinders ejected from the tubes no longer rushed directly up the cinder bank and into the atmosphere via the chimney. Instead, the draught drew them into the angle of the V-plate and to the bottom of the 3 in. pipe to be sucked up the pipe into the chimney. The cinder drift no longer provided a rapid, direct route for the sparks. The observer noticed that the sparks progressed from the cinder bank to the foot of the pipe in a series of jerks with each pulsation of the engine, and had cooled to invisibility in 10 seconds after having entered the smokebox. By the time they were ejected they had cooled considerably. Several variations of the V-plate were tried before the final form was decided on.

In 1911 Reid had Robert Stephenson and Co. build a further six Atlantics, but apart from that Cowlairs did not try to emulate the St Rollox big engine policy. Instead, Reid turned out a series of extremely neat, workmanlike 4—4—0s, the best known of which were the Scotts and Glens. These were the favourites of my boyhood days; I grew up with them. There were few days in the year when I did not see some of their number. The Scotts had the usual 6 ft 6 in. driving wheels, and the first six engines were built in 1909 by the North British Locomotive Co. Then more followed from Cowlairs in 1911 and later on a further 27 superheated engines were built, making a total of 43. The Glens were 6 ft versions of the Scotts and there were 32 of them. Reid named the Scotts after the colourful characters from Sir Walter's Waverley novels, and the Glens took their names mainly from West Highland glens which they were destined to serve. I knew a North British goods guard who could put all the Scott names in their proper context. And what names! How I enjoyed listening to his stories of Caleb Balderstone, Simon Glover, Bailie Nicol Jarvie, Cuddie Headrigg and the rest. Looking back I have often thought how Scott, such a bore in the classroom, became such a delight in the bothy. (On the other hand it was heartening during a geography lesson on the West of Scotland to be confronted with a map bristling with engine names.) I like to think of some forgotten employee of the North British with a list of numbers at his elbow thumbing through the Waverley novels and putting names to them. I can hear him chuckling after he had written the name of that great divine Peter Poundtext against No. 497 and saying to himself, 'Och, we may as well gie the minister a priest to keep him company.' And then he inscribed Father Ambrose against No. 498. I have no record of No. 497 and No. 498 double-heading a train although they might well have done for they were at Eastfield together. What fun there would have been if they had turned out *Father Ambrose* to work one of the specials on the day of the Orange Walk!

In the first week of October 1911 J. F. McIntosh received an official letter commanding him to be present at Perth on the arrival of the Royal Train on 11 October. A similar letter was received by David Deuchars, superintendent of the line, North British Railway. The letters did not explain their purpose, but their recipients had a good idea of what was in the wind. The occasion was the return of the royal family from Balmoral to London by the West Coast route. McIntosh rode on the train from Aberdeen in the course of his duty and at Perth he joined Deuchars on the platform. Both men were seen to enter the royal day saloon and some minutes later they emerged wearing the insignia of the Royal Victorian Order. Contemporary accounts of the event throw some light on the importance that was attached to royal railway journeys in those days. Not only was Perth platform thick with Caledonian officials, but there were representatives present from the Midland, the North Eastern and the Great Northern with, for good measure, a director of the Highland Railway. All hurried forward to shake hands with the distinguished railwaymen who had just left the presence of the King and Queen. McIntosh later told how they had entered the royal saloon and the King had shaken hands first with Deuchars and then with himself. The Queen was sitting at a table strewn with magazines. King George thanked the railwaymen for their

231

P

long and devoted service (Deuchars had just retired) and formally presented them with their decorations.

McIntosh retired in February 1914, and his chair was filled by William Pickersgill. The last locomotive superintendent of the Caledonian Railway was in the same mould as the first. He was an Englishman, reserved by nature, who had served his apprenticeship on the Great Eastern and in 1894 had gone to be locomotive superintendent of the Great North of Scotland Railway with strong recommendations from William Dean and James Holden.

Pickersgill's first design for the Caledonian was a large 4—4—0 in the McIntosh mould, but in the same year—1916 —he broke new ground by producing the first main line Caledonian outside-cylinder engine since Brittain's bogie of 1882. This was the '60' class of 4—6—0, six of which were built at St Rollox. In the following year Pickersgill designed and Hyde Park built an extremely handsome 4—6—2 passenger tank, and the twelve engines of this class worked for many years on the Clyde coast trains. Meanwhile at Cowlairs Reid went on adding to his stud of 4—4—0s, and producing still larger and heavier 0—6—0 goods engines.

During the war years the North British Locomotive Co. carried on its normal home and export trade in locomotives and also produced war materials from wooden legs to heavy tanks. A total of 1,412 locomotives were built during the war period, ranging from a 15-ton tank for the Darjeeling Himalayan Railway to a 128-ton Mallet compound for the South African Railways. Of the total, 695 engines went to the war area, among them four-cylinder compounds for the State Railways of France and massive 91-ton tanks for the Paris— Orleans Railway. While this considerable locomotive production was in progress the works also turned out 497,125 shells of various sizes, 6,000 sea mines, 82 sets of double revolving torpedo tubes, a large quantity of trench howitzer carriages and several single-engined aircraft. Perhaps Hyde Park's proudest wartime product was the great Mark VIII tank. This new type of heavy tank was built, except for the petrol engines, entirely at Hyde Park and tested on ground adjacent to the works, Winston Churchill being present at the initial tests.

When Walter Chalmers had succeeded Reid at Cowlairs in 1920 he ordered two more Atlantics from the North British Locomotive Co., No. 509, *The Lord Provost,* and No. 510, *Duke of Rothesay.* They differed little from their predecessors of the same class, except that they were superheated. Pickersgill prepared for the anticipated boom in post-war traffic by turning out 43 heavy 0—6—0s, and in 1921 he built four large three-cylinder 4—6—0s, an innovation for the Caledonian. But by then the writing was on the wall for both men.

Chapter 7

RUSHY REMINISCENCES

Pickersgill and I arrived in Springburn in the same year. By the time I was able to get my chin on the sill of my bedroom window the locomotive superintendent of the Caledonian Railway was beginning to think about his 956 class of 4—6—0. I spent a lot of time at that window. My bedroom was on the top flat of a tenement at the NB end of Springburn and from the window I could look out across the serrated roofs of Cowlairs works and miles of open country beyond to where the distant mountains peeped over the horizon. In the yard directly below my window there was magic. For a spell, morning and afternoon, the Wee Puggie pushed and pulled wagons loaded with timber and barrels of oil along rails that creaked and groaned. For hours on end I watched the performance of the Wee Puggie; at a more mature age I was to identify it as a Holmes 0—4—0.

The view from our front parlour was even more intriguing, for the window looked out on Cowlairs Incline. The railway came up from Queen Street and crossed my line of vision at an angle, eventually to pass under our street. I could tell when a train was coming because a fountain of smoke and steam erupted from a hill face half a mile away. A minute or two later the train would come into view, a big dark green engine, a string of red carriages and a little black tank pushing for all it was worth at the back. What a thundering there was when the engines plunged into the rock cutting and passed under the bridge that took our street over the railway. At night the

234

labouring banker shot a thick column of sparks as high as the tenement roofs. Just before it passed under the bridge, which was near the top of the Incline, it would give the train a final kick in the back and red-hot coal would come spattering down on the roadway, sending pedestrians scurrying for shelter.

I have a crystal-clear picture of the earliest railway recollection to which I can put a precise date. It was wintertime, but the day was sunny and the sky was blue, and there were washings flapping from ropes in the backyards below my window. Suddenly the Wee Puggie began to emit wild blasts on its whistle, which was baffling and unusual, for it seldom gave more than a perfunctory toot. Workmen began to pour out of various doors and stand about in groups in the yard. Somewhere a church bell began to ring. Then my mother burst into the room and told me that my uncle would soon be back from the war. It was eleven o'clock on the morning of 11 November 1918.

The last signature was affixed to the Treaty of Versailles at 3.55 on the afternoon of Saturday, 28 June 1919. It was precisely then that Thomas Black, a fitter on the back shift at Eastfield shed, spotted something burning outside the machine shop. I would like to say that I remember the Eastfield fire; I certainly joined the pilgrimage of Springburn folk who went to view the burnt-out shed on the Sunday. A fire engine still pumped water on to the debris, but I was of an age when no railway engine—not even nineteen burned railway engines— could compete with a fire engine.

Thomas Black found that a heap of discarded waste alongside the machine shop had caught alight. He ran for a hose, but before he could get it in action the flames were crackling across the timber roof of the shop and licking round the oil store. A barrel of paraffin exploded and the flames swept over the main shed. By the time the fire brigade arrived, smoke was curling from under the slates and burning timbers were falling on the engines below. Every available driver was rounded up to assist in getting out as many engines as possible.

235

Many were dead, and the shed pilots had to be run into the seat of the fire and coupled up to them. In forty minutes East-field was ablaze from end to end and nobody could get near it. One by one the towers of the ventilators crashed through the remains of the roof, and the boilers of the engines were heaped with embers. At the height of the fire locomotives could be seen with the coal in their tenders blazing furiously, their boilers glowing bright red. Nineteen were badly damaged, among them two Glens Nos. 100 and 405, an Inter-mediate 4—4—0 No. 332, and the Holmes 4—4—0s Nos. 215 and 600.

The emancipation that came with my enrolment in our local primary school meant that I could visit the Rushy Park. 'The Rushy' was an area of waste ground that lay between Cowlairs Incline and the Caledonian main line out of Buchanan Street. Throughout my boyhood the Rushy was my playground. What a playground, and what a pageant of trans-port moved along its boundaries as the years unrolled! The school bell signalling the end of the day rang exactly when the 4 p.m. Leeds, now the 'North Briton', was leaving Queen Street. Every day it was a race between me and the Leeds to my vantage point in the Rushy. I was down the school stairs like a tornado and in place to see the train come storming up the slope. There would be a Scott on the front end. I can hear yet the strong, measured beat of the Scott's exhaust and the staccato bark of the banker. Hard on the heels of the four o'clock came the 4.7 Thornton. *Peter Poundtext* No. 497 had a regular turn on that. I liked *Peter Poundtext,* for I knew George Pringle, its regular driver, and he always looked for me and gave me a wave. Pringle lived in a tenement overlook-ing Cowlairs Incline and when he came down the hill at the end of a run gave a special whistle to let his family know that he was safely home. In the same tenement lived another East-field driver, Archibald (Sandy) Deuchar. His engine was *Father Ambrose* No. 498 on the Edinburgh run. He had a long beard and looked immensely old—he was in fact 69—as

I saw him framed in the cab window of his Scott when he took his train down the Incline. Sandy Deuchar had a family code whistle too, but there came a night when it failed to sound.

It was 27 May 1922, a Saturday night, and Sandy Deuchar was on the 8 p.m. express from Edinburgh to Glasgow. Pringle that day was on a Fife train that was due in Queen

A COMMON HERO

" An engine driver, Alexander Hay Deuchars, of Springburn when the boiler of his engine burst at Manuel, cried to his fireman : ' Jump, mate ; one life is enough!' and busied himself in the scalding steam, shutting off the brakes, until he died. But for his sacrifice the train would have been wrecked."
—Daily Press.

Not there alone upon the plains of strife
Where martial music cheers the quivering nerve ;
But even in the common walks of life
There heroes prove that they can bravely serve.

In Britain's mills and deep in Britain's mines,
Upon the railways and the mighty sea ;
There is the field where common courage shines,
Where humble toilers prove their chivalry.

Think, now, of ALEX. HAY DEUCHAR, who cried
" Jump, mate, one life's enough," and then
He sprang into the scalding steam, and died,
Giving his life to save his fellow men.

No V.C. will adorn his breast ; no spoil
Of victor with his loved-ones screen,
But there upon the Cenotaph of toil
We'll carve his name and keep his memory green.
FRED EASTON.

ALFORD STREET,
SPRINGBURN.

Memorial card for Driver Deuchar. It was a common custom for memorial cards to be issued. The verse on this one was composed by a neighbour of Deuchar's. The name as quoted in the newspaper article is wrongly spelled

Street on the tail of the Edinburgh. This was a turn that led to friendly banter between the drivers, for if Deuchar did not clear Winchburgh Junction promptly Pringle on the Fife could be checked. From Winchburgh the Fife pursued the Edinburgh through the sections all the way to Queen Street.

That night the signals were clear for Pringle at Winchburgh Junction, but as he came up to Manuel Junction the home was against him. He was not entirely displeased for he concluded that his neighbour had been tardy in getting through the section ahead. But when he had been standing for several minutes and the signal did not clear he became apprehensive, especially since the sound of escaping high pressure steam came to him from some place ahead. Pringle told his fireman to climb on to the roof of a lineside hut, and the fireman reported that he could see a column of steam shooting high into the air near Manuel station. Just then the signal cleared and Pringle eased forward to Manuel Junction.

The Edinburgh was standing in the down platform. *Father Ambrose* was wreathed in steam and red-hot coal was piled knee-high on the footplate. Deuchar had been having trouble with 498 since he left Edinburgh and he had told his fireman that he intended to stop at Manuel Junction to examine the engine. But before he got there the big end pierced the firebox, into which live steam roared in a sudden scalding torrent driving incandescent coal before it. In seconds the footplate was a hell of fire and high pressure steam. Deuchar pushed his fireman on to the steps. 'He told me one life was enough,' the fireman was to say later. And then Sandy groped through the steam for the regulator and the Westinghouse brake valve and brought the train to a stand. When Pringle found him, he was lying in the waiting room at Manuel station cruelly burned and scalded, and two doctors from his own train were doing what they could for him. They lifted him into a compartment in the Fife and Pringle resumed his journey to Glasgow. 'Tell them at home I'll be all right, Geordie,' he said.

Deuchar died on the following Wednesday. They buried him in Sighthill Cemetery close by Cowlairs Incline and in full view of his home. Footplatemen all over the North British system contributed to a memorial to commemorate his brave deed. It is a handsome stone in Aberdeen granite and it bears the inscription

He gave his richest gift, his life,

On the altar of honour.

I last saw it a week or two after the 41st anniversary of Deuchar's death, and was pleased to notice that somebody had placed a vase of fresh flowers before it.

The school holidays provided long days of sheer delight in the Rushy. Most days I was there from breakfast time until dusk with reluctant breaks for meals. The engines became part of my young life. *Dominie Sampson, Hal o the Wynd, The Pirate, Meg Dodds, Glen Dessary, Glen Spean;* how I revelled in those romantic names. The traffic on Cowlairs Incline was varied. The Edinburgh's were the prestige trains. They had Scotts pulling them, and very occasionally a great North British Atlantic. There were Scotts and Glens on the Fifes and Glens, often in pairs, on the West Highlands. Little Holmes 4—4—0s came up with the Aberfoyles (the trains were made up of a dozen or so four and six wheelers) and smart 'C15' tanks went to places like Lennoxtown, Kilsyth and Bonnybridge Central. Alas, not only are the engines gone, but the very rails have disappeared from many of the places they once served. The best moment of the day came about 3.15 in the afternoon when a long cavalcade of engines (six or seven coupled together) went gliding down the hill to take charge of the late afternoon traffic. Two Glens would be leading, one each for the West Highland and the Lothian Coast Express, then would come a Scott for the Leeds and another Scott for the Thornton, a Reid Intermediate for the Grangemouth and a Holmes 4—4—0 for the Alloa. Within an hour they all came up the hill again with their respective trains.

During my early schooldays I gave little thought to the

239

Caledonian. Indeed, I was bound by a parental injunction not to go near the Caley. This was not due to family partisanship but to certain physical hazards which faced a small boy at the approaches to the Caledonian main line. The Rushy, inviting and verdant at the North British side, degenerated into a wilderness of slag heaps and turgid pools at the Caledonian side. There came the day when, greatly daring, I ventured over to the Caley. The railway lay at the bottom of a deep gorge cut out of the mounds of grey gritty alkali waste that had been spread over the ground by the Tennant brothers a hundred years before. I watched from the lip of the gorge, and as I watched there was a rumble, and sweeping down the line came the biggest and most beautiful engine I had ever seen. It was brilliant blue, its boiler was of enormous length and it had more wheels about it than I had ever seen on one engine. It had a train of *white* carriages. I have never forgotten the sight of that glorious blue engine soaring down the slope between the dingy slag heaps, and disappearing into the tunnel with a roar like an ocean liner. Secretly, I wished that we could have something as good on *our railway*.

Of Sunday traffic on Cowlairs Incline I can tell you nothing, for I did not watch trains on Sunday. The power of Presbyterianism, which the Edinburgh & Glasgow knew in the first days of railways, was still very much in evidence in the Springburn of the twenties. Sunday was a day of dignified quiet when the railway families went to church. Many of the footplatemen and shopmen were elders of the kirk and took their duties very seriously. There was a church in Edinburgh not far from Haymarket and Dalry Road sheds, the congregation of which consisted largely of North British and Caledonian men. The minister was Bell Nicoll and his son, Dr J. T. Bell Nicoll, has left a wonderful account of railwaymen and their attitude to church. He was writing of Edinburgh, but his words describe perfectly the Springburn Sunday as I knew it. In his *The Span of Time* Bell Nicoll said:

'There were between 30 and 40 Elders, and though I

have met many men in all walks of life I have yet to meet a finer body of men. They were working men. Their Christianity was not a mere symptom of neurasthenia as it is with so many. They were men whose Christian faith made them finer individuals in every way. They carried the stamp of their manliness and dignity as naturally as noblemen wear the insignia of their rank. There was John Sinclair, who on weekdays drove the express from Edinburgh to Aberdeen. John might be seen walking to his engine any day of the week clothed in the pale blue dungarees and glazed peak cap which are worn by those on the footplate. When he wasn't driving the express he was to be found doing some job or other in connection with the church. I have never met any man to whom the immediate presence of Christ was such a reality. His face was always beaming with smiles, and it gave one the impression of perpetual polish just as he kept his engine polished with a greasy rag. The satisfactoryiness of a sermon could always be told by the nodding of John's head.'

John Sinclair drove a North British Atlantic.

I remember coming across a railway drawing in a local newspaper. An engine was the centre piece, and inside a balloon emanating from its whistle was the inscription, 'Too too—too—too too.' I had to seek parental guidance on the significance of this, and the date at the top of the page was pointed out to me. It was 22 February 1922; 22.2.22. Ominous year! Little did I know that my world of green and blue engines was soon to be swept away and that sombre changes were in store for Springburn.

One day about two years after the cartoon incident my mother announced that we were to have *English people* to tea. This was an event, for up to that time I had never met an Englishman nor, to the best of my knowledge, had I seen one. I had listened to Englishmen on the crystal set on the mantelpiece, and was well aware that they had a peculiar way of speaking. I was given to understand that our guests had had to leave their English home because of a sinister thing called The Grouping, and my parents were offering hospitality to these strangers within the gates. Our visitors duly arrived, father, mother and boy of my own age, stiff and prim in their Sunday best, but speaking not at all like the people in our crystal set, which would have something to do with the fact that our guest was a displaced Hull & Barnsley iron moulder. We never saw them again. The father persevered at Cowlairs for a year or so, but his wife took fright at Springburn tenement life and hurried back to Yorkshire.

My route home from Sunday School took me across the railway bridge in Springburn Road, and one Sunday afternoon in 1924 I saw a crowd peering over the bridge parapet —something very unusual for a Sunday. In Hyde Park sidings was an engine—of sorts. To the schoolboy of a later generation its shape would have occasioned no wonder. It was a long metal box with a chimney at one end and a cab in the middle. I was looking at the Reid-McLeod turbo-condensing locomotive which had just returned from a trial spin on the Edinburgh main line.

As far back as 1909 the Hyde Park Reids had plans for a turbine locomotive. The highlight of Hugh Reid's presidential address to the Glasgow University Engineering Society in October 1909 was his revelation that, in conjunction with D. McNab Ramsay of the Ramsay Condensing Locomotive Co. Ltd. of Glasgow, he was building at Hyde Park a turbine locomotive with electric transmission. This was the Reid-Ramsay locomotive. The engine was completely enclosed, coal was carried in internal bunkers and water in side tanks. Superheated steam from a conventional boiler was used to drive a turbine at 3,000 r.p.m. and a continuous-current variable voltage dynamo coupled to the turbine supplied current to four series of traction motors, the armatures of which were built on the four driving axles. Exhaust steam was condensed and returned to the boiler by means of a feed pump. Hugh Reid stressed the fact that all the components incorporated in the engine had proved their efficiency in other spheres; the novelty lay in combining them in a locomotive. The Reid-Ramsay locomotive was built and tested on the Caledonian and North British main lines, but little is known of the results. High initial cost of construction was said to have been the biggest snag, and the engine was put into store at Hyde Park.

Immediately before the first world war two young Glasgow engineers, separately, came to Hyde Park with new ideas for locomotives. One was Mr C. R. H. Bonn, who put before the North British Locomotive Co. the idea of a diesel-propelled locomotive. Hugh Reid, by now Sir Hugh, his brother John and Mr Frame devoted an entire day to discussing the project and examining Mr Bonn's model of his gears. Bonn was to say many years later that he was received with great patience, interest and courtesy. But the Hyde Park hierarchy could see no future in the diesel. The other candidate for the Reids' attention was James McLeod, who had been investigating the application of the geared steam turbine to locomotives. The North British Locomotive Co. was soon overwhelmed with war work, experiments with new forms of traction were shelved for the time being, and it was 1921 before Sir Hugh Reid and James McLeod took out joint patents and the Hyde Park drawing office staff got down to work.

The Reid-McLeod locomotive used the frames and boiler of the earlier experimental locomotive. The engine was a 4—4—0 + 0—4—4, each of the compound bogies having four driving wheels and a four-wheeled bogie. The condenser was at the leading end of the engine and the boiler supplying steam at 180 p.s.i. superheated to 700 deg. F. was at the trailing end. The impulse-type turbines were coupled to the driving wheels by double reduction gears. The motive power unit was contained in an oil-tight casing and oil at a pressure of 20 p.s.i. was circulated continuously to all bearings and rotating parts. The cab interior was like the engine room of a ship. Instead of a regulator there was a horizontal wheel which was set in the mid position for *stop*. A turn one way produced forward motion, a turn the other reverse motion. The NBL had high hopes for the Reid-McLeod. As exporters of locomotives they had potential customers for the new engine in torrid sandy climates with little water but plenty of dust. Railway managements in such places would welcome a successful condensing locomotive that had all its gears and working parts sealed. The builders made great play of the enclosed gearing, even celebrating it in verse in official advertising literature.

Though open forms of slide-valve gears on Models we display,
These tend to harbour grit and grime, and grind themselves
away.
So on our Turbine Loco closed gears must be the rule,
With forced oil lubrication to keep them clean and cool.

To those who ask to see its works we are obliged to state
On High-Speed Balanced Engines seen gears are out of date.
And though the movements thus concealed leave less to make
one stare,
When'er you ride behind her you'll know the goods are there.

The Reid-McLeod turbo-locomotive was exhibited at the British Empire Exhibition of 1924. But it was its conventional sister exhibit, the Gresley Pacific, *Flying Scotsman*, that was to make history. The Reid-McLeod came home to Springburn and oblivion.

The great thing about the grouping for me was the appearance of familiar engines in new liveries. The first LNER engine I saw was a Holmes 4—4—0 that came scudding down the hill one afternoon with the Alloa. It looked grand in apple green. Then a few Scotts appeared in green. Never had a North British engine looked more handsome. Over at the Caley the position was less happy. One can imagine the feelings of the St Rollox painters when they had to obliterate the matchless blue beneath drab Derby-decreed maroon. 'We nearly came out on strike,' an old painter told me years later. New engines appeared on Cowlairs Incline. The first of these were the soft-voiced Directors. They took *Peter Poundtext* away from my old friend George Pringle and gave him a Director. He hated it. Then there were the Gresley tanks that we nicknamed 'teddy bears'. An occasional North Eastern Atlantic turned up on the Edinburgh trains—usually 714 or 721. I remember them chiefly for the song they made about coming up the Incline. Later on came the Shires. Gradually North British engines were ousted from the best trains. What I did not realise was that no more designs would be produced at Cowlairs and St Rollox.

I think I was enjoying my tenth summer when a colleague informed me that a big American engine had gone down the hill. 'It has five wee puffs and one big puff,' he explained to me with, as it turned out, commendable accuracy. I remember the great green shape pounding past me when it came back up the hill at the head of a train. I had a vision of a great boiler with a bulge in it, an incredibly small chimney and bowler hats bobbing on the footplate. A polished curved splasher bore the name *William Whitelaw*. Thus did I set eyes on my first Gresley Pacific. Many a time in the years to come I was to hear Pacifics hammering up the hill. Nowhere was the Gresley voice heard to better advantage.

There was a rumour that the LMS were planning a big new engine and that Hyde Park was working on the design. The LMS named the class after the oldest regiment in the British army. I saw the first of the fifty Hyde Park Royal Scots in the works siding. The railway company did not go so far as to write poetry about these engines but they did the next best thing when they got S. P. B. Mais to compose a eulogy about them. Mais saw in the maroon livery a 'dawn-like blush that suffuses her whole surface'.

In the early summer of 1926 my train-watching was interrupted for more than a week while the nation indulged in the novelty of the General Strike. The strike started at midnight on a Monday and all that evening I was in the Rushy watching train after train go up; specials mostly taking home people who wanted to get to their destinations before the big shut-down. It was an evening of high entertainment, but I could sense the undercurrent of disquiet among the adults around me. Yet they had no doubt that the drastic course on which they had embarked was right.

There was a Sunday quiet about the place on Tuesday morning. The works horns sounded at the appropriate times, but no one answered their call. There were no trains in the Rushy, and by the end of that first day the rails were rusty. The strike was several days old before I saw anything exciting. As I came out of school one afternoon a tramcar driven by a civilian volunteer came lumbering up the road. At the sound of its approach people poured from the tenements and blocked its path. Presently a bag of flour came sailing over the crowd and struck the hapless driver on the shoulders. He stood there on the driving platform, his trilby hat pulled down on his head, flour spattered over his raincoat. More flour bags followed. All this was sheer delight to a schoolboy—the Keystone Cops come to life. Almost alongside the tramcar was a large heap of stones from a demolished house. It is significant that the Springburn revolutionaries, rather than throw stones, preferred to queue up at the local shop to buy flour bombs at their own expense.

One day a rumour gained currency that a train was about to come up from Queen Street, and crowds flocked to the Rushy, armed this time with margarine which they rubbed on the rails. We waited gleefully to see what would happen, but no train came. Next day Baldwin announced on the wireless that the strike was over, and there was great relief in our street.

On the evening of 12 October 1928 there occurred a frightful disaster in Queen Street tunnel. An unbanked Edinburgh express got into difficulties and ran back down the tunnel to crash into the engine of a train that had been making a shunt move, but was then stopped. A great mass of wreckage was compressed into the narrow confines of the tunnel, and several people died among it. The signalman at Queen Street was arrested and tried on a charge of culpable homicide, it being asserted that he had permitted the shunt movement too soon after the entry of the express to the tunnel. The arrest was as unpopular with the LNER as it was with the public. There was a sensation at the trial when the express driver admitted that the sanders on his engine were defective, and that he would not have run back if they had been working properly. The chief running superintendent, although warned by the Judge that he need not answer incriminating questions, frankly informed the court that the sanders had indeed been reported as defective on three occasions in the week before the accident. When the jury returned a not guilty verdict for the signalman, the Ministry of Transport accident inspector who was in Court rose from his seat and shook the signalman by the hand.

Towards the end of 1929 it became known that both the LNER and the LMS were building engines of an unusual character. Glasgow had much to do with both. The LMS engine was taking shape in Hyde Park, the joint venture of Sir Henry Fowler and the Superheater Company; it was the ill-fated *Fury*. Externally the engine differed little from the conventional Royal Scots, but it was fitted with a Schmidt high pressure boiler delivering steam at 900 p.s.i. A high pressure boiler, too, was the main feature of the rival LNER engine. No. 10,000 was built at Darlington, but she was boilered at Yarrow's on the Clyde, the boiler being the joint patent of Harold Yarrow and Nigel Gresley, and Cockburn and Co. of Glasgow, specialists in high pressure mountings, provided the safety valves, regulator and water gauges. The secrecy surrounding No. 10,000 resulted in the popular press naming the engine the 'hush-hush', a description that made her all the more exciting to her potential schoolboy admirers.

On 22 October 1929 a paper by James McLeod, of the Reid-McLeod venture, was read to a meeting of the Institution of Engineers and Shipbuilders in Scotland on the subject of the steam turbine locomotive. On display at this lecture was a drawing of a high pressure boiler which was presented as being McLeod's own invention. It was plain to everyone in an audience that included Harold Yarrow that the drawing was that of the Yarrow-Gresley boiler tested only two weeks previously. 'I am quite sure,' said Yarrow, 'that it was misapprehension on Mr McLeod's part to take credit for the design of the boiler that he illustrates and with which he had nothing whatever to do. The drawing so far as the boiler installation is concerned seems to be a copy of the drawing that is attached to the patent specification which was taken out a year ago.' Unfortunately, McLeod was absent at a Power Conference in Japan, and his paper was read for him by Mr Frame of Hyde Park. A formal apology was expected from McLeod at the next meeting of the Institution. Instead, McLeod revealed that he had designed his engine, including the boiler, quite independently of Gresley and Yarrow. But the third high-pressure locomotive was never built.

On 10 February 1930 *Fury* left Hyde Park for a trial run. It got as far as Carstairs when there was an explosion in the firebox and the inspector of the Superheater Company who was on the footplate was killed. I saw the engine still in works grey and with part of its motion lying on top of the tender outside Hyde Park next day. No further attempt was made to run *Fury* as a high pressure locomotive, and it eventually emerged from the works as *British Legion,* No. 6170, the first taper boiler Scot. No. 10,000 had a longer run for its money before being rebuilt on conventional lines. In June 1931 the 'hush-hush' was installed in Cowlairs paint shop and members of the public were invited to inspect it. The visitors included large numbers of Springburn housewives who had no interest in the engine but who grabbed at the chance to penetrate the forbidden gates to catch a glimpse of their menfolk at work.

The men at Cowlairs and St Rollox did not take kindly to the relegation of their workshops to mere repair shops, and chagrin turned to alarm when even repairs fell away in volume and men were dismissed. There was a feeling among the former North British men that they were being sold down the river Don. The following entry appears in the minutes of a meeting of the Cowlairs Central Works and Agreement Committee held on 1 July 1929:

'The position in the sawmill was brought up for consideration. Bro. O'Brien opened the discussion explaining that the position was of a serious nature and that it was not only the sawmill that was affected but that the wagon and carriage shops were in much the same position. He believed that they were centralising the work and most of it was going to England. He then moved that we approach the St. Rollox committee with a view to having a joint meeting of both committees. Bro. Duthie in seconding the motion stated that the carriage shop was at one time a first class shop, but was now reduced to a repair shop, and was not getting what he thought was a fair share of the work.' A pencilled note in the minutes suggests referring the matter to the Secretary of State for Scotland and the local Member of Parliament.

There were misgivings too when it was said that no new boilers would be made at Cowlairs. When the men protested the official answer was 'Doncaster can build a boiler for £71 and at Cowlairs the same boiler takes £121 to build'.

The minute books of the Works Committee are unique and valuable social documents, giving as they do an unusual slant to the railway scene. Thomas Heywood, formerly locomotive superintendent of the Great North of Scotland Railway, was in command at Cowlairs at the time, and he appears throughout the minutes as the villain of the piece. On one page he is ordering the dismissal of a slinger who has allowed his squad to stand under a boiler while it was being raised, on another he is sacking apprentices who have been caught smoking in the lavatories during working hours. At one point he is brusquely refusing the request of a boilermaker to be paid early on Friday so that he can attend classes at Glasgow University, in another he gives a take-it-or-leave-it ultimatum to a tradesman who has lost an eye in the railway service and has been offered a job as lavatory attendant at 27s per week. However, it was well known in Cowlairs that Heywood's dismissals were not taken too seriously. It is said that only one man ever accepted dismissal, and nobody was more surprised than Heywood himself.

Some of the entries are commendably blunt. When the question of contributing to the retirement testimonial of a works manager came up 'Bro. Arnott moved a motion to the effect that Mr. —— is not a Fit and Proper person to receive a Testimonial and we advise others not to contribute'. The Works Committee received with scepticism a request from Friends of the Soviet Union to send a delegate to a railway gathering in Moscow. The Committee would have nothing to do with the matter and the workers were left to decide for themselves whether a delegate should be sent to Russia. Votes were taken on a departmental basis, and ten departments voted for and seven against appointing a delegate. The total votes cast throughout the works amounted to 3,136 and the majority for the motion was only 44. A delegate was duly appointed, but Heywood refused him leave of absence to visit Russia. Gresley was appealed to, and he upheld Heywood's decision.

In the end Cowlairs and St Rollox did not do badly out of the aftermath of the grouping. Both were reorganised and equipped to handle heavy repairs. If the glory of the past had departed at least a steady flow of repair work was assured. A generous share of the new engines that Cowlairs and St Rollox might have built came to Springburn in any case, for large batches of the new designs turned out at Doncaster and Derby were built at Hyde Park. The depression days of the thirties brought short time and unemployment to Springburn, but there was none of the destitution that resulted from the empty berths in the shipyard districts of Glasgow. Between repair work and new orders the railway skills of Springburn were usefully, if not always fully, employed.

Epilogue

SPRINGBURN TWILIGHT

In 1951 the Festival of Britain heralded what was thought
to be the dawn of a bright new era in the story of British
achievement. To represent the booming British locomotive
industry the North British Locomotive Co. sent an engine to
the South Bank. It was one of a batch of W.G. class 2—8—2s
on order for India. The Festival year was indeed one of prosperity for the company. Steam engines in prodigious batches
were building or were on order to equip railways the world
over that had been starved during the war years; 70 'R' class
for the Victorian Railways, 16 big 4—8—2s for New Zealand,
100 metre-gauge Pacifics for India, 100 class '25' 4—8—4s for
South Africa. Hyde Park was open seven days a week, and
most days shifts worked round the clock. It was little wonder
that in 1953 the NBL, in presenting their jubilee brochure (its
cover had a replica of the plate on No. 28,000) could say:
'This record is regarded by the board of directors more as a
stimulus to the future than a nostalgic glory of the past.'

The future! Ten years later the North British Locomotive
Co. had ceased to exist. In 1963 the deserted, derelict, broken-
down buildings of the Atlas and Hyde Park works stretched
like an abcess over acres of ground in the heart of Springburn.
To those who had known the throbbing, vital days of not so
long ago the landscape of rusting ironwork and broken glass
has an air of unreality. Springburn is no longer a great railway
community. Its skilled tradesmen go out of the district to jobs
along Clydeside or in the new industrial estates. And it was

251

Springburn Railway Workshops
CAMPAIGN COMMITTEE

INVITE THE RAILWAY AND NON-RAILWAY PEOPLE OF SPRINGBURN TO TAKE PART IN THE GIGANTIC DEMONSTRATION THAT WILL LEAVE GOURLAY STREET ON WEDNESDAY, 3rd OCTOBER, AT 1.30 p.m. THEN MARCH TO NTH. HANOVER STREET WHERE PROMINENT T.U. AND POLITICAL LEADERS WILL ADDRESS THEM ON RAILWAY CLOSURES.

WE THE RAILWAY WORKERS OF THIS AREA ARE LOOKING FORWARD TO SEEING THE HOUSEWIVES AND SHOPKEEPERS TAKE PART IN THIS DEMONSTRATION.

GONE—N.B. LOCO, CABLE WORKS, BRABY'S !
GOING—COWLAIRS, SARACEN FOUNDRY ! ! !
MARCH—STOP THIS ROT!

Handbill issued in 1962 during march of 7,000 Springburn railway employees to protest against projected closure of works too much in an age of retrenchment to expect that British Railways would retain two large factories within half a mile of each other. Cowlairs is doomed, and when the final pattern emerges only a truncated St Rollox will remain. The steam engine made Springburn. It was 1946 before Springburn began to dabble in diesels; the experiment was not happy. When the steam engine died, Springburn died with it.

This chronicle began on a New Year Day. It ends with a Hogmanay reminiscence. Hogmanay was a grand night in the Springburn of my boyhood. Soon after teatime on 31 December you would see the womenfolk cleaning and polishing their windows, for it was unthinkable that the first light of the New Year should shine through dirty glass. Then in the last minutes of the old year there would be a scurrying of feet on the tenement staircases as the women, carrying their kitchen ashpans, ran to the dustbins to discard the last ashes of the dying year. Meanwhile the men at Eastfield and St Rollox were preparing to welcome the New Year in their own special way. I liked to bring in the New Year standing at the top of Balgray Hill. That was a marvellous vantage point on which to hear the New Year arriving—for it was an aural occasion. There was an unnatural stillness during the final minutes of the old year. The city lay shining but silent below. Then at midnight there would be a solitary tentative blast on a ship's siren down by the Clyde, and near at hand the bell of the parish church would start its clamour. Instantly, Springburn exploded in a glorious cacaphony of railway sound, as fifty Eastfield whistles shrieked a welcome to the New Year and over the hill from the direction of St Rollox came the distant deep Caley roar. Above it all was the steady crack of a dozen detonators spaced at regular intervals on the rail and now being exploded by an engine crew delegated for the task.

But now the voices of the Scottish engines are silenced, and Hogmanay can never be the same again. All we can expect are a few feeble Doncaster *wheeps* augmented by the devilish discord of the diesel horns.

APPENDIX

Table showing the number of men employed in the British locomotive trade between 1890 and 1899

	1890	1891	1892	1893	1894
Neilson & Co.	2,505	2,584	2,307	1,396	1,510
Dübs & Co.	1,960	1,940	1,697	1,775	1,465
Beyer Peacock	2,159	1,565	1,507	1,359	1,239
Sharp, Stewart	1,336	1,971	1,292	1,246	1,145
Kitson	1,255	1,270	1,268	1,079	1,143
Robert Stephenson	679	666	561	486	320
Vulcan	530	659	455	344	610
Manning Wardle	474	419	377	320	236
Nasmyth Wilson	493	477	257	293	349
Hunslet	236	282	240	245	234

	1895	1896	1897	1898	1899
Neilson & Co.	1,617	2,360	2,600	2,937	3,275
Dübs & Co.	1,773	1.868	2,004	1,931	2,017
Beyer Peacock	1,196	1,727	1,756	1,792	1,866
Sharp Stewart	1,178	1,333	1,432	1,435	1,561
Kitson	915	1,192	1,192	1,357	1,440
Robert Stephenson	387	586	885	894	1,047
Vulcan	514	770	792	713	820
Manning Wardle	314	370	483	335	590
Nasmyth Wilson	337	459	443	517	526
Hunslet	242	245	271	270	300

ACKNOWLEDGMENTS AND SOURCES

I owe much to Mr C. W. Black, City Librarian of Glasgow, and Mr Robert S. Clark, Deputy Librarian, for their enthusiastic help. It is specially fitting that Mr Clark should have been associated with the preparation of this book, for I first met him many years ago when he was District Librarian at Springburn and I was a schoolboy finding my way in the world of books. (The library building itself stood in the immediate shadow of Hyde Park works on ground gifted by the Reids.) I am grateful to the Mitchell Library staff for their unfailing efficiency and courtesy, and especially to Miss Glass of the photographic department who was responsible for extracting the library treasures and preparing them in a form acceptable to the printer. Many thanks also to Campbell Cornwell, James McEwan and Montague Smith for their much-appreciated scrutiny of the manuscript or proofs.

THE ILLUSTRATIONS

The chief merit of the illustrations is that most of them have not been seen before. Old photographs that have been mouldering in albums or drawers for years perhaps lack the technical perfection of prints freshly made from agency plates, but they do have originality. I am greatly indebted to the many people (and especially to railwaymen's widows) who let me see photographs in their possession. Many promising subjects, alas! were impossible to use because of their physical condition.

Photographs and prints from the Mitchell Library Collection: page 19 *top*, page 20 *top*, page 37 *top*, page 109 *top* and *bottom*, page 127 *top* and *bottom*, page 145, page 146 *top*. William Graham photographs in the Mitchell Library Collection: page 20 *bottom*, page 56 *top*, page 73 *top*, page 91, page 128 *top*. Of the portraits on page 74 *top left, top right* and *bottom left* are from The Bailie, and *bottom right* is from the Wotherspoon Collection, all by courtesy of the Mitchell Library. Page 37 *bottom,* The Institution of Engineers and Shipbuilders in Scotland. Page 38 *top,* Wm Hennigan Collection. Page 55 *top,* a William Graham original by courtesy of Wilson Tennant, *middle,* courtesy J. Deuchar. Illustrations of page 55 *bottom,* 110 *bottom,* 181 *bottom* and 182 *top* are by courtesy of Montague Smith. Page 56 *bottom* Mrs Riddel, pages 73 *middle* and 163 *top* and *bottom,* Mrs Jardine; page 92 *top,* R. Allan, *bottom* courtesy Mrs Douglas; page 110 *top right,* Douglas McMillan; page 164 *top,* William Teacher & Sons Ltd, *middle,* British Railways. *Frontispiece,* North British Locomotive Company Ltd. Photographs by the author appear as follows: page 19 *bottom,* page 38 *bottom,* page 73 *bottom,* page 110 *top left,* page 128 *bottom,* page 146 *bottom,* page 164 *bottom,* page 181 *top,* and page 182 *bottom.*

Sources of line drawings and documents:

Mitchell Library	Davidson's electric locomotive, announcement of Promenade in Queen Street tunnel, cartoon 'The Rivals'
Institution of Engineers and Shipbuilders in Scotland	Spark arrester diagrams
Mrs Williamson	Neilson Certificate of Apprenticeship
J. Deuchar	Memorial card

BIBLIOGRAPHY

Springburn, Its Church and Parish. Burnett, A. L. 1942.

'Some Reminiscences of Springburn Forty-Fifty Years Ago.' Text of a lecture delivered in Cowlairs Parish Church Hall on 26 February 1940 by Charles Forsyth.

Life of James Beaumont Neilson, F.R.S. (West of Scotland Iron and Steel Institute.) 1928.

Edinburgh & Glasgow Railway Rule Book. 1846.

Edinburgh & Glasgow Railway Guide. Willox, J. 1842.

Documents relating to railways and canals around Glasgow. (Mitchell Library Collection.)

Hill's *Views of Glasgow.* (Garnkirk & Glasgow Railway.) 1832.

Industries of Glasgow. 1888.

The Hyde Park Dinners. After-dinner speeches reported in the *St Rollox and Springburn Express.* (The main speakers were railway personalities, and they had interesting things to say on current railway trends.)

Transactions of the Old Glasgow Club.

Various papers in the *Transactions* of the Institution of Engineers and Shipbuilders in Scotland, 1857, onwards.

Transactions of Institution of Locomotive Engineers.

Exhibited Machinery of 1862. Clark, D. K.

Railways of Great Britain and Ireland. Whishaw, F. 1840.

Cowlairs Co-operative Society Jubilee Book.

Caledonian Railway Centenary. Stephenson Locomotive Society. 1947.

Caledonian Railway Christmas Annual, 1909.

North British Locomotive Company Ltd. *Record of War Production.* (1914-1918.)

North British Locomotive Company. *History.* 1953.

North British Locomotive Company. *Catalogue.* British Empire Exhibition. 1924.

Glasgow Exhibition, 1901. *An Engineering Record.*

Scottish Railway Strike. Mavor, J. 1891.

'History of the Electric Locomotive,' Haut, F. J. G. *Transactions* of the Newcomen Society, Vol. 27.

Institute of Transport Congress. St Rollox, 1930.

Newspapers and Periodicals: *Glasgow Argus, Glasgow Courier, Glasgow Herald, The Scotsman, St Rollox and Springburn Express, Springburn Advertiser, Cassier's Magazine, The Ironmonger, Practical Mechanics and Engineers Magazine, The Engineer, Engineering, Railway World, Railway Herald, Railway Times, Railway Gazette, Railway Engineer, The Locomotive, Herepath's Railway Journal.*

INDEX

Italic figures indicate illustrations

GILBERT THOMAS & DAVID ST JOHN THOMAS

DOUBLE HEADED

Two Generations of Railway Enthusiasm

THIS unique book will give the railway enthusiast hours of pleasure. It might even convince the uninitiated that there is more in trains than a mere means of transport. Britain's railways are portrayed as seen by father and son over a period of 65 years. It is a many-faceted portrait, serious and entertaining, with glimpses of trains past and present in all parts of the country, and more solid contributions, too, especially on a number of lesser-known aspects. Branch lines, and narrow gauge, steam and even model railways find their place.

We see the Midland Railway at the turn of the century, the building of the Great Central, and the rise and fall of cross-country trains. City stations like Bristol Temple Meads and wayside ones deep in the country are brought to life. Railway management is scrutinised in the Lake District, County Donegal and the Westcountry. There is an evocative article on 'Highland Luxury', a trip on the Highland Railway to Inverness with a deviation up the Aberfeldy branch.

'The book has three main objectives . . . it succeeds in all these; yet there is a good deal more . . . better than the general level.' —*Railway World*

'This delightful collection.'—*Railway Magazine*

'Gay as well as serious, engaging as well as penetrating, and very well illustrated.'—*Country Life*

'Although I have been reading railway books and magazines since about 1894, I don't think I have ever *enjoyed* one quite so much as DOUBLE HEADED.'—A Glasgow reader's letter

105 illustrations   25s *net*

DAVID & CHARLES, DAWLISH
and
MACDONALD, LONDON

TWO STANDARD HISTORIES

H. A. VALLANCE

THE HIGHLAND RAILWAY

THE Highland's popularity with those who love railways arose from the scenic charm of its terrain, and also from the way in which the small company succeeded in working its traffic in the face of natural difficulties, and with limited financial resources, over routes that were largely single-track.

'The writing is clear and concise and the pages are enriched by miscellaneous illustrations which add authentic "background" to the story of one of the most delightful of the pre-grouping railways . . . this book is excellent value'.—*Stephenson Locomotive Society's Journal.*

66 *illustrations*   *Second impression*   25s *net*

H. W. PAAR

THE SEVERN & WYE RAILWAY

(A History of the Railways of the Forest of Dean: Part One)

THE railway history of the Forest of Dean stretches from 1800 to the present day. Horse tramroads, tramroad locomotives, the broad and standard gauges, the Foresters have seen them all. This volume describes the Severn & Wye and Severn Bridge Railways; its successor will cover the other Forest lines. The many difficulties of those who built the Severn & Wye and its branches are described against the background of the collieries and industries the company sought to serve and of the laws and traditions of the Forest itself.

'The author certainly succeeds in compiling an interesting narrative and brings together some remarkable illustrations of the equipment employed, from horse vehicles on tramplates to unusual steam locomotives.'—*Modern Transport*

56 *illustrations*   **30s** *net*

DAVID & CHARLES, DAWLISH
and
MACDONALD, LONDON